MAN AND HIS MUSIC

VOLUME THREE

This book is published also as Part III in a
one-volume, illustrated, bound edition containing
all four volumes. The cross-references to page
numbers, Parts, and Plates, refer to that edition
and should be disregarded here.

MAN AND HIS MUSIC

THE SONATA PRINCIPLE

WILFRID MELLERS

SCHOCKEN BOOKS · NEW YORK

First SCHOCKEN PAPERBACK edition 1969

Copyright © 1962, 1969 by Wilfrid Mellers

Library of Congress Catalog Card No. 77-75744

Printed in Great Britain

CONTENTS

PREFACE

To WRITE about the past, which we call history, is difficult, for the obvious reason that we cannot experience it at first hand. To write about music is also difficult, because although we may experience it at first hand we are forced, in the act of writing, to translate our experience into another language. To write about history and music simultaneously is therefore a task which one ought to approach with both circumspection and humility. It is not enough to write a bit of potted European history and then to cite musical parallels; nor is it adequate to write about music as though it could exist apart from the context of human life. One has to experience music 'from within'; and in so doing to see it as historical evidence of a more inward kind than the documents with which historians usually have to deal.

One can hardly begin to experience music as historical evidence until one has faced up to a more fundamental question: if music 'conveys' experience as a language does, what kind of a language is it? The language of poetry is basically the same as the normal means of communication between human beings. The poet may use words with a precision, a cogency ,and a range of emotional reference which we do not normally find in conversation. Yet though the order he achieves from his counters may be more significant than the desultory patterns achieved in talk by Tom, Dick, and Harry, at least the counters (words) are the same in both cases. Even with the visual arts there is usually some relationship between the order of forms and colours which the artist achieves and the shapes and colours of the external world. The relationship between the formal and representational elements is extremely complex and not easily susceptible to analysis; but it is at least usually clear that some such relationship exists.

With music, the relationship between the forms of art and the phenomena of the external world is much less readily apprehensible. It is true that composers have always made attempts to imitate the sounds of nature—from the bird-calls and clattering water-mills of Ars Nova down to Strauss's bleating sheep. But no one would claim that the imitative aspects of Rameau's hen or Beethoven's cuckoo were the essential experience with which the music was concerned; the 'Pastoral' Symphony was not composed to do what cuckoos and quails can do much better. Yet if music is not imitation, there would seem to be uniform agreement that it does express, or at any rate mean, something. Charles Avison could find plenty of support, down the centuries, for his contention in his *Essay of Musical Expression* (1751) that 'the force of Sound in Alarming the Passions is Prodigious'. When he goes on to speak of the 'pleasing sorrows' and 'grateful terrors' we experience in listening to music he implicitly suggests that music is not synonymous with self-expression. It is neither the whoop of joy nor the yell of pain or fright: though it may include such manifestations. This is equally true of *King Lear:* for we are in a profound sense 'pleased' and 'gratified' by a sorrow and terror that in life the humanity of Lear, let alone our puny selves, can scarcely bear. So music as a language is perhaps, after all, not radically distinct from poetry and painting. All the arts are an order made out of reality. Music differs from the other arts only because it embodies its reality not in words, nor in shapes and colours, but in sound. It can do this because certain properties of sound are correlatable with some aspects of our physical and mental lives.

Thus we all live in time; and music essentially involves movement. Any sequence of two notes implies a progression in time: a sense of direction either up or down or, if the two notes are the same, in a straight line. The intervals of octave and fifth—whether sounded in sequence (melodically) or simultaneously (harmonically)—suggest stability because the vibration rates of the two tones bear to one another a simple arithmetical relationship. The intervals of major seventh, minor ninth and tritone* suggest unrest and tension because the two wave motions are in complex vibration ratio to one another: they therefore agitate the diaphragm of the ear and, in turn, the nervous system. All melody consists of alternations of tension and relaxation existing in time. Big leaps, jagged rhythms, tend to imply agitated movement; stepwise progressions, in even rhythm, suggest repose. Pentatonic† melodies come as close as is possible to a tensionless state, because their formulae are

* The augmented fourth or diminished fifth, i.e. F♭ to B♭ or B♭ to F♭.
† For an account of the pentatonic scale see Vol. I.

most directly derived from the prime members of the harmonic series. Chromatic melodies tend to be most emotionally disturbing because they disrupt the melodic formulae which, for scientific reasons, the human voice most naturally sings.

The tenser a melodic progression, the more it is apt to carry harmonic implications. The major sixth (for instance, C to A) may suggest the harmonic centrality of the triad, or it may be absorbed into floating, pentatonic-like arabesques, as it is in the opening of Dvorak's 'Nigger' Quartet. The minor sixth (C to A*b*), however, always seems to be 'seeking resolution' in the fifth. It tends to feel like a suspension, which is essentially a harmonic concept. Such harmonic concepts too have a precise relationship to physiological and psychological facts. Thus the suspension—the tense or dissonant note which resolves by a stepwise droop on to the relaxed or consonant interval—is a literal musical equation for the sigh. The major triad (C, E, G) is a musical symbol of natural order because its relationship to the fundaments of the harmonic series is simple: while the tritone has always been a symbol of disorder because its relationship is ambiguous and complex. The minor triad (C, E*b*, G) is less final, less resolved, than the major triad because the vibration ratio of the minor third is complicated by the presence of lower partials or combination tones.

Sometimes the presence of words in a vocal composition makes clear the relationship between these—and many other— sound symbols and our physical and mental experience. Consider, for instance, the conventional stepwise movement of the classical operatic *scène de sommeil;* Bach's scalewise floating angels; his chromatic crucifixions; his weeping appoggiaturas.*
Yet whether or no words offer a verbal gloss, the language of music always speaks in the same basic terms. Bach's last chorale prelude and the D sharp minor fugue from Book I of the *Forty-eight* are 'about' the same experience, as we can demonstrate from an analysis of their technique, though we have an implicit verbal commentary on this experience in the first case, none in the second.

Whether or no a musical composition has verbal associations, our comments on it will be valid only in so far as they have reference to the fundamental symbols of sound, as outlined

---

* APPOGGIATURA: a dissonant 'ornamental' note on the strong beat which resolves on the weak. See Vol. II.

above. In the course of this book I refer, for instance, to a melodic phrase as 'caressing'. Of course, the adjective is a metaphor; but is it valid and relevant? When I looked at the score I decided that just possibly it was valid; for the contour of the phrase describes a curve that looks like the curve of a caressing hand; it is a physical gesture in time. None the less, the word 'caress' is not purely descriptive; it introduces an emotional overtone that may or may not be pertinent. We can decide whether or not it is pertinent only when we see this phrase in relation to the composition of which it is a part. For although our comments about music are invalid unless they are based on the facts of sound rather than on those of another medium, we are not concerned with those facts in themselves. For us, such facts exist only within the context of particular pieces of music; and this context is at once personal experience and an aspect of history.

For instance, the acoustical distinction between the major and minor triad is of crucial significance in Schubert's music. But that the minor triad is, scientifically speaking, less resolved than the major triad does not take us far in understanding the extraordinary, and highly personal, poignancy of Schubert's use of alternating major and minor. We need to know not only that the alternation happens, but why it happens when it does. In the slow movement of Schubert's last piano sonata in B flat the ultimate appearance of the theme in the major is heart-breaking. But why this major transformation proves, in apparent paradox, to be so much sadder than the minor version is something we can understand only in reference to the complete movement and, indeed, sonata—or even to the context of Schubert's work as a whole. Though we have started from a fact of musical technique, we have found that the facts become significant only in relation to the whole of which they are a part. In the long run, this whole involves the strange, fascinating phenomenon of Schubert's psychology—his human experience, which becomes part of our experience while being at the same time unlike that of any other human being.

If this seems a matter of 'personality' rather than of 'history,' another example will reveal how inseparable the two concepts are. The chord of the dominant seventh* has certain specific

*See Vol. I.

acoustical properties which depend on the fact that it involves both a stable major triad and a tense tritone that seeks resolution. Yet the effect of the chord when it appears in the Agnus Dei of Byrd's five-part Mass is utterly different from its effect in the sequential modulations* of Chopin's C major Etude (opus 10, no. 1, bar 24, et seq.). There is a historical reason for this: Byrd and Chopin lived in different worlds both temporally and geographically. Byrd's 'suspended' seventh is a harmonic catch-in-the-breath, a sob, approached as a movement of independent vocal lines; Chopin's dissolving sevenths are an effect of harmonic 'colour' in part suggested by the movement of his hands on the keyboard. But this technical distinction is not merely a difference between two epochs: it rather comes to us as a distinction between two human beings who were, inevitably, representatives of the worlds in which they lived. Nor is the emotional and intellectual life of a single personality ever absolute and constant. Chopin's treatment of the dominant seventh is different from Byrd's because the nineteenth century is not the sixteenth, and because Chopin is not Byrd. But his treatment of the chord also varies, within the basic assumptions of his age, according to the context. Whenever we talk about music we are discussing two things simultaneously. We are concerned with the fundamental assumptions of an age about the way in which (say) a dominant seventh ought to behave; this is the technical complement to some part of the values by which a society lives, or thinks it lives. We are also concerned with the way in which this dominant seventh does in fact behave at a given moment in a given context; this is the experience of the individual artist.

No work of art can be 'explained' by reference to its historical connotations. Every artist self-evidently 'reflects' the values and beliefs of his time; he has no choice in the matter, even though he may, like Swift, express them largely in negative terms. At the same time, any truly creative artist is also making those beliefs. It is true that we cannot fully understand Beethoven without understanding the impulses behind the French Revolution. It is equally true that we cannot fully understand the French Revolution without some insight into Beethoven's music. We can see in his music those elements which are

---

* A SEQUENCE is the repetition of a passage at a different pitch.

conditioned by his time (for they could not be otherwise) and yet are beyond the topical and local. Beethoven is a point at which the growth of the mind shows itself. He is a part of history: and also the human spirit making history.

This is fairly obvious in the case of an artist who, like Beethoven, deliberately wanted to be an 'epoch-making' force. It is hardly less true of a relatively small, marginal figure such as César Franck. There can be no distinction between Franck's curious psychological make-up and the equivocal quality of his music—the contradiction between the fluidity of his tonality and the disintegration of his harmony on the one hand, and on the other hand the nagging reiteration of his metrical patterns and thematic contours, oscillating obsessively around the mediant.* Yet this element of frustration in both technique and personality is also what makes him historically representative. Even with composers living in more stable and homogeneous societies it is impossible to separate personal from historical significance. In the sixteenth century there was a common European idiom which we now know as Palestrina style. This was music's common denominator for certain assumptions of the Catholic Church and of Renaissance society. Yet it matters to us because it was the framework within which men such as Byrd, Lassus, Victoria, and Palestrina himself expressed very different attitudes to those assumptions. Handel's basic idiom was so universally accepted that he could lift into his own work large sections of other people's music without anyone noticing, or caring if they did notice. Yet what we remember of eighteenth-century baroque music is the revivifying experience of creative minds. We respond to the profound equilibrium between acceptance and protest, tradition and revolution, lyricism and tonal drama in the music of Haydn and Mozart; while we have forgotten the innumerable symphonic hacks who exploited the small change of rococo style as an easy way of passing the time—and making money. Most of all, perhaps, we see Bach's crucial position in European history in relation to his independence of time. Firmly rooted in what was then present, he philosophically and even technically harked back to a medieval past, while looking forward not merely to nineteenth century romanticism, but still more to the twentieth century.

* The third degree of the scale.

So in talking of Music and Society we should not think we are saying anything worth saying in pointing out that there are connexions between what has happened in music and what has happened in the external world. That is, or should be, a truism. We should, however, in listening to the music which great and less than great men have created at different times in the past, learn to experience that music as the deepest kind of evidence as to the ways men have thought, felt, and acted. In order to do this we need a historical sense: but only because— or in so far as—the past is relevant to the present. Before the nineteenth century any musician would have thought it odd to listen to music of the past rather than of the present. We take it for granted that we listen to more music of past ages than of our own. But if we are all historically minded, we are learning to understand that the historian's task is both to apprehend the significance which past music had when it was still present: and to differentiate between those elements of the past which have lost, and those which retain, a meaning.

The delicacy and complexity of the historian's task is thus only too pointed. Nothing he says is valid unless it is based on concepts related to the nature of sound, and on the particular ways in which a composer has used these sound-symbols at a given moment. Yet the historian has also to see these given moments in relation to the composer's personal experience, in the context of his life and in the wider context of history. Above all, he has to be able to distinguish between those elements of history and biography which are relevant to the musical experience and those which are not; and to do this no amount of accumulated learning will help him. Indeed, learning may hinder as much as help him; for the amount of music which one man can know—in the real sense of experiencing it from within —is restricted both by the limitations of human understanding and by time. This historian, at least, would claim no more than that he has approached his task with humility, and that he has tried not to lose sight of the living reality of history: which is the point of intersection between the private and the public life.

WILFRID MELLERS

I TRADITION AND REVOLUTION

THE BIRTH OF SONATA

THE second half of the eighteenth century is a crucial turning-point in the history of European music. During this period a revolutionary principle of composition was created. We call it Sonata Form, though the term is misleading because it suggests that 'form' can exist independent of the musical 'content'. Sonata, like fugue, is not so much a form as a principle, an approach to composition. The sonata movements of Haydn, let alone Beethoven, resemble one another in their approach, but not in the details of the pattern. One might even say that there is no such thing as sonata form; there are only sonatas. Sonata is a way of composing which grew out of a particular set of circumstances: which is apposite to those circumstances and not necessarily to others. A new approach to composition grew out of new human needs and desires. Certain conventions were, of course, gradually deduced from this new approach and hardened into cliché and dogma; social small talk which could be used by composers who had nothing to say as an agreeable way of passing the time and making money. But for the masters style never becomes dogma; form remains principle which perpetually renews itself under the pressure of experience.

At the outset, therefore, we have to enquire what were the social and philosophical circumstances that created a new musical style; and how did this new music differ from previous kinds of composition. Let us first look at two pieces of music which were composed before this great new epoch. The first is J. S. Bach's last chorale prelude, *Vor deinen Thron tret'ich allhier* (the 'Eighteen' Chorale Preludes).* This piece is founded on a chorale or hymn which was not Bach's own creation, but was the property of his Church; the tune enters intermittently in comparatively long note values. When we examine the music more closely we find that the other parts, which might seem to

* For a detailed analysis of this piece see Hermann Scherchen, *The Nature of Music.*

be accompanying the melody, are in fact thematic. Each phrase of the chorale is treated in diminution as a fugue subject, the answer usually being in inversion. The concluding phrase appears in its original hymn-tune time values, in diminution and in double diminution simultaneously, and both ways up. It is almost true to say that there is not a single note in the piece which is not derived from the liturgical melody.

Moreover, the progression of the parts is mainly by step or by small, smooth intervals, moving at about the speed of the human pulse. The persistent answer by inversion creates an equilibrium of emotion, each rise being balanced by a fall; and though the harmony which the parts create is often tensely dissonant, this pathos dissolves away in the measured flow of the lines. Bach's personal feeling is powerful (he knew he was dying as he dictated this piece); but it is absorbed into something greater than himself. All this we can deduce from the technique of the music itself. In this case it also happens that the implicit words of the chorale corroborate what the music is telling us in its own terms. Into Thy hands I commend my spirit; in the fragmentary disintegration of the theme during the extended plagal cadence* of the concluding bars man is united with the infinite.

Bach [1685–1750] was in many ways an archaistic composer, and the thematic and fugal unity of this last chorale prelude is more typical of earlier creative periods than of his own. At least we may say that there is some connexion between fugal unity as a principle of composition and an age dominated by religious faith—by belief in something more than human potentiality. Now let us look at another piece of music, this time by Handel [1685–1759], a contemporary of Bach, but a man who, unlike Bach, was progressive in his time. The well-known air from *Messiah*, 'How beautiful are the feet', is again an expression of unity; but it is not fugal. The unity this music achieves is architectural. There is again only one theme which falls, however, into a number of clearly defined segments. The first half modulates from tonic minor to relative major; the second half returns to the tonic by way of related keys. The purpose of these modulations is to emphasize the grouping of the clauses, not to provide a dramatic contrast. Bach's chorale

* The cadence formed by the progression from the subdominant chord (that on the fourth degree of the scale) to the tonic. See *Cadences*, Part I.

prelude is an instrumental piece constructed on principles which are inherently vocal. Handel's aria is a vocal piece which is constructed on principles derived from the architecture of the dance.

Perhaps one might say that a general principle is involved: Bach tends to think fugally even when he writes dances; Handel thinks in terms of the dance even when he writes fugues. Bach's unity is the growth of the single melody in all the parts; Handel's unity is imposed on his tunes by periodic dance metre and by the definition of tonality. And Handel is the representative musician of the baroque era; for whereas Bach reveals the order inherent in melody, Handel creates order by a balance of clauses and keys—just as the architects and gardeners of his age established order through the symmetry of shapes and contours. Bach still expresses a theocratic —a God-centred—view of the universe, while Handel's attitude is humanistic. Bach wrote for the Church, even in his instrumental music. Handel writes for the opera-house, even in his church music: and the opera-house was the symbol of King and State, of the man-made autocracy in which the King became God. The importance of the chaconne form in baroque music is not fortuitous; for the chaconne is a longish piece constructed over the regular repetition of a dance rhythm and of a harmonic bass. This periodic pattern disciplines the music's passion in much the same way as the conventions of aristocratic society aimed to control personal feeling in the interests of the community. Couperin's terrific *Passacaille* in B minor is an extreme example of this. The chromatically violent harmony reaches its climax in the penultimate couplet; but the emotion is dammed up by the relentless repetitions of the rondeau (Ex. 1). The vehement passions of the individual seem to be

Ex. 1. Couperin: *Passacaille*

desperately struggling against the conventions that make civilization possible. In so well ordered a world there is never any doubt that civilization will triumph.

We have commented on two kinds of unity in music previous
to the sonata epoch: that of Bach, which is at once melodic and
harmonic, and religious in impetus; and that of Handel, which
is primarily rhythmic and tonal, and based on a ritual of the
State. Both kinds of unity imply reference to a central authority
outside the self; and it is not surprising that the relationship
between social ritual and art which we find in Handel, and still
more in the composers of Louis XIV's France, should have
been precarious. It depended on the existence of a public small
and unified enough for a system of values to be universally
intelligible. The decline of the aristocracy meant its end; and
we can observe the beginnings of a change even in the work of
Rameau [1683–1764], who regarded himself as an heir to the
classical baroque tradition. Although many of Rameau's later
operas were presented at the court of Louis XV, we may say
that he, unlike his predecessor, Lully [1632–1687], wrote with
the Parisian public in mind. It is significant that his patron was
Le Riche de la Pouplinière, a financier and one of the wealthiest
members of the new bourgeoisie.

Rameau starts from the old heroic operatic conventions,
yet repeatedly he recreates them for new ends. In place of ceremonial grandeur, he offers a still more voluptuous harmony
and a richer orchestral colour. Whereas the style of Lully and
Couperin [1668–1733] had depended on melodic continuity
and harmonic order, there are many passages in Rameau
which depend solely on instrumental figuration and on rhythm
to make a sensational effect. Consider, for instance, the earth-
quake in *Les Indes Galantes*, or the *bruit de mer* in *Hyppolyte* with
its shooting scales, percussive rhythms, and picturesque orchestration (Ex. 2). This is a deliberate attempt to make an im-

Ex. 2. Rameau: *Hyppolyte et Aricie*

mediate impact on a relatively large and untrained public. It
was a new style of composing; but its implications were not yet
to be explored in France, where the aristocratic central authority was strong enough to suppress internal dissension. The more

sensitive spirits of the classical age—such as Fénélon and La Bruyère—had been painfully aware that their autocracy occasioned misery among those less fortunately placed. None the less they believed in their world with an almost religious intensity. It was not until many years after Louis XIV's heyday that the undercurrent of revolutionary fervour came to the surface.

In Austria and Germany, however, the Thirty Years' War had left in its wake a legacy of chaos and disintegration, and had established the dominance of a foreign power. In these conditions the petty princelings attempted to maintain an oppressive feudal serfdom, while they themselves emulated the fashionable French and Italian models in their palaces, their art, their music, their codes of etiquette. Austrian culture became cosmopolitan; the Catholicism and Italianate elegance of the Habsburgs could not provide a unifying force comparable with that of the *Roi. Soleil* in France. By the middle of the eighteenth century the conflict latent in society had become patent. The split was noticeable even within the nobility itself, for the Emperor Joseph II, who opposed the Papacy, attempted to abolish serfdom, and established an Edict of Toleration, came into bitter conflict with the patriarchal feudal landlords, such as Haydn's patrons, the Esterházys. The fantastic dream-world of the Esterházy palace in the marshes was a conscious attempt to transplant Louis XIV's glory into Austria—an oasis, even a mirage, in a desert of misery, for it depended on serfdom for its existence. The reformist's zeal was defeated; Joseph had to withdraw his Edict. Revolutionary aspirations broke out again, and were again defeated, innumerable times down to the twentieth century.

Yet the victory of the feudal landlords was more apparent than real. Their sun was setting, and a new aristocracy was arising in their midst. This aristocracy was bourgeois and middle-class, and rational rather than Catholic. Its power is exemplified in the rise of Freemasonry; for although the Masons were an elect, they did not come from the landlord or the military classes. While many Masons were formally Catholics, the Church (and with it the State) was suspicious of the movement in so far as it encouraged equalitarian ideas. The Church traditionally distrusted Reason; the Masons believed that society could be regenerated through the exercise of Reason, which would bring Enlightenment—without, presumably, the intervention of Grace. Haydn, ostensibly a pious Catholic, got into hot water with the Church because of the Masonic implications of his oratorio, *The Creation*. Mozart's Masonic opera, *The Magic Flute*, was regarded with suspicion by the Church as a subversive manifestation. These facts alone indicate how powerfully democratic ideas permeated the work even of artists who had been aristocratically nurtured. The growth of eighteenth-century sonata style is the musical expression of this new democracy. Indeed, the symphony orchestra itself reflected a democratic ideal; Joseph von Holzmeister, in a speech delivered on the occasion of Haydn's admission to the Masonic Order, pointed out that Haydn had created a new order in the orchestra, 'for if every instrument did not consider the rights and properties of the other instruments, in addition to its own rights, if it did not often diminish its own volume in order not to do damage to the utterance of its companions, the end—which is beauty—would not be attained'.

When the Austrian composers began to feel around for a style that would be appropriate to a changing view of the world, they were able to profit from the Italian domination in Vienna. For the rage of the moment was the *opera buffa*, which while taking over many conventions from the degenerating *opera seria*, was in part a reaction against the heroic view of life. The *opera seria* dealt with figures larger than life: humans swollen to gods or monsters, as were the monarchs of the great autocracies. The *opera buffa* debunked the sublime and dealt with the low life of Tom, Dick, and Harry—and, of course, that of their young women. The musical style of the *opera buffa* was related to urban popular music; and the instrumental sections, especially the overtures, most significantly modify the techniques of classical baroque music.

The basic formal conventions of the baroque had been the binary dance movement and the *aria da capo*. In the former, as we saw from our example from Handel's *Messiah*, a single melody is divided into two sections, the first of which modulates from tonic major to dominant or from tonic minor to relative, the second moving back to the tonic by way of related keys. In the *aria da capo*, there is an extended melody in dance rhythm, which may itself be in binary form; then a middle section based on a different aspect of the same theme, and often in the tonic minor; then a repeat of the first section, with elaborate ornamentation. Except for the intensifying ornamentation the theme is not *changed* by what happens in the middle section, for the *da capo* aria, like binary dance form, is architectural, not dramatic. It is obvious, however, that the modulatory sections in both binary and ternary aria *could* be exploited as an effect of dramatic contrast. This begins to happen in some of the later examples of the concerto grosso.

This form was a reduction into instrumental terms of the conventions of heroic opera: the soloistic group took the place of the singers, the *tutti* that of the operatic orchestra. The alternation of *soli* and *tutti* suggests the use of different, even contrasting material in association with the two keys—tonic and dominant, or tonic and relative—which are the orthodox props of binary structure. When once the idea of contrast is admitted, modulation may be used as a shock tactic, rather than for architectural reasons. In the concertos of Vivaldi [1675–1741], for instance, the slow movements are always based on continuous melodic growth, in the heroic manner of Handel or Bach. But the quick movements, especially the finales, already suggest a dualistic rather than a monistic principle of construction. They exploit the exciting effect of tonal and rhythmic contrast; and that they do so is inseparable from the fact that their themes are no longer heroic, but popular in style.

If this is true of Vivaldi's concerto movements, which grew out of the baroque heritage, still more is it true of the stock operatic overture, which was in part a reaction against that heritage. Here, if the modulatory sections are not dramatic, or at least momently surprising, they are nothing: for there is no melody, as Bach or Handel conceived it, to extend. In Paisiello's overture *Nina*, for instance, there is no lyrical theme. There are little tootling arpeggio phrases and prancing scales in perkily periodic rhythms. The props of tonic and dominant are established only in order to be contradicted, so that the music moves in short, contrasted sections punctuated by cadences, rather than with the continuity and unity which Bach and Handel, in their different ways, sought after. The music is heterogeneous in effect and, as a noise, superficially exciting: consider Paisiello's use of a new instrument, the clarinet. But although the surprises—in modulation, dynamic contrast and tone-colour—arouse expectation, expectation remains unfulfilled. The composer shows no capacity to organize his multifarious material, nor was he much concerned to do so. His overture was to be chattered to rather than listened to. If it created a general feeling of ebullience, it sufficed.

There is no real difference in principle between many of Vivaldi's finales to his concertos, an Italian operatic overture, and the quick movements of the innumerable works which, after about 1740, appeared in Austria under the designation of symphony. Sometimes the link with the concerto grosso is direct, since the symphonies are in four movements, slow, quick, slow, quick. Only the rapid movements are in the new popular manner, though the slow movements are becoming pretty rather than heroic. Sometimes the symphonies have three movements, quick, slow, quick, in the fashion favoured by the Italian theatre; again, the two allegros are in *buffo* style, with a prettified aria in the middle. At other times symphonies may have five or even six movements, since reminiscences of the suite suggest the inclusion of more than one dance movement, either in binary form or in ternary style, like the minuet and trio.

The four movements into which the symphony finally settled down involved a medley of all these elements. First movement allegro came from the *buffo* overture, though it might still be prefaced by a slow introduction derived from the concerto grosso and from French heroic opera: this introduction was habitually preserved by Haydn, exceptionally by Mozart and Beethoven. Slow movements were always derived from the operatic aria. The third movement, the survival from the dance suite, became traditionally a minuet, though its aristocratic elegance gave way to a rustic vigour. The finale might again be in the *buffo* binary style which we have come to call 'sonata', though it too might betray a dance origin by being in rondo— a symmetrical tune intermittently repeated, with varying episodes between each repetition. Whatever form their symphonies assumed, the Austrian composers had found in the Italian *buffo* overture and the popular elements of the concerto grosso just the materials they needed to create a 'democratic' instrumental style. These Italianate features could easily be reconciled with the urban and rustic popular music of their own country.

If one listens to the music of Johann Stamitz [1717–1757], who was an Austrian by birth, but worked for Rameau's patron, Le Riche de la Pouplinière, and for the Elector Palatine at Mannheim, one can observe how he is using theatrical elements to create an easily intelligible dramatic style in purely instrumental terms; one contemporary chronicler significantly remarked that Stamitz makes the instruments sing *'so that one forgets that such things as voices exist'*. In addition to the new type of melody and rhythmic accompaniment, Stamitz introduces many devices intended to excite and astonish his audience. In his orchestration he concentrates all his attention on getting the tune across. The harpsichord continuo, which in baroque music supplied the harmonic background to the interweaving melodies, disappears; ostinato string figures and sustained notes on the horns now fill in the middle parts since melodic definition in any part except the top is unimportant. The crescendo and diminuendo, tremolos, sudden changes of dynamics, marks of expression and nuance—all the effects which in Rameau's operas had grown from theatrical exigencies (such as earthquakes), become an end in themselves. The bouncing upward arpeggio figures 'across the strings' (known as the Mannheim sky-rocket), the twiddling figurations (the Mannheim birdies), the long crescendo over a reiterated bass, to which the audience rose to its feet as one man (the Mannheim steam-roller) became famous or notorious all over Europe. Stamitz vigorously expressed the feelings of a growing public which had been unrepresented in the aristocratic art of the previous generation. The bourgeois forces in the Age of Enlightenment knew that the future was with them. Their self-confidence is reflected in the jaunty vitality of Stamitz's music.

Stamitz's recipe for excitement may seem to us, as it would have seemed to Bach or Couperin, a little crude; yet, since he was a composer of personality and talent, the recipe worked. It was, however, fatally easy to imitate; and the thousands of rococo symphonies that appeared in the second half of the eighteenth century are a phenomenon comparable with commercial dance music to-day, except that, being less mechanized, they were less synthetic. If the formulae were mass-produced, they were at least in no particular, rather than in offensive, taste. The contemplation of these countless symphonic corpses is the more depressing because depressing is the last thing they were meant to be; nothing is more dismal than jokes that have

lost their savour, or thrills that have become routine. Even in
the eighteenth century, however, truly creative spirits began
to feel that this eupeptic middle-class style could not be permanently satisfying. Their sympathies were with Feeling and
the Enlightenment; but they wanted to express themselves at a
deeper level than would be likely to appeal to a mass audience.
The new aristocracy will depend neither on birth nor on
acquired riches, but on innate ability and sensitivity; Tom,
Dick or Harry might be the architect of a new world. So there
grew up, alongside the popular manner, a style of Sensibility
which finds its most distinguished expression in the work of
J. S. Bach's most talented son, Carl Philipp Emanuel [1714–
1788]. To his music there are two aspects which are at once
independent and complementary.

Consider the first movement of the F minor Sonata from the
series which he composed in 1763, not for *hoi polloi*, but 'for
Connoisseurs and Amateurs' (amateurs in the strict sense, of
course). This is in orthodox binary form, like most of his father's
dance pieces, and has no contrasting second subject. The initial
figure is a bounding Mannheim sky-rocket (Ex. 3); and the

Ex. 3. C.P.E. Bach: Sonata in F minor

interest of the music lies not in the themes, which as melody
do not exist, but in the tonal conflict which is generated from
them. The point of the movement is the dramatic crisis which
occurs in the middle section—we can now legitimately call it
a development—on the surprising chord of F flat major: a
'Neapolitan' relationship to the minor of the relative (A flat)
(Ex. 4).* Here the popular manner of Stamitz has not lost its

Ex. 4. C.P.E. Bach: Sonata in F minor

* The 'Neapolitan' cadence substitutes a minor for a major sixth over the sub-
dominant root, in the conventional progression from subdominant to dominant to
tonic. The 'minorish' feeling of a cadence in the minor key is thus greatly intensified.
Neapolitan opera composers were especially partial to this harmonic piquancy in
moments of dramatic pathos.   See Part II.

vitality; but it has gained a personal urgency. C. P. E. Bach reveals that the surprises and explosive contrasts of the new style become significant only when they achieve a new kind of order; and this order, depending on oppositions of tonality and harmony, is inherently dramatic. The drama is no longer projected on to a stage; it is embodied in self-contained instrumental form.

C. P. E. Bach's creation of dramatic order within the popular manner can thus be reconciled with the mode of Sensibility which he explores in his slow movements. The remarkable E flat largo from the second sonata of the fifth book (1784) achieves by way of its broken, limply ornamented melody, its chromatic harmony and enharmonic transitions a brooding, introspective pathos (Ex. 5); it could be adequately realized

Ex. 5. C.P.E. Bach: Adagio from Sonata in B♭

only on an instrument, such as the new piano, capable of nuance and tonal gradation. One can see a similar quality in his church music, as compared with that of his father. J. S. Bach uses operatic techniques in his cantatas without ceasing to be liturgical in spirit: acutely dissonant harmony and elaborately expressive ornamentation are absorbed into the flow of the lines. In the church music of Carl Philipp harmonic and decorative pathos take—to use an appropriate metaphor—the centre of the stage, disrupting continuity of line. The effect of the music is powerful, but more subjective, less devotional, than J. S. Bach's. This is especially evident in the intimate solo songs or *Geistliche Lieder*, like the beautiful *Tag und Nacht, du Heil der Frommen*. There is no melodic or harmonic element in the song which could not, considered by itself, be found in the music of J. S. Bach; but whereas in J. S. Bach the weeping appoggiaturas

and stabbing Neapolitan chords would intensify a continuously
evolving line, in C. P. E. Bach they are the essence of the music.
There is a comparable distinction between the texts set by J. S.
and C. P. E. Bach respectively. J. S. Bach's texts tend to deal
dramatically but impersonally with liturgical dogma or biblical
history. The poems of Carl Philipp's *Geistliche Lieder* deal with
the relationship between God and Myself.

The music of another of Bach's sons, Wilhelm Friedmann
[1710–1784], suggests a similar comparison. Consider, for
instance, J. S. Bach's E flat minor Prelude from Book I of *The
Well-tempered Clavier* alongside W. F. Bach's Polonaise in the
same key. Both pieces are in binary form, and intensely passionate. But in J. S. Bach's Prelude the dissonant harmony reinforces the wide soaring and declension of the melodic line:
while in W. F. Bach's Polonaise the melody is broken, fragmentary, subservient to details of harmony, ornamentation,
and sequential modulation. J. S. Bach's piece sounds like a
Passion aria: the suffering is Christ's, which happens also to be
Bach's and ours because Christ died for us. W. F. Bach's piece
is a passion aria, which is about his own suffering, because he
was an eccentric and a misfit who became, before his time, the
typical artist of romanticism.

The creation of a Popular style and a style of Sensibility
means the beginning of a split between artists' music and
'people's' music. We can observe an interesting example of this
in the career of another of Bach's sons, Johann Christian
[1735–1782]. He started his musical life as a composer of
Italian opera; after he settled in London as a composer of
instrumental music for the drawing-room, he was normally
content to exploit rococo elegance in a manner that was superficially entertaining. His tunes are pretty if short-winded,
his texture pleasing, his harmonies and modulations mildly
titillating to the senses without being disturbing. But he also
wrote a few works, notably a piano sonata in C minor, which
hint at a different and a deeper world. The first movement
opens with dissonant suspensions, accompanied by a surging
arpeggio bass, which suggest the liturgical grandeur of Johann
Sebastian; while the second movement begins as a fugue which
has something of the power of J. S. Bach and of the dramatic
energy of Carl Philipp. The surging arpeggios of the prelude
degenerate, at the appearance of the second subject, into an

Alberti figuration* as footling as it is inconsistent; and the fugue soon relapses into comically automatic sequences. But though Johann Christian was no longer able to realize the potentialities of the baroque idiom, he still respected it. Such is the way Bach would write—he once said, speaking of this sonata—if he did not have to address himself to the children.

This must be the first instance of a composer admitting that the style which he adopted for commercial reasons was distinct from that in which he would naturally express himself. This 'split personality' was to have far-reaching consequences later on, and we shall have much to say about it. For the moment, we are concerned with the way in which the Popular style and the style of Sensibility interacted on one another to produce the mature sonata idiom of the Age of Enlightenment. We have already indicated how in the sonatas of C. P. E. Bach the dualism between the two modes came to exist within the works themselves; we may even see a hint of it in W. F. Bach's E minor Polonaise, which begins with a lyrical, J. S. Bach-like cantilena and then introduces an abruptly contrasted arpeggio motive that fulfils, within the space of a few bars, the function of a second subject, with a miniature 'development' after the double bar. This conflict grows increasingly intense throughout the sonata forms of the eighteenth and nineteenth centuries, for it is related to a conflict in society itself. In tracing its course through the work of Haydn, Mozart, Beethoven, Schubert to Bruckner, Brahms, and Mahler, we shall observe that although Tradition and Revolution are variously interrelated in their music, the thread of a creative principle links both their art and their lives.

---

* A keyboard device whereby the player's left hand spreads out chords into rhythmic arpeggio figures, usually rotating on the bass note of the harmony.

U

HAYDN

JOSEPH HAYDN [1732–1809] was a revolutionary composer without conscious volition, perhaps even without conscious awareness. His crucial position in European music is related not only to the nature of his genius, but also to his mere longevity. When he was born in 1732, J. S. Bach had still to write many of his greatest works; when he died, in 1809, Beethoven had already begun to create some of the music which marked the end of the classical sonata as Haydn and Mozart had conceived it. He was writing music himself as early as 1750; he was still vigorously creative in the first decade of the nineteenth century.

We think of Haydn as a representative of an urbane civilization, and rightly so. Yet we misunderstand his society if we fail to see how closely it was interlinked with the countryside. His parents were musical in that they were country people who spontaneously made music, singing to the harp. Haydn's early consciousness was permeated with folk music, as one aspect of the everyday activities of an Austrian village. His tranquillity of soul was based partly on the peasant's simple acceptance of nature, rather than on the romantic cult of Nature as a refuge from humanity.

When, as a boy, he moved to Vienna to the choir school at St. Stephen's Cathedral, he did not lose this awareness of country life, for Vienna was a small city by our standards. If it was small, however, it was highly sophisticated and cosmopolitan. Traders of all nations and constellations of Italian singers and composers abounded in this stimulating, glittering world. If it was already corrupt, the young Haydn was emotionally too direct to be aware of its corruption, as Beethoven and Schubert were later to be.

At St. Stephen's, Haydn would have become familiar with a certain amount of counterpoint, in the old-fashioned manner of Fux [1660–1741]; his brother Michael [1737–1806], who was primarily an ecclesiastical composer, never lost touch with this style throughout his career. But most of the music Joseph sang and played would have been 'modern', in spirit as well as in date: and most contemporary church music was operatic in style, since Italian opera was the central expression of rococo sensibility. The difference between baroque art and rococo art may perhaps be summed up by saying that in baroque art the ornamentation is an integral part of the 'expression', closely related to structure: whereas in rococo art—whether visual or aural—ornamentation tends to be an end in itself, a delight in profusion and sensory adventure, related loosely, if at all, to structure. Yet the Viennese, in Haydn's day, were right to worship God according to their own lights, which were brilliant, if unstable: for they had no others. They were not mystical or devotional; it was well that they did not pretend to be so. Their very frivolity helped Haydn to discover his own profundity. Even after he left St. Stephen's, his training remained Italianate. He became accompanist for singing lessons given by an Italian opera composer and singer, Niccola Porpora [1686–1766]; receiving in return a modest stipend and lessons in vocal composition.

But the greater part of Haydn's working life was spent outside Vienna as household musician to the Esterházy family. Living in seclusion in this dream-palace in the marshes, Haydn was a feudal dependant to several generations of Esterházys. He wore livery, dined with the servants, produced quantities of music for the entertainment of the court, and directed the band and singers in the performance of it. He was a servant of autocracy, as the baroque musicians had been; unlike Mozart, he never consciously resented his position. Such troubles as he had were personal—his marriage was unhappy, and his belated love-affair with one of the singers could not offer the secure serenity he needed. In his professional existence, he was comfortable and uncomplaining. He was able to compose music as a full-time occupation, and to hear it performed; even his remoteness from the centre of civilization had compensations, for, as he said: "My Prince was always satisfied with my works; I not only had the encouragement of constant approval, but as conductor of an orchestra I could make experiments. I was cut off from the world, there was no one to confuse me, and so I was forced to become original."

No doubt, in this 'originality', there was an undercurrent of

revolutionary resentment, of which Haydn was no more aware
than his master. Certainly, after he had become an international
celebrity, Haydn relinquished his post as household musician
and became a free-lance. Lully, court composer to Louis XIV,
also came of artisan stock, but he would never have said with
Haydn: "I have had converse with emperors, kings, and great
princes and have heard many flattering praises from them;
but I do not wish to live on a familiar footing with such persons,
and I prefer people of my own class." It is significant that Haydn
formally entered the Masonic Order only after he had left the
Esterházys' service; and that when, at the instigation of the
impresario Salomon, he made his triumphant visits to London,
he took with him his greatest symphonies and brought back,
from a study of Handel and English oratorio, a new conception
of religious music. Henceforth he was able in his church music
to express, not liturgical dogma, but his deepest ethical
convictions.

Indeed, Haydn's long development may as a whole be described as a gradual discovery of his own nature. In his earliest
works he is preoccupied with formal problems: how convin-
cingly to integrate his heterogeneous material—the Mannheim
quirks and quiddities—by means of a developed sense of
tonality. He is not at first greatly concerned about the significance of his structures as human experience: so that the music
is Entertainment in no discreditable sense. One can see this in
his approach to both string quartet and symphony, which to
begin with were for him interchangeable.

The most important form in baroque chamber music had
been the trio sonata, as the concerto grosso had been in music
for a band. The trio sonata was again a distillation of operatic
conventions into instrumental terms. The two sustained singing
voices of the solo violins were poised over the string bass and the
harmonic filling in of the continuo instrument; this might be
organ or harpsichord, according to whether the sonatas were
to be played in church or at home.

Whatever its subsequent development, the birth of the string
quartet was once more a democratic process; music moved not
merely from church and court to the chamber or living-room,
but even into the streets. Vienna was a-jingle with serenading
parties playing in the open air. If this music was to be effective,
its style had to be even simpler than that of *opera buffa*. It called

for perky tunes at the top, easily recognizable rhythms, and a
rudimentary accompaniment filling in the harmony with
repeated notes and arpeggios, since it was hardly practical to
carry around a continuo instrument such as harpsichord or
piano. These *quadri*—pieces in four parts of which only one had
melodic significance—could be played either on a quartet of
solo instruments, or by small bands with the parts doubled.
Even in the solo quartet medium Haydn often writes in only
two parts, each doubled at the octave—a primitive technique
which can sound delightfully fresh in open-air performance.

Haydn himself composed a large number of trio
sonatas, usually involving the baritone, an obsolete stringed
instrument favoured by Prince Esterházy. These charming,
trivial pieces were a *galant* simplification of baroque style;
Haydn's first quartets differ from them mainly in discarding all
traces of the heroic. These divertimenti, cassations, and serenades, the earliest of which were composed around 1750, still
show the influence of the suite. They are always in the major
key, with five dance-like movements, including two minuets.
The trios of the minuets, which are peasant Ländler* rather
than courtly dances, are sometimes in the tonic minor; dominant, sub-dominant, or relative are occasionally employed for
the slow movements. While almost all the sonata movements are
different, and diversified in their material, Haydn makes no
more attempt at thematic development than did the stock
composer of *buffo* overtures. The slow movements are usually
operatic arias sung by the first violin to an accompaniment of
pizzicato chords or the like. They are not convincing, for
Haydn seems to have relinquished the grand manner without
knowing what to put in its place. The unequivocally 'low'
movements are the best, and much more stimulating in performance than they look on paper. Haydn was a practical
musician, who wrote music to be heard, in given conditions.
The crudities of his first works in part reflect the change in
music's social status.

Haydn was composing these works—whether one regards
them as rudimentary quartets or rudimentary symphonies—
between 1750 and 1760. It cannot be said that he approaches
Stamitz in fire or precision of effect: nor that he adds anything

---

* An Austrian country dance in slow waltz time, usually in regular two-bar
periods and with simple (mainly tonic and dominant) harmony.

substantial to his other models—the Austrians Monn [?1717–
1750], Wagenseil [1715–1777] and Richter [1709–1789], and
the Italian Sammartini [1701–1775]. But it is not long before he
begins to acquire character as a symphonist. The twenty-
second Symphony, known as 'The Philosopher', is especially
interesting in that its transitional position—half-way between
baroque and rococo—is clearly evident. Its four-movement
structure—slow-quick-moderate-quick—follows that of the
baroque concerto grosso, with a peasant Ländler minuet substituted for the aristocratic sarabande. Moreover, Haydn's
method of handling the orchestra recalls the chamber style of
the baroque rather than the modern symphonic manner of
Stamitz; the wind instruments, in particular, are given solo
parts to play.

The first movement is grave and austere, an archaic *canto
fermo* which seems to look backwards to Bach and forwards
to Mozart's Masonic works—a significant re-creation of outmoded techniques. The second movement, on the other hand,
is rococo and symphonic, briskly popular, but without Stamitz's
energy in key contrasts, since Haydn allows himself no contrasting subject matter and almost no time for development. The
minuet is a rustic Ländler, which introduces a vestigial counterpoint in the trio. Counterpoint, we have seen, was rigorously
avoided by the early symphonists, who wished to make the
easiest possible appeal. Haydn reintroduces it, not as a basic
principle of construction, as did Bach, but to avoid empty
passage-work and thus to assist his search for symphonic
coherence. We shall note a much more important development
of this in his and Mozart's mature music. The last movement
returns to *buffo* style, with an episode in the minor which is at
once witty and dramatic.

This is by no means the only one of Haydn's early symphonies
in which he attempts to enrich the musical significance of the
quadri by a compromise with old-fashioned techniques. In
Symphony No. 31 ('*Auf dem Anstand mit dem Hornsignal*') he treats
the wind instruments in the concertante manner of the solo
group of the concerto grosso: though he emulates Vivaldi
in creating by means of them sound pictures of everyday life,
rather than a refined, relatively abstract music for the court.
The quick movements, replete with shooting scales and repeated notes, and even a faint suggestion of a contrasting

'lyrical' idea, are much more dramatic than the comparable movements in 'The Philosopher'. The slow movement has difficult concertante parts for violin and 'cello, with four obbligato horns. The seductive melody sounds like an Italian operatic duet, its sophistication modified by a popular Viennese lilt; Italian elegance has come within the reach of ordinary rustic folk. The presto conclusion to the final variations has a Stamitz-like ferocity, and is full of surprises both in figuration and in scoring.

These two symphonies, and the triptych describing country life at Esterházy called *Le Matin, Le Midi,* and *Le Soir,* were composed during the 1760s. Despite their originality and their musical substance, they still come into the category of the 'entertainment' symphony: they are half-way between symphony and serenade. With the approach to the 1770s a remarkable change comes over Haydn's music. There are a number of external reasons that help to account for this. He may have become familiar with the anticipatory romanticism of the poets and prose writers who were known collectively as the *Sturm und Drang* group; he had certainly embarked on his love-affair with Luigia Polzelli; and he had certainly made a renewed study of the music of C. P. E. Bach. But these are only superficial causes. The real reason was the complex of impulses which had given rise to the fashion for 'Storm and Stress' in the first place: that had prompted C. P. E. Bach to create a a music based on conflict between Sensibility and popular feeling. In any case, in his music written during the '70s Haydn exploits the dramatic potentialities inherent in rococo style. In the G minor Symphony, No. 39, for instance, all the stock rococo features—shooting scales, repeated notes on the horns, sudden breaks, contrasting dynamics, dissonant appoggiaturas—are used not as a pleasing titillation of the senses, but for their dramatic intensity (Ex. 6). The panting, repeated

Ex. 6. Haydn: Symphony No. 39 in G minor

quavers of the opening are almost hysterical, while the whirling scales of the last movement (also in sonata form) have a frightening energy. The music is fiercer, if less melancholy,

than Mozart's G minor mood; indeed, there is little lyricism in
the whole work. The modulations jump to extravagant keys;
though Haydn still likes to derive his second subjects from his
first. In opposition to rococo variety, he feels a need to give his
music cohesion. Seeking unity in diversity, he relates his subject
groups ever more intimately, without sacrificing the dramatic
tension which we have seen to be the essence of sonata style.
The majority of these stormful symphonies are in minor keys
or, if in the major, in outlandish keys, such as B. Many of them
have descriptive titles, '*La Lamentazione*', '*La Passione*', 'The
Farewell'; all the slow movements show the influence of the
affetuoso manner of C. P. E. Bach.

The tempestuous features in these works strike one's attention
immediately; one should not overlook the fact that they also
represent a significant development in Haydn's humour. The
funny elements in his earlier work were in the main a simple
buffo frivolity. Such comic movements as occur in the *Sturm
und Drang* works tend—in an abrupt contrast of key, a melodic
ellipsis, a sudden pause or contraction of rhythm—to startle as
much as to amuse. Procedures that may in some contexts be
drama are in other contexts wit: an intense levity that entails
a recognition of 'other modes of experience that are possible',
and therefore an awareness of instability. Consider the approach
to the coda of the presto in his Symphony No. 52 in C minor
(Ex. 7). All through Haydn's mature music—and in a more

Ex. 7. Haydn: Symphony No. 52 (Presto)

poignant way in Mozart's also—one finds this precariousness: the sudden defeat of expectation, the interruption
of a norm of behaviour, whether of tonality or of melodic,
harmonic, or rhythmic formula. One does not usually find this

quality in composers who lived before the Age of Reason, in an age of Faith, whether in God or the State. Bach and Handel are sometimes comic, seldom if ever witty.

At about the same time as he was composing these first 'Storm and Stress' works, Haydn was also achieving a genuine quartet style. His opus 9 and opus 17 appeared in 1769 and 1771 respectively. Both collections—especially the quartets in minor keys—show signs of the conflagration of *Sturm und Drang*; while for the first time Haydn writes for each instrument as an independent entity. It would be impossible to play these works as band pieces, for they are already, in Goethe's words, a dialogue of 'four sensible people conversing with one another'. The key contrasts are much more enterprising than in the earlier quartets, and the developments, instead of being perfunctory, tend to be longer than the expositions. The D minor quartet of opus 9 and the C minor of opus 17, with their chromaticisms, sforzandi, syncopations, and passionate declamatory passages in particular suggest the influence of C. P. E. Bach, while attaining a more convincing continuity of line and of dramatic evolution.

The 'Sun' quartets, opus 20, dating from the following year, 1772, intensify all these features and add another, which we have already referred to in the symphonies. Many of them have fugal finales; and in all of them counterpoint is used in a manner remote from the conventionalities of *style galant*. The F minor quartet ends with a fierce fugue on a theme that was almost a stage-property of the baroque—the two most famous examples are 'And with his stripes' from Handel's *Messiah* and the A minor fugue from Book II of Bach's *Forty-eight*. The re-creation of the baroque fugue was not, however, the solution Haydn was seeking. He wanted to give the quartet dignity and coherence, and counterpoint was a means to that end; but the counterpoint he wanted to evolve was not baroque, but symphonic, and therefore reconcilable with the pathos of a movement such as this quartet's opening allegro. Here the second theme, though related to the first, is unmistakably also a lyrical contrast, and the development, with its remote modulations, is as long as it is dramatic. The recapitulation is itself modified and extended; and a final consummatory development occurs in the strange coda, with its remote transitions (Ex. 8).

Haydn's phase of overt passion and protest did not, however, last long. In his music of the 1780s, passion is absorbed into acceptance; and while his own creative development was the fundamental reason for this, the example of Mozart had

Ex. 8. Haydn: Quartet opus 20 No. 5

something to do with it. The mature Mozart taught Haydn how both counterpoint and themes of lyrical contour could be adapted to the dramatic purposes of the symphony. The D minor Symphony, No. 80, shows Haydn in the process of discovery. Apart from the wittily syncopated finale, all the movements have melodies which are more Italianate, lyrical and Mozartian than those of Haydn's previous works. But Haydn has not yet learned to create a lyricism appropriate to his own kind of symphonic thought. Here the contrasts of mood between the lyrical phrases are queerly abrupt, in the operatic adagio even more than in the allegro: so that the music reminds one of Mozart's slightly revered D minor mood without the resolving power of his cantabile melody. The work is enigmatic and disturbing: and a critical stage in Haydn's career.

When, in the sequence of symphonies he wrote for his first visit to England, Haydn finally achieved his synthesis of protest with acceptance, he had solved the problem of writing themes which have lyrical amplitude; which are at the same time susceptible of treatment in sonata style; and which no longer sound in the least like Mozart. The search for unity in diversity, which must be attained without impairing dramatic tension, here reaches its apotheosis. This remains true though Haydn's treatment of sonata form in his mature works is unpredictable, no two movements being quite alike in structure.

If one compares Symphony No. 104 in D with the earlier

symphonies the most immediately striking difference is the power and serenity of the opening theme, which is a singing melody, moving mainly by step, rather than a rhythmic 'motive' (Ex. 9). The second subject is a modified version of the

Ex. 9. Haydn: Symphony No. 104

first; out of it grows a little rhythmic figure in the codetta* of the exposition (Ex. 10). The development is based mainly on this little motive, combined with fragments of the main themes.

Ex. 10. Haydn: Symphony No. 104

A tremendous dramatic intensity is generated without disturbing the continuity of the texture. In the recapitulation the material is creatively modified; it has been born afresh in the course of the development. Indeed, one might say that Haydn's mature movements are all development, which starts in the exposition, since the second subject is a development of the first. Whereas Bach and Handel—in their different ways—are concerned with states of Being, Haydn's sonata movements already deal with growth and change—with Becoming.

The andante is based on one of those measured, spacious melodies which are the unique creation of Haydn's later years (Ex. 11). Their lyricism is utterly different from Mozart's:

Ex. 11 Haydn: Symphony No. 104

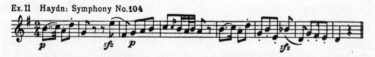

non-chromatic, less operatic; more homely, one might say, if the tunes were not also sublime. Yet this movement, which opens with a theme so tranquil of soul, turns out to be a dramatic sonata movement, with weird modulations in the development, proceeding from G to D flat, and home by way of C sharp minor and F sharp minor and major. Here Haydn has

* A coda in a classical sonata movement is a peroration which rounds off, and gives finality to, the recapitulation. A codetta is a 'little coda' which occurs, not at the end of a movement, but at the end of a section of a movement—usually the exposition.

indeed attained a new resolution of the conflict between the artist and his world; and it is not extravagant to say that Haydn's true religion is enshrined in this prophetic music. He celebrates the Enlightenment's Discovery of Man. Democratic man had to find himself in order to rebuild civilization in the light of Reason: thus his passions were important, but were not the be-all and end-all of existence. They were a means towards the Apollonian equilibrium which became the classical ideal: which is epitomized in Haydn's late symphonic allegros and hymn-like andantes, as it is in Mozart's Masonic style. It is present too in the apparently slighter scherzo and finale of this Symphony No. 104; for the minuet, with its sudden breaks and trills, attains an almost Beethovenian power, and the rustic joviality of the finale, with folk-like theme and bagpipe drone, grows through its symphonically developing counterpoint into a paean of praise. It is at once comic and majestic.

If Mozart's example helped Haydn to reach maturity as a symphonist, Mozart admitted that the appearance of Haydn's opus 33 was a turning-point in his own development. Haydn said that in these quartets he was composing in 'an entirely new and special manner'. This was not strictly true, for we have seen that there was already plenty of 'thematic development' in the quartets of the 'Storm and Stress' period. It is true, however, that by his opus 33 Haydn has learned how to achieve concentration in sonata style, using counterpoint as a means to an end, without returning to baroque techniques. The quartets written in the '80s, like the symphonies of the same period, show a Mozartian leaning towards a more lyrical type of melody: in slow movements, for instance, Haydn tends to abandon sonata form in favour of variations, or a simple song tune in ternary form, with a minor episode in the middle. Even the most melancholy of the quartets comprising opus 54 or 64, such as the F sharp minor or the B minor, have not the fever-ishness of the 'Storm and Stress' years; they are mellowed by their lyricism. On the other hand, the wit of the comic pieces is enriched by touches of Mozartian chromaticism in the harmony.

Haydn attains his Apollonian equilibrium in the last series of quartets, opus 71, 74, 76, and 77. If one compares his last completed quartet, the F major of opus 77, with one of the early *quadri* or even the well-known 'Serenade' quartet from opus

3, it seems as though the composer has not so much developed a technique as created a new world of thought and feeling. As in Symphony No. 104, the finale is a superb piece of symphonic counterpoint; and the first movement opens with a theme rich, ample, cantabile. The second subject is a creative development from the first, but in consolatory inversion. The development, again like that of the allegro of the symphony, is based not on the cantabile melody, but on a rhythmic figure which appears in the codetta of the exposition. The repeated quavers of rococo convention are no longer cheerfully footling; nor are they frenzied, as they were in the stormy and stressful works. They become, as the music modulates flatwards through remote keys and with an ever acuter dissonance, pregnant with wonder and mystery (Ex. 12) : so that the movement can be succeeded

Ex.12. Haydn: Quartet opus 77 No.2.

inevitably by the hymn-like andante with variations. The melody remains almost unaltered, being an entity complete in itself; the variations are arabesques embroidered around it. The same is true of the treatment of the most celebrated of all these great andante tunes—that from the C major quartet of opus 76. In this case the tune is in fact a hymn, for it is the most noble national anthem ever written.

The development of Haydn's piano sonatas follows a pattern almost identical with his symphonies and quartets. A little work like the A major of 1762 is in the orthodox binary structure of Bach's or Handel's dances. It is quite different in spirit, however, because it has almost no melody. Its appeal depends on its superfices—its twirls and twiddles. Then Haydn discovers how to extract drama from these frolics. For instance, in the F major Sonata of 1776 the first movement has nothing worth calling a melody. There is a rhythmic figure (tum-ti-tum): a percussive series of repeated notes in the bass: and some pathetic sighing appoggiaturas: all these being presented in the tonic key and its relative minor (Ex. 13). After a modulation to the dominant we have two other little figures, one based on a rapid arpeggio, the other on a scale (Ex. 14). Thus instead of baroque unity and continuity we have contrasting and heterogeneous material associated with two different key centres. The

Ex.13. Haydn: Sonata in F

Ex.14. Ibid.

structure of the piece is no longer the unfolding of melody, but the conflict between two groups of material and between different keys. The development begins with some sensationally rapid modulations; all the material is presented in startling oppositions of key, often with false starts and changes of direction (is there a faintly comic undertone to the equivocal use of the natural or flat second?). When the recapitulation happens we can at last appreciate the dramatic significance of the apparently innocuous fragments of tune and rhythm from which we had started. This dramatic purpose is still more marked in those sonatas which, like the fierce B minor, are directly influenced by the mood of 'Storm and Stress'.

In the late sonatas, particularly those written after the first English visit, both the themes and the keyboard writing acquire a new ripeness; again the themes tend to be closely interrelated. The great sonata in E flat, with its lyrical adagio in E major (approached as a kind of Neapolitan F flat) is a worthy pianistic counterpart of the London symphonies and the opus 76 and 77 quartets. In sonatas, symphonies, and quartets equally the dramatic urgency is increased rather than diminished, as compared with earlier works; only the drama is now resolved in a structure radiant with light. Apollonian order implies a new kind of belief. Haydn's God was not the mystical divinity of Bach, nor the Lord of earthly glory of Handel; but all his later music is religious in the sense that it reflects the beliefs that had meaning for him—an ethical humanism based on reason and the love of created nature. The development of his own ostensibly religious music shows him gradually discovering, in ecclesiastical terms, the religion that is implicit in his later instrumental music.

In his youth, Haydn composed a great deal of church music on commission, in the accepted rococo style. To object to the frivolity of this style is irrelevant; as we have seen, it was appropriate to the garishly decorated churches, and to the spirit of the people who worshipped with its help. In the sixteenth century, church motet and secular madrigal were basically the same in idiom, and the liturgical manner dominated the secular. In Haydn's day it was the other way round; the opera-house dominated the church to such a degree that even ecclesiastical buildings began to look like opera-houses. The style of Haydn's early masses is related to the secular operatic cantata and to the concerto grosso, with solo voices and choir fulfilling much the same functions as the concertino and ripieno instruments. One of his first pieces, a *Salve Regina* for soprano, contralto, two violins, and bass, is treated like a baroque trio sonata. It was written while he was a pupil of Porpora, and pays Italianate homage to his master.

Haydn felt no qualms about the frivolity of the masses he composed in the 1750s. On the contrary, he revived the first mass of all quite late in his life, considering that it merited the addition of wind parts: "What I particularly like about this little work", he said, "is its tunefulness and a certain youthful fire." But Haydn regarded these early masses in much the same way as he regarded his cassations and serenades for instruments. His carelessness in setting the text is significant: hardly ever does he attempt to interpret the words; sometimes he makes nonsense of them. Although late in life he was profoundly shocked at the imputation that he was not a pious Catholic, he never had any interest in the mysticism of Catholic dogma. In his youth he was content to say: "Since God has given me a cheerful heart, He will forgive me for serving Him cheerfully. Whenever I think of the dear Lord, I have to laugh. My heart jumps for joy in my breast." When in his mature years he discovered the nature of his own faith, it was profound enough, but it had nothing to do with mysticism or dogma.

During the 1770s the passions of 'Storm and Stress' effect a

change in Haydn's church music comparable with that in his
instrumental works. Two pieces contain the essence of this
transformation: the *Stabat Mater*, in which C. P. E. Bach-like
chromaticisms, sighs, syncopations, and sforzandi are obviously
appropriate to the text; and *Tobias*, ostensibly a return to the
baroque oratorio which resembles the more symphonic style of
Rameau's or Gluck's operas, rather than the monumental
grandeur of Handel. Both choruses and orchestral writing are
impressively dramatic.

During the early 1780s Haydn composed a number of large-
scale festival masses. Though these hardly suggest the direct
influence of Mozart, they are Mozartian in that their theatrical
manner is no longer a cheerful noise existing in its own right,
like a symphony or a serenade: the music now underlines the
meaning of the words. At least this is true of movements such as
the Crucifixus of the 'Mariazell' Mass, in which Haydn can
regard Christ not as a superhuman divinity, but as a man,
suffering. In 1783, however, the progressive Emperor Joseph
banned complicated church music; and Haydn wrote no more
officially liturgical music for fourteen years. The only exception
to this is the wonderful *Seven Last Words from the Cross*, a series of
orchestral meditations on Christ's words which Haydn composed, at the instigation of Boccherini, for performance on
Good Friday at Cadiz Cathedral. These seven adagios all, like
the andante of Symphony No. 104, combine a sublime lyrical
serenity with intense tonal drama. The themes are, however,
more Italianate than the Masonic hymns of Haydn's last years.
Perhaps for this reason the music has a meditative ecstasy
which makes it seem more Catholic in spirit than any music
Haydn wrote.

However this may be, when he turned to church music again
his approach had been transformed—partly by his experience
as a symphonist, partly by what he had learned, on his visits to
England, of Handel and English oratorio. He had no moral
objection to the theatrical manner; he merely felt that it was no
longer capable of expressing his deepest thoughts and feelings.
Handel himself had re-created heroic baroque conventions in a
more middle-classical manner; Haydn, in *The Creation*, fuses
Handelian oratorio with the dramatic thrust of his own symphonic style. Rococo affectations disappear; instead, Haydn
celebrates ethical humanism and the glory of God in Nature.

Baron von Swieten's text was a re-hash of a re-hash by Linley of Milton; it is utterly un-Miltonic in that it divests God of spirituality and man of the sense of sin. "An object must be found", said von Swieten, "for music which, by its fervour, its universal sufficiency and perspicuity, may take the place of the pious emotions of former days"; and he turned God into a working mechanic, the story of the Creation into a Masonic parable. 'Now vanish before thy holy beams The spirits of the ancient Night.' Light triumphs through Reason, darkness is vanquished; but what makes the victory significant is precisely mankind's 'fervour, sufficiency and perspicuity'. Haydn's genius, in this case, stands for mankind.

The Creation falls into three parts. The first describes the birth of Order from Chaos; the second deals with Created Nature; and the third with human love (the Adam and Eve story). From this account it is clear that the story of *The Creation* is simply an explicit statement of the experience we have seen to be implicit in all Haydn's mature symphonies, sonatas, and quartets. The creation of Order from Chaos—Unity from Diversity—is the impulse behind the marvellous prologue to *The Creation*, in which the lucidity of C major emerges from the mysteriously veiled tonality and the chains of dissonant suspensions, with their romantic orchestration. It is also, we have seen, the motive force behind Haydn's greatest symphonic music. The famous blaze of C major at the words 'Let there be light' implies a large-scale symphonic architecture, for such an assertion of tonality has point only in reference to the ambiguities that have preceded it; one cannot recognize order unless one has first seen chaos. Similarly, the realistic portrayal of Nature in the second part is an extension of the simple acceptance of Nature as a background to human life which we have commented on in the symphonies: Nature is to be valued for its relation to human conduct, not romantically for its non-humanity. Similarly, again, in instrumental music no less than in the third part of *The Creation*, it is through the agency of human love that life is redeemed. So *The Creation*, like creation itself, forms a circle and ends at the point where it began. Life is perpetual renewal; the alternation of Light and Darkness, Order and Chaos, is perennial—as Beethoven was to discover in a more deeply subjective sense. Thus Haydn and the Enlightenment inherited the Christian doctrine of redemption,

while believing that the agent of redemption was man become
God, not God become man.

After returning from his first trip to England, Haydn
composed several more masses for the Catholic Church. The
spirit of them is distinct from that of the early masses. The
rococo perkiness has gone. Instead, we have the dramatic power
of Haydn the symphonist, reconciled with the monumental
counterpart of the baroque: and thus translated into the relative
impersonality of liturgical style. The *Missa in Tempore Belli* was
composed while Napoleon's armies were pressing across the
Styrian border. The trumpet-calls and kettledrums of the slow
introduction to the Kyrie have the dramatic solemnity of one
of Haydn's, or even Beethoven's, symphonic openings; and the
Kyrie theme is a symphonic rather than operatic motive. The
orchestra is handled with powerful independence throughout,
in the same style as the last symphonies; the choruses, on the
other hand, have a contrapuntal grandeur which suggests
Bach even more than Handel. A movement such as the Miserere
Nobis is a liturgical act which is also a personal utterance.
Haydn's true religion has burst through the façade of dogma.

This is still more evident in the masses that post-date *The
Creation*. The 'Nelson' Mass of 1798 is a humanistic mass with
a tremendous Kyrie in full sonata form, combined with magnificent counterpoint, especially in the Credo. The 'Theresa'
Mass of the following year is remarkable for the way in which
elements of sonata and of opera are absorbed into a *dramatic*
fugue to the words '*Et vitam venturi*'. The last of the masses, the
Harmoniemesse of 1802, is perhaps the greatest of all. The large-
scale sonata of the Kyrie and the majestic use of the wind band
almost suggest the Beethoven of the *Missa Solemnis*: on the
other hand, the counterpoint of the Qui tollis comes closer to
the spiritual essence of Bach than did any other composer of
a later generation. Mozart only once attempted anything comparable with this in church music; and the work remained
unfinished. He was no longer a man of faith. Haydn's faith was
changing in ways of which he was but obscurely conscious; yet
he came just in time to make the best of two worlds.

In a work such as the *Harmoniemesse* he rebuilds the Church
in the spirit of the Enlightenment which he celebrates in his
greatest instrumental works. The serenity he attains may not be
mystical; it certainly entails what one can only call Belief,

"Often", he once said, "when I was wrestling with obstacles of every kind, when my physical and mental strength alike were running low and it was hard for me to persevere on the path on which I had set my feet, a secret feeling within me whispered: 'There are so few happy and contented people here below, sorrow and anxiety pursue them everywhere; perhaps your work may one day become a spring from which the careworn may draw a few moments' rest and refreshment.' And that was a powerful motive for pressing onwards". His prophecy has been fulfilled; and we find his music increasingly valuable to-day, when belief in life, and in man's potentialities, is subject to much discouragement.

3

MOZART : MUSIC FOR HOME AND CHURCH

Haydn's career covers a long tract of time and a still wider range of experience. He was twenty-four when Mozart [1756–1791] was born, and had written none of the music by which he is remembered. When Mozart died Haydn was nearly sixty. He had another eighteen creative years before him, in the course of which he learned from Mozart while becoming more deeply himself. Mozart had less than half as long as Haydn to live. By the time he was twenty-four he had advanced about as far in his creative development as Haydn had at the age of forty. It is as though he knew he had but little time, whilst Haydn knew that he need not hurry. This temperamental difference is a deeper matter than a distinction between personalities; it has reference too to the sense in which Mozart is the more 'modern' composer. Like Haydn, he was aristocratically nurtured; but the elements of protest in his temperament were more strongly marked, if not less strongly disciplined.

Haydn was a countryman who could move easily among the great in centres of sophistication, while being content to spend most of his life in seclusion; his character, like his music, is a mingling of peasant horse-sense, feudal gallantry, and middle-class Masonic morality, all reborn in his creative fire. Mozart was born in 1756 in rococo Salzburg, a smaller town than Vienna, but perhaps for that reason more exquisite, more precious. Haydn remained in some ways a countryman all his days; Mozart was from early youth a townsman and cosmopolitan. At the instigation of an ambitious father, who was a professional whereas Haydn's father had been an amateur musician, the young Mozart was launched on a musical career at an age when Haydn had scarcely become aware that he was a sentient being. Mozart's career as virtuoso and child composer carried him all over Europe; whereas Haydn for sixty years did not move further than a few miles from Vienna. As a result, Mozart never acquired a settled position, either as a household musician like Haydn, or as director of an opera-house or church. Such jobs as came his way he found increasingly irksome. A turning-point in his career came when, in 1781, he quarrelled finally with Colloredo and was kicked out by the Archbishop's secretary. This incident used to be recounted in the history books as evidence of the composer's noble nature rebelling against the odious tyranny of service. But there is nothing intrinsically wicked about patronage, so long as one believes in the system that supports it. From a material point of view, Mozart's action was silly; it was his own fault that he was buried in a pauper's grave. None the less, from another point of view, the history books are right. Mozart's action was inevitable, given the kind of man he was, the kind of music he was writing, and the conditions under which he worked. At that particular moment it was what he had to do: a symbolical gesture against a world in which he was ceasing to believe. No more than Haydn was he a conscious revolutionary. Indeed, unlike Haydn, he believed passionately in aristocracy, though in an aristocracy of the spirit. He was painfully aware that the reality was remote from his ideal; and he was seeking for that ideal in his subjective interpretation of Freemasonry during his last fevered years. Though he never found it in the outside world, he left it, for us, in his music.

The one fundamental quality which Mozart has in common with Haydn is his humanity. Belief in human nature excludes all other interests except music; and for Mozart the two can hardly be separated. Haydn saw human beings against their environment and in relation to Nature and a humanistically inclined God. But we know from Mozart's extraordinarily vivid letters that even as a young man—one might almost say as a child— people and music absorbed his whole being. Travelling through Italy, he makes scarcely a reference in his letters to art, architecture, or the beauties of scenery. His pen-pictures of people— celebrities, intimate friends, and chance acquaintances—and his comments on the music he heard are, on the other hand, astonishingly acute—and neither bitter nor sentimental. We should not therefore be surprised that Mozart was fundamentally an opera composer, whereas Haydn was fundamentally a symphonic and instrumental composer. Haydn wrote operas, but himself said that in this field he was a nonentity compared with Mozart. Mozart's operas are the core

of his work, though his notion of what opera was differed from
that of any previous composer. His changed conception of opera
is associated with the fact that he was a composer of the sonata
epoch; it is also true that his conception of sonata was modified
by the fact that throughout his life he thought in vocal and
operatic terms.

In a superficial sense this is evident even in Mozart's boyhood
training. Any composer brought up in eighteenth-century
Austria would have been nurtured on Italian opera; but we
saw that the music which first fired the young Haydn's imagination was rather the instrumental vitality of Stamitz, and the
northern passion of C. P. E. Bach. The first music Mozart knew
well was naturally that of his father. Leopold was a typical
Salzburg composer; his music was in the popular middle-class
manner, but prettily elegant, without the Mannheimers' power.
As soon as Mozart was old enough to know what he felt, he
liked the prettiness in his father's music, but despised the
popular element: just as he came to hate the bourgeois Salz-
burgers in whose bovine pranks he had played his part. Unlike
Haydn, he could never accept the middle-class style without
transforming it into the spiritually aristocratic. As for rural
folk-song, for him that was something to be parodied.

Most of the music which Mozart heard on his Continental
travels was operatic and Italian. As a boy composer he willingly
acceded to his father's ambition that he should become a
successful creator of Italian operas, both serious and comic.
His childhood operas did, indeed, achieve a considerable
measure of acclaim, by no means entirely due to the fact that
they were written by a child. They show evidence of a command
of vocal technique and of lyrical melody which conditioned his
approach to all kinds of music-making. One would not expect
them to be distinguished by originality or depth.

Among sonata composers Mozart would, as a youth, have
studied the music of C. P. E. Bach, who was accepted as one of
the great masters. He admired but did not love Carl Philipp's
music. Nordic introspection did not spontaneously appeal to
a composer who, thinking operatically, preferred to objectify
his passion. This is one reason for the apparent lack of connexion between Mozart's music and his biography.

There were, however, two sonata composers who made a
deep impression on the young Mozart. One was Johann

Schobert [1720–1767], a composer from the Polish border who had settled in Paris, where Mozart met him while on tour. Schobert's music is emotional and instinct with Sensibility; but, unlike C. P. E. Bach's, it is also elegantly urbane. Mozart probably relished its rococo charm rather than its nervous intensity. That the intensity was there, however, must have been a subconscious reason for the appeal; for as he grew only a little older Mozart was to discover his own passion beneath the rococo façade.

There was another composer whom the boy Mozart met on his travels: that was J. S. Bach's youngest son, Johann Christian [1735–1782]. In him Mozart found a kindred spirit; for J. C. Bach was a German composer who had turned from the Protestant north and settled in Milan, where, having become a Catholic, he composed innumerable operas and cantatas in a prettified version of Italian baroque. He also composed much instrumental music in the new *style galant*, especially after he moved to London and became a leader of musical fashion. His music in sonata style was always modified by his early love of and training in Italian lyricism; this suited a public that liked their music to be superficially enlivening so long as it did not ruffle complacency. Only very occasionally, and in spite of himself, did he allow the dualistic energy of sonata style or the gravity of the Bachs' Protestant heritage to disrupt the rounded pleasantries of his art—as in the C minor Piano Sonata we referred to earlier. Like his brother Carl Philipp, he wrote for the new public of 'connoisseurs and amateurs'; but whereas Carl Philipp regarded this public as an intellectual élite, for Johann Christian it was a source of revenue—and no doubt of pleasant social intercourse. "My brother lives to compose," remarked Johann Christian. "I compose to live."

The appeal of Johann Christian's music to the young Mozart is easy to understand. It was 'modern', and in that sense superficially youthful in spirit; it was also instinct with a cantabile lyricism which seemed antipathetic to sonata style. Again, Mozart's inclinations were prophetic in a way deeper than conscious understanding. For if Stamitz—and Haydn in his early days—achieved symphonic drama by sacrificing lyricism, and J. C. Bach preserved lyricism only by refusing to realize the dramatic implications of sonata, in Mozart's mature music lyrical melody and tonal drama are to be accorded equal rights. The equilibrium between lyricism and drama which Haydn so gloriously achieves in the music of his last years is evident in Mozart's music almost from the moment he becomes a person. In his instrumental works the parts sing, as do the voices in his operas; and both create an interplay of character and motive. One might almost say that the two elements of vocal lyricism and instrumental drama in Mozart's sonata movements are synonymous with acceptance and protest.

It is mistaken piety to maintain that Mozart's boyhood compositions are intrinsically very valuable; though by adolescence he must have attained a stage of emotional development that few reach by the age of thirty. Certainly, he had a greater technical assurance at fourteen than Haydn had at twenty-four. Haydn's earliest works are, in their popular virility, sometimes wilfully uncouth. Mozart's early works—whether he writes serenades for weddings of the local bourgeoisie or symphonies which are not radically distinct from them—have always an Italianate sweetness and polish. Even street tunes acquire a courtly grace. At about the age of puberty—an important experience for everyone, though not many are at that age blessed with the faculty of creative expression—Mozart begins to adapt the clichés of *opera buffa* and of J. C. Bach to his own modest purposes. The little symphony, K.22, contains a chromatic andante which is more than an evocation of fashion; and even Mozart's accompanying figurations become cantabile.

It is interesting too that almost the first group of works to betray a Mozartian personality is a set of violin sonatas, K.55-60. Now whereas in the baroque violin sonata string melody had been the music's life-blood, which the keyboard succours and supports, in the rococo period the functions of the two instruments had been reversed. The early violin and piano sonatas of Haydn make sense if played as piano solos—a violin part is provided should a fiddle and sociable fiddler be handy; for the idiom of the classical sonata, being at first harmonic and rhythmic rather than melodic in approach, was in some ways radically opposed to the genius of the violin. This is why Haydn favoured the piano sonata and more or less ignored the violin as solo instrument. But with Mozart, even in early youth, the violin comes once more into its own as an instrument allied to the singing voice. His piano sonatas are relatively insignificant. His mature violin and piano sonatas are neither accompanied song-without-words, like the baroque sonata: nor dance action with a few perfunctory tunes thrown in, like rococo sonatas for piano 'with violin accompaniment': but real *duos* that achieve an equilibrium between symphonic drama and song.

In the 1770's Mozart, like Haydn, went through a phase of 'Storm and Stress'. Haydn was in his forties at the time; Mozart was adolescent. A symphony such as K.133 is still wittily poetic in its lyricism; but its grace becomes imperceptibly dramatic, especially in the subtly modified recapitulation and coda to the first movement. The influence of the genius of Haydn—and of growing up—is beginning to deepen the rococo charm he learned from J. C. Bach. The next year brings a still more remarkable development. The little G minor Symphony, K.183, is fascinating both for its resemblances to and differences from Haydn's minor moods in his *Sturm und Drang* compositions. It has the same passionate repeated notes and brusque changes of dynamics which we noticed in Haydn's G minor Symphony (No. 39). But whereas Haydn is fierce, Mozart is melancholy; and the difference consists in the sweetly singing quality of Mozart's themes as compared with Haydn's explosiveness, and in the persistently sighing appoggiaturas (Ex. 15). This does

Ex.15. Mozart: Symphony in G minor K.183 (last movement)

not mean that Mozart's melancholy is limp. It is acute, because it is already inherently dramatic. It is worth noting that whereas Haydn and C. P. E. Bach and Beethoven—who were not *primarily* lyrical composers—prefer to unify their material as closely as is consistent with their dramatic intentions, Mozart and J. C. Bach, who naturally think lyrically, can afford to introduce more obvious contrasts between their themes. Even Mozart's A major Symphony, K.201, which is a radiant piece, places sinuously chromatic melodies alongside airily dancing *buffo* tunes: and contains the longest and most exciting development that Mozart had yet created.

'Storm and Stress' was, however, an element inherent in Mozart's temperament, rather than absorbed from without.

His equilibrium between lyricism and drama involves too a
balance between joy and sorrow; nor are we ever quite sure
whether his music is happy or sad. This characteristic of mature
Mozart is already evident in the E minor Violin Sonata of
1778. The first of the two movements is passionate in its
soaring themes, tense in its chromaticism and modulations:
the excitingly re-harmonized recapitulation is itself a further
development. It is followed by a little minuet with a trio in the
major which ought to be consolatory, but is in effect more
heart-breaking than the minor allegro (Ex. 16). This is partly

Ex. 16. Mozart: Violin and piano sonata K. 304 (second movement)

because the exquisite singing melody is harmonized with an
unexpectedly seductive richness; partly because each phrase
dissolves away in a sigh—a falling dissonant appoggiatura. The
sigh and the chromatics imbue the theme with a sense of
yearning. The bliss of such a melody seems seraphic: and so
unattainable in this world.

Mozart's growth to full maturity occurs in the early 1780s.
If Haydn's development was soon to be profoundly influenced
by Mozart, we have the younger man's word that his own
development was decisively affected by Haydn's opus 33.
Mozart's first quartets, modelled on the Milanese style of
Sammartini and J. C. Bach, were simply three-movement
Italian symphonies without wind. The quartets composed
between K.155 and K.172 approach the *galant* quartet style of
Schobert; they manifest some of the emotionalism typical of the
early violin sonatas, along with a half-hearted attempt to
emulate the fugal discipline with which Haydn had experi-
mented in his opus 9 and 17. After that, Mozart wrote no more
quartets for ten years—a long time in so short and crowded a
career.

In 1783 Mozart composed—after long and wearisome toil,
he tells us—a set of six quartets which he dedicated to Haydn.
The older man had shown him how to compose for four stringed

instruments in dramatic dialogue. Yet although these quartets
contain movements which were obviously intended to be
modelled on movements by Haydn, they at the same time
attest Mozart's independence. The opening theme of the E flat
Quartet, K.428, with its tritone and sinuous chromaticism, is
as personal and un-Haydnesque an utterance as the hauntingly
seductive andante. Even the last movement, which opens with
a Haydn-like wit, develops elements of chromatic pathos.
Haydn's great lyrical melodies are never chromatic; when he
does use melodic chromaticism it is usually for a parodistic
effect. Mozart's melodies are always liable to acquire chromaticism, even if they are not chromatic to begin with. Again, his
irregular phrase lengths and his emotional use of contrasting
dynamics are almost always, as here, associated with the articu-
lation of melody. Haydn's tend to be associated with rhythmic
and harmonic surprises.

Perhaps the most profoundly representative quartet of the
group is the D minor K.421. All four movements have the
slightly fevered intensity which seems typical of Mozart's D
minor utterances. The last movement, a variation-set in siciliano
rhythm, is an instance of Mozart's ability to invest an apparently innocent pastoral with the force of tragedy: partly by
means of violent syncopations, of a subtle ambiguity between
major and minor, and of a cadential use of the Neapolitan sixth
which introduces an uncannily strange perspective into the
tonality (Ex. 17). In the coda the repeated Ds high up on the
first violin send a chill down the spine; and the frightening

Ex. 17 Mozart: Quartet in D minor K. 421 (last movement)

quality of this music is inseparable from its restraint. It is devoid
of rhetoric, yet more dramatic music has never been created.

In the first movement of this quartet, all the themes sing,
and much of the figuration is chromatic. The melodies seem to
be complete in themselves, like the vocal themes of opera. Yet
the modulations of the development are powerfully dramatic,
and the continuity of the texture is assured by masterly counterpoint: fragments of the themes are bandied about between the
four instruments as they might be in an operatic ensemble.
The slow movement is another of Mozart's idylls in the major
key, which appear to be relief from the stress of the minor, but
are in fact still more melancholy. Here the pathos springs from
the way in which the caressing curves of the melody and the
warm harmony are intermittently broken by abrupt sequential
modulations. Again, the movement suggests an operatic situation: the love scene in which a transitory bliss hides heaven or
hell knows what perturbations of spirit. The overlapping
asymmetry of the phrases emphasizes this hint of dramatic
dialogue; the speakers interrupt one another in the urgency of
their passion (Ex. 18):

Ex. 18. Mozart: Quartet in D minor K 421 (slow movement)

The C major Quartet, K.465, is a still more remarkable
instance of this quasi-operatic instrumental technique. The
notorious slow introduction which so alarmed Mozart's contemporaries is a subjective rather than ceremonial re-creation
of the old baroque overture: its chromaticisms and dissonant suspensions possibly suggested to Haydn the mysterious

Prologue to *The Creation*. In the development of the first movement, Mozart treats quartet style in a manner comparable
with his handling of an operatic ensemble. It is worth noting
that although all these quartets contain magnificent contrapuntal writing, the counterpoint is always symphonic and
dramatic. Even the fully-fledged fugue at the conclusion of
K.387 is an immensely invigorated *buffo* finale.

Naturally enough, this approach which Mozart brought to
quartet-writing invaded too his symphonic style. K.425 (the
'Linz') is the first of his symphonies to acquire something of
the urgent grandeur, as well as the wit, of Haydn's mature
works. More surprisingly, we find this new approach also in the
'occasional' music which Mozart still composed in the manner
of the divertimento. The C minor Serenade for wind instruments of 1781 is one of the darkest and most serious of his works:
so much so that Mozart later arranged it for string quintet, a
medium which he normally reserved for his most personal
utterances. It sounds magnificent in its original form—as
worthy a companion to the solemnity and power of *Idomeneo* as
the string quintets are to the later, less heroic operas. Mozart
was probably justified in thinking that it would disturb rather
than satisfy the folk at whose commission it had been written.

It was some time before Mozart followed the 'Haydn' set
with further quartets. He rather turned to experiment in the
combination of strings, and sometimes wind instruments, with
piano, producing in the G minor piano Quartet one of his most
passionate instrumental works, and in the Trio for clarinet,
viola, and piano one of his most enigmatically profound. For
this kind of dialogue between melody instruments and piano
Mozart had virtually no models: even C. P. E. Bach had
attempted in this manner only works of rococo charm. Mozart
did not consider these hybrid combinations entirely satisfactory,
because the contestants were not equally balanced. But it is easy
to see why he devoted such care to these works. They were
studies towards his great cycle of piano concertos; and in this
medium Mozart was to discover the consummate form of his
fusion of operatic techniques with sonata. It is significant that
the cycle of piano concertos was composed during Mozart's
greatest period of operatic creation; and that in these years he
wrote only one symphony.

It is hardly extravagant to say that Mozart created the classical

concerto—created and fulfilled it, for his concertos have no
successors. Before him, the rococo concerto had been even less
pretentious than the rococo symphony. It was a not very taxing
display piece for a soloist with instrumental accompaniment.
It whiled away idle moments with a pleasing euphony, but its
wayward and improvisatory nature hardly lent itself to the
dramatic urgency of sonata style. Mozart's own Flute and Harp
Concerto, written on his visit to Paris, is a more than normally
distinguished example of such rococo entertainment; it exploits
the sonorities of the instruments to woo the senses, and highly
effective is its courtship. Even Mozart's early violin concertos,
written (at Leopold's instigation) to show off his virtuosity, are
unambitious; and the beautiful Sinfonia Concertante for violin
and viola, which directly emulates operatic aria in instrumental
terms, remained an isolated experiment.

Mozart did not enjoy composing his violin concertos, and
found the Flute and Harp Concerto a sore trial. When he
took up concerto form in earnest he ignored melody instruments
and turned to the piano. We have seen that as an instrument
for solo sonatas Mozart preferred the cantabile violin to the
piano. As a concerto instrument, he preferred the piano to the
violin, because in its power and contrasting timbre it could be
a worthy opposite number to the orchestra. He sees the piano
concerto as a duality in unity: was subconsciously fascinated by
it because it offered an allegorical expression of the separation
of the individual (the soloist) from society (the orchestra). But
this separation is made in order that the soloist and orchestra
can, in the course of the music, evolve a new relationship. The
Mozartian concerto threatens, only in order to vindicate, civilization. So Mozart remains a classical artist, even though his
preoccupation with this new medium is indicative of a romantic
strain more developed in him than in Haydn. The older master
composed no concertos of significance in comparison with his
greatest symphonies and quartets.

Composers before Mozart had written piano concertos, some
of which—notably those of C. P. E. Bach and Schobert—
contain fine music. But the impressive passages are intermittent,
for these composers were content to accept the origins of the
style in improvisation. The boy Mozart wrote many concertos
on the model of C. P. E. Bach and Schobert—and of Wagenseil
and J. C. Bach—for himself to play on his Continental tours.

But in 1776 (significantly during the 'Storm and Stress' phase) he produced a concerto which gave intimation of the importance which the form would later have for him. It has been said that this concerto, K.271, was a step forward in Mozart's development comparable with that which Beethoven took in proceeding from the Second Symphony to the 'Eroica'. The claim is hardly too extravagant.

The most immediately striking point about this concerto is that Mozart is clearly trying to give the form a stature comparable with the most serious kind of symphony he knew of. Compared with rococo concertos, it is long, and very difficult; and although in the orthodox three movements of the concerto, the last telescopes the symphonic rondo and minuet. While this rondo tune is itself comic, the interjections of the minuet as episodes are deeply disturbing: as is the passionately operatic slow movement in the relative minor, in which the pianist emulates the operatic singer by breaking into recitative. All the cadenzas reveal their operatic origin; and they were all carefully written out by Mozart. The concerto was too much for Mozart's public, who considered it noisy and overburdened with notes.

The cycle of mature concertos begins in 1782, alongside the cycle of operas. If his violin concertos are based on the principle of operatic aria, the piano concertos are founded on the principle of operatic ensemble; his first-movement form in concerto is almost always more complicated than it is in symphony. Soloist and orchestra always have equality of status. The orchestra makes its statement with independent matter in a long prelude. The soloist enters, often with different material. There are thus two complimentary expositions with four, five, or even six subjects, which can be interlinked in constantly changing sequence. All these themes may be developed simultaneously in ensemble, creating a new clarity out of complexity. This technique implies a new conception of orchestration. Mozart's scoring is not purely linear, like the baroque, nor purely harmonic, like the rococo: it is a mixture of both, in which all the parts are volatile, whether they be themes or melodic figurations that support the harmony. There is nothing in music to which this technique may be compared, except Mozart's own mature operatic ensembles in which a number of characters sing together phrases different in mood and psychology: yet the result is not chaos, but understanding.

Mozart's slow movements in his concertos are varied in form.
They may be simple A-B-A song forms (which he often calls
romanza),* serving as a relief from the first movement's clear
complexity. They may be in adagio sonata form, with the evolution of aria-like melody more important than dramatic
development: as in the wonderful F sharp minor *napolitana*†
from K.488. Or they may be in variation style with or without
coda. His finales are usually rondos crossed with elements of
sonata, in that the episodes may introduce dramatic modulations which carry the rondo tune with them. When the rondo
theme returns to the original key it has the effect of a recapitulation: though rondo style remains more easy-going and improvisatory than first-movement form. For Mozart, and still more
for Beethoven later, sonata has become the dynamic principle,
variation the static; while rondo is a hybrid between the
two.

The great Mozartian cycle begins with two lightweight concertos, K.413 and K.414. Perhaps Mozart felt that in presenting his new kind of ensemble-concerto, he should let his public
down gently. These amiably pastoral works reveal unsuspected
depths which the listener may bypass if he wishes. But K.449
he can only take or leave. It is grand, powerfully melancholy,
and full of intimate associations with *Figaro*. So is K.459, with
its nocturnal slow movement which reconciles the popular and
the learned in fusing symphonic homophony with fugato and
operatic ensemble. K.482 has a comparable relationship to *Cosi
fan tutte*, and the 'demoniacal' D minor to *Don Giovanni*, whose
tragedy is likewise rounded off in *buffo* merriment.

. The peak point of the Mozartian concerto is, however, the
C minor, K.491, which has all the D minor's passion, ennobled
with a classical grandeur. The long orchestral prelude is based on
material most of which is creatively modified in the concertante
sections; the effect of the soloist's entry, with a new (and
pianistic) theme, is extraordinarily telling. The final variations
are again grand and sombre in their resilience, endlessly
resourceful in their handling of dialogue between soloist and
tutti. The last concerto of all, the B flat K.595, is as different in

---

* For Mozart's generation the *romanza* was a short movement in song style, in
single binary or ternary form, moderate in tempo, intimate and sentimental (in
the strict sense) in mood.

† Originally a popular song for several voices, in lilting 6–8 time, allied to the
sixteenth-century Villanella, and much cultivated in Naples.

mood from the severity of K.491 as could be imagined. It sounds childlike only because its subtleties are so lucent. Yet this exquisite music was composed in conditions of appalling mental and physical suffering; and when we have heard it we find ourselves wondering whether this concerto or the C minor is the sadder.

The rondo finale of this B flat Concerto is based on an early song of Mozart which sounds like a nursery tune. Its significant title was 'Longing for spring'. Spring is still present in the transformed version it assumes in the concerto; in the modulatory episodes longing wellnigh breaks the heart. Yet the work as a whole seems to glitter with light. It is never self-regarding music; the melancholy inherent in its chromatic figurations and poetic felicities of scoring is absorbed into the precision of the music's structure. So the sadness within its gaiety seems to be not Mozart's, but the mutability in life itself.

This concerto seems to be gay; the G minor Quintet, written a few years earlier, is the most melancholy piece Mozart ever wrote. But the percussive repeated note accompaniment, the dissonant suspensions, the yearning lift to the sixth and the minor ninth in the second subject, have none of the feverishness of the youthful G minor Symphony, or the violent passion of the G minor Piano Quartet. In both concerto and quintet, whether gay or melancholy, the passion is purged: realized so consummately in musical terms that it is beyond either our laughter or our tears.

We have observed that counterpoint, half operatic, half symphonic in character, plays a conspicuous part in Mozart's mature music. There is a further aspect of this: for in his last years Mozart made a detailed study of the music of Bach, remarking that here at last was something from which he could learn. Some of the works which Mozart deliberately wrote in a Bachian manner—notably the Adagio and Fugue for string quartet, K.546—are very odd in their emotional effect. Mozart so crams in his contrapuntal devices of inversion, augmentation, diminution, and stretto, and thereby so coruscates the harmony that the music produces an impression of a driving energy strained almost to breaking-point. These 'monistic' pieces of Mozart are thus more agonized than his most dualistic sonata movements: exactly contrary to Bach in spirit, however they may follow the letter of his technique.

But the Bachian exercises are interesting not only because they helped Mozart to perfect the kind of counterpoint that was valuable for him; they were also one of the elements that went to create the Masonic style of his last years. We can see this in the great trio of symphonies which were Mozart's last word in this form. The only symphony he had composed during the period of his piano concertos was the 'Prague', which is full of 'operatic' polyphony and is, like the D minor Concerto, related to *Don Giovanni*. But the last three symphonies he wrote to please himself; and he made in them the affirmations about life and death which he had embodied in his emotional reinterpretation of Freemasonry. He has transformed the symphony from rococo entertainment into a personal testament.

The key of the first of the group is E flat; and this key has a symbolical significance in all the works Mozart wrote for Masonic ceremonies. Woodwind instruments were also associated with Masonic rites; and they play an important part in this symphony, especially in the *passionately* ceremonial introduction. The G minor Symphony,* like the Quintet in the same key, is a distillation of suffering: all the 'properties' of 'Storm and Stress' are divested of rhetoric, so that the drama is pure music and the music drama, and the suffering is neither Mozart's nor ours, but mankind's. The C major is an assertion of order. In the last movement Mozart's masterly fusion of sonata conflict with operatic-ensemble counterpoint triumphs over pain and darkness. The last three symphonies are not 'better' than the great concertos, but they mark a new development. The concertos are the instrumental epitome of the operatic Mozart; in the last symphonies he offers a purely musical expression of what he had discovered to be his religion.

His spiritual career thus follows a path in many ways parallel to that of Haydn, though the point at which he arrived is different. Neither man could have put into words what he had come to believe, and as much of Mozart's beliefs as found its way into the libretto of *The Magic Flute* distorts by oversimplification. Since Haydn and Mozart were musicians, not poets, this is of little consequence: from their music itself we can see that there is a distinction between their attitudes both to the orthodox creed of their time, and to the religion which they had discovered in the course of their creative lives. Haydn

* For a detailed analysis see Rudolf Reti, *The Thematic Process in Music*.

modified traditional Catholicism in the light of his and his age's rational humanism; the qualities distinguishing his last ethical works such as *The Creation* also make an imprint on his last masses. But he never wilfully broke with Catholic dogma, nor had any conscious desire to substitute for it a new ideal.

In his youth, both at Salzburg and during his Italian travels, Mozart composed a considerable amount of church music because it paid him to do so. Like all rococo church music, it is completely theatrical in style, except for a few archaic, undigested survivals of baroque counterpoint. As music, it is best when unashamedly simple and sensuous, as in the tender Lorettine Litanies and the *De Profundis*, K.93: exquisite music which has no more connexion with mysticism than the ludicrously lilting setting of the words 'Miserere Nobis' in the *Litaniae de venerabili altaris sacramento* of 1772.

It is significant that Mozart gave up composing church music as soon as his official duties no longer called for it. The only exceptions to this are the Mass in C, K.337, and the *Kyrie*, K.341, written while he was working on *Idomeneo*: very beautiful works which, like the opera, manage to reconcile some of the ceremonial majesty of the baroque with symphonic drama; and then the big C minor Mass, K.427, and the *Requiem*, both of which he left unfinished.

These two supreme climaxes of Mozart's church music were both composed for personal rather than for dogmatic reasons. The Mass he wrote at the time of his marriage, as an avowal of praise and gratitude. Its models are the great baroque masters, Handel, Caldara, Alessandro Scarlatti, and above all the polyphony of Bach, in whose music Mozart found so much to fascinate him. It interprets its baroque models symphonically and dramatically, however, as Haydn had done in his last masses; and relates the Italianate vocal style of the baroque to Mozart's own type of operatic lyricism. The Qui Tollis, like that of Haydn's *Harmoniemesse*, is especially Bachian, the Et Incarnatus especially operatic; but there is no longer any confusion of genres.

We do not know why Mozart left this superbly powerful work unfinished. Perhaps the reality of his marriage proved less inspiring than his ideal conception of it; very probably he had to put the Mass aside to meet commitments which brought in more immediate financial return. In any case, this was not

the kind of music in which he was most interested. The *Requiem*
is a different matter. The Mass, written for Constanze, is still
ostensibly Catholic in spirit. The *Requiem* he wrote for himself,
and its spirit is personal and Masonic. The story of the Dark
Stranger who came to commission the work is well known.
There was a rational explanation of his presence; he was the
emissary of a Count who wished to preserve anonymity in
order to pass off the work as his own composition. To Mozart's
sick imagination he seemed an emissary from another world.
He wrote the Mass feverishly, conscious that death was over-
taking him.

The elements of Mozart's Masonic style are all present in the
Requiem. One of them is still Bachian counterpoint; but although
this may sometimes be thrillingly monumental, as in the Rex
Tremendae, its habitual manner is more intimate and restrained
than in the Catholic Mass. It has a tense serenity such as we
can observe too in the profoundly lovely fugal movements that
Mozart included in his Masonic works for mechanical organ.
In the *Requiem*, especially the Introit, the suspensions, tied notes,
and syncopations create a suppressed agitation beneath the
solemnity. This is enhanced by the dark Masonic orchestration,
with pairs of clarinets, basset horns, and bassoons (Ex. 19):

Ex. 19. Mozart: *Requiem*. opening of Introit

There is another style in the *Requiem*, however, which is as
purely homophonic as the Bachian movements are contrapuntal. The Hostias is a hymn-like melody—in the 'Masonic'
key of E flat—harmonized with the utmost simplicity (Ex. 20):

Ex. 20. Mozart: *Requiem*. Theme of Hostias

Melodies such as this occur in instrumental works (for instance the slow movement of the clarinet concerto) as well as in Masonic motets like the *Ave Verum* and in *The Magic Flute*, where they are associated with the triumph of Light. They are quite different in effect from the grander melodies of Handel and Gluck that may have been their prototype; though we may consider them alongside the hymn-like themes of Haydn's last years, and regard them as anticipatory of a type of theme to be developed by Beethoven (for instance, the slow movement of the Violin Sonata, opus 96). In any case, the significance of these melodies in relation to Mozart's 'religion' is unmistakable. He associated them with the triumph of Light: but only in the negative sense that their consolatory gravity robs death of its power. This is why Mozart's Masonic music is so different in effect from Haydn's. Haydn celebrates life; in the orthodox religion on which he had been brought up death was accounted for, and it is unlikely that he often thought about it. Mozart lives so intensely that the consciousness of death can never be far off; he increasingly sees death, not as a mystical release from the sufferings of his and our life, but simply—or profoundly —as the context in which we exist. On this theme he wrote a most remarkable letter to his father:

"I need not tell you with what anxiety I await better news from yourself. I count upon that with certainty, though I am wont in all things to anticipate the worst. Since death (take my words literally) is the true goal of our lives, I have made myself so well acquainted during the last two years with this true and best friend of mankind that the idea of it no longer has any terrors for me, but rather much that is tranquil and comforting. And I thank God that he has granted me the good fortune to obtain the opportunity (you understand my meaning) of regarding death as the key to our true happiness. I never lie down in bed without considering that, young as I am, perhaps I may on the morrow be no more. Yet not one of those who know me could say that I am morose or melancholy, and for this I thank my Creator daily and wish heartily that the same happiness may be given to my fellow men."

Mozart never lost his belief in the potentialities of the human heart; but he came to accept man's natural limitations.

Can we see something of this acceptance of life and death as complementary even in the smallest works of Mozart's last years? Although his life was so short and so intense, the completeness and perfection of his music leave nothing to be said. Had he lived longer, he would presumably have added something to a musical experience that seems already all-inclusive, but it is impossible to imagine what. Even Mozart's slightest works appear, in his last years, to exist independent of time or place. The little works for glass harmonica, not to mention the great E flat Divertimento for string trio, are poles apart from the serenades and cassations of his youth. They diverted Mozart himself, no doubt, and they would divert a company of angels; but they are no longer music to eat or to chatter to. It almost seems as though Mozart has given up the attempt to write music for a society in which he only half believed. He now writes in a celestial drawing-room, where the only audience is himself and silence (and he does not need to listen): just as Bach in his last years, composing *The Art of Fugue* in an outmoded fashion, played to himself in an empty church.

4

BEETHOVEN

I T IS the essence of the personality of Beethoven [1770–1827], both as man and as artist, that he should invite discussion in other than musical terms. We cannot begin to understand him unless we recognize that for him music was not merely a pattern of sounds nor even merely an aural means of self-expression; it was also a moral and ethical power. On the other hand, if we do recognize this we may be tempted to talk about what we imagine to be Beethoven's message rather than about his music; and Tovey properly deplored this tendency in pointing out that remarks about the French Revolution do not help us to listen to Beethoven's music more sensitively or more intelligently.

Yet the case is not as simple as Tovey makes it seem. There *is* a connexion between Beethoven's music and the French Revolution, since even in so strikingly personal a work as the Fifth Symphony he was directly influenced by French revolutionary music. This—and the related fact that one of his first works was a cantata dedicated to the progressive Emperor Joseph—may not be very important. But the general relationship between Beethoven's music and the *idea* of revolution certainly is: for if Haydn and Mozart were incipiently revolutionary composers, Beethoven is overtly so. The Fifth Symphony revolutionizes the then accepted notion of symphonic form, and its technical revolution is inseparable from the fact that it conveys in musical terms a message—a new approach to human experience. If we ignore that message we cannot claim to understand Beethoven; but we must be sure that the message we discover is Beethoven's, and not our own or someone else's. It must be a deduction from the nature of the musical technique, not something tacked on to the music fortuitously.

We have seen that both Haydn and Mozart achieved a classical equilibrium between acceptance and protest; in Mozart's case one can almost equate the two sides of the balance with lyrical melody and tonal drama. His equilibrium, we said, is at once a threat to and a vindication of civilization: so that we do not, in listening to his music, consciously think of change. But from the start Beethoven desired change. He wanted to build a new world; and he thought of his music as a means to that end. Mozart's art, as we can see most readily from his operas, is based on acceptance, tolerance, and understanding. This does not preclude stringent criticism; but he has no ethical intentions. Beethoven was probably the first composer consciously animated by a desire to do good. Religious composers of the past presumably wrote for the good of man's souls, but they did not consciously aim to promote good actions. Beethoven disapproved of Mozart's *Don Giovanni* because he thought it promoted bad actions; even as early as 1792 we find him writing in a friend's album:

> To help wherever one can.
> Love liberty above all things.
> Never deny the truth
> Even at the foot of the throne.

If change is necessary—and it is—it will come only through individual effort. In the fight for truth one will always be opposed to convention; one must rely on oneself because there is nothing else to rely on.

Haydn, Mozart, and Beethoven were all men of middle-class provincial origin. Haydn was content to remain socially, though not spiritually subordinate; Mozart became himself cosmopolitan and sophisticated; Beethoven insisted that fashionable society should remake itself in his image. We saw that the very perfection of Mozart's last works entails a kind of spiritual isolation; and though he was so interested in people, he was hopelessly incompetent in dealing with practical affairs. But he was never a wilful misfit, like Beethoven, who as a schoolboy had been "shy and taciturn, observing more and pondering more than he spoke"; who as a young man was clumsy and gauche in his movements, "an unlicked bear;" and who in mature years "found the world despicable, but did not thereby render it any the pleasanter either for himself or for other people". At school, Beethoven had learned to read and write easily and was, of course, musically precocious. That, however, was the extent of his intellectual attainments; he

never learned to accomplish the simplest arithmetical calcula-
tion. Though the sordid conditions of his childhood had something to do with this, they were not the main reason. From
earliest youth Beethoven was a dedicated spirit. He was alone,
and he had a purpose. Anything which distracted him from
that purpose—including arithmetic—he rejected. In Vienna,
his rudeness to members of the aristocracy and to any persons in
authority was a calculated gesture. "*My* nobility," said Beethoven, "is *here* and *here*"; and he pointed to his head and heart.

Beethoven's attitude to life is inevitably reflected in his
approach to his art. As he was the first composer to wish to
change the world, so he was the first composer to believe that
originality in a creative artist was an asset. He once said that
he did not often listen to other people's music, for fear it might
impair his individuality. Although the remark was a gruffly
characteristic joke, it was a significant joke for Beethoven to
make. Another story is relevant enough to recount. A reveren-
tial friend, examining a new score of Beethoven's, ventured to
point out to the master that in one passage hidden fifths had
crept in.* Beethoven truculently demanded what was wrong
about that. The timid answer was that 'the rules' do not permit
them: to which Beethoven retorted, "Then *I* permit them." In
musical technique, as in life, the ultimate authority is the self.

But though Beethoven believed that change was essential,
he also still believed in civilization. He was born into a great
musical tradition which he respected; for with all his disrespect
towards people and things he considered unworthy, he had the
true humility of the great. So the subversive tendencies of
his music are not immediately evident. He accepts the conventions which he inherited from Haydn and Mozart: but emphasizes the revolutionary at the expense of the traditional features
in them. It is interesting that when, having moved from
provincial Bonn to Vienna, Beethoven took a course of composition lessons with Haydn, they were a failure. From a great
master of the previous generation he could learn nothing. The
Viennese tradition he absorbed, as it were, with the air he
breathed; the only lessons he ever found profitable were

---

* Parallel fifths are forbidden in the orthodox grammar of the harmonic period
of European music (roughly the sixteenth to the twentieth centuries) because they
weaken independent part-writing. Hidden fifths are parallel fifths which are
less apparent to the *eye* in that they are disguised by passing notes in one or more of
the parts.

studies in strict counterpoint with Johann Albrechtsberger [1736–1809]. These taught him facility in his craft, while having no reference to problems of creation. Such problems were his own concern, exclusively.

If one considers the piano trios that comprise Beethoven's opus 1—and still more the string trios of opus 3—it is clear that although they establish a strong personality and contain remarkable audacities, they are music which Haydn would have recognized as having a kinship with his own. But the piano sonatas of opus 2 are already a new world of feeling. The dimensions of the first sonata, in F minor, are those of a normal classical sonata; indeed it is shorter than Haydn's later sonatas. Nor is there anything unorthodox about the treatment of sonata form; indeed, the first movement is more orthodox than most of Haydn's mature works, with a Mannheim sky-rocket for first theme, a free inversion of it for second subject, and a not extravagant modulatory scheme in the development. It differs from Haydn, and still more from Mozart, in the almost complete subservience of the melodic element to a dynamic treatment of piano technique. This is even more strongly marked in the last movement, also in sonata form. This ferociously whirling toccata is an assault on the listener's nerves. When a relatively lyrical theme occurs at the opening of the development, it is of so primitive a nature that it has, intentionally or not, an effect of parody. One can imagine the explosive violence of the young Beethoven's performance of this movement: the truculence of its abrupt conclusion. If the piece seems crude both melodically and rhythmically in comparison with Haydn and Mozart, it already shows complete self-assurance. Beethoven knows what effect he is after, and is willing to sacrifice much in its interests.

Though apparently a cheerful work, compared with the F minor's vehemence, the second sonata of the group (in A major) is subversive in an altogether subtler way. According to rococo convention, the exposition of a sonata was supposed to establish the basic tonalities of tonic and dominant, associated with the first and second subject groups respectively. Beethoven here opens his second subject in the minor of the dominant—a slight but not extreme abnormality often found in Haydn and Mozart. Then, in the space of twenty bars, the theme develops sequentially through no less than eight keys,

touching on tonalities as remote from home (A major) as G
major and B flat major (Ex. 21). Such extreme modulations,
if permitted at all, were normally reserved for the climax of the

Ex. 21 Beethoven: Piano Sonata in A opus 2 No. 2 (first movement)

development. Here they occur in the exposition, the point of
which is conventionally to establish tonality before development
begins. Yet the effect, though startling, is not anarchic, because
the whole of this passage has a bass line which rises by step
from E up an octave; and then finally establishes the dominant
in which the exposition concludes. The passage is a boldly
expanded but logically convincing dominant preparation.
Beethoven then attains his climax in the development by building his modulations not on step-wise progressions, but on a
series of descending thirds.* Such passages are an exact counterpart in musical terms to the young Beethoven's flouting of
social etiquette—his rudeness to duchesses and his uncere-
monious hurling around of crockery. Although these latter
examples may seem frivolous, it is not too much to say that the
same motives prompted both Beethoven's musical and his social
bad manners.

At first, Beethoven's fashionable audience enjoyed his
truculence. Up to a point, they liked being shocked by his
boorish behaviour; and they found his music exciting, while
at the same time it was based on premises they could understand. It is significant that the most representative music of
Beethoven's youth is in his piano sonatas. His early fame was as
pianist and improviser; and we have seen that the piano was
becoming, for him, a dynamic rather than a melodic instrument.
His early violin sonatas are much less aggressive than the piano

* For a detailed analysis, see Tovey's commentary on this sonata.

sonatas of the same date. The subversive qualities of his opus 12
sonatas for violin and piano consist in their ironic modulations,
and the pawky wit of their rhythmic surprises. Yet they preserve
an almost aristocratic elegance in the spare keyboard texture
which Beethoven considers a fitting complement to violin tone;
and they include no real slow movement, no outburst of
rhetorical passion. His opus 12 remains domestic entertainment music of a personal distinction; his opus 13—the C minor
Piano Sonata—is a call to arms.

One can appreciate the force of this if one compares Beethoven's C minor mood in this 'pathetic' sonata with the C
minor of Mozart's late Fantasia and Sonata, K.475 and 457,
Mozart is fiery, but classically disciplined, even in the improvisatory Fantasia. Beethoven cracks sonata form with a passion
that is almost melodrama. The sonata allegro is prefaced by
a slow introduction deriving from the French operatic overture,
even to the detail of the dotted rhythm. But this introduction
is no longer ceremonial, but even more passionately subjective
than C. P. E. Bach in its accented appoggiaturas, enharmonic
modulations, and sequences: indeed, it forcibly suggests
Wagner's *Tristan* (Ex. 22). Moreover, it is not merely an introduction; it reappears in different keys at crucial points in the

Ex. 22   Beethoven: Sonata in C minor opus 13 (introduction)

development, preceded and followed by dramatic silences. No
composer before Beethoven had exploited silence in this way,
so that it becomes a part of the musical argument. And although
the structure of the sonata allegro does not itself depart from
classical precedent, except for the tremendous stroke in the
recapitulation when the syncopated minims are screwed up
from C to D flat, it is true that the music demands a new technique of performance. It is not merely facetious to say that this
is the first music to be composed for ten fingers and a lock of
hair. Physical gyrations of the limbs, tossings of the head, are
unavoidable if one is to play the piece as though one believed

in it. While it may be melodrama to Mozart's tragedy, its
implications were prodigious.

We do not have to wait long to see the shape the prodigy will
assume. In opus 13 the classical mould is still evident, though
the way in which the introduction is used threatens to break it.
By the time we get to opus 27—the two sonatas which Beethoven described as being *quasi una fantasia*—subjective experience has completely remoulded the mould. The so-called
'Moonlight' Sonata no longer even looks like a sonata. Indeed,
the only sonata movement is the last; we might term its three
sections Prelude, Interlude, and Sonata. The slow prelude
appears to be calm because its movement is smooth; but
beneath the surface hides a tremendous intensity. Its binary
structure is like a miniature sonata movement without a second
subject. We get a hint of its subterranean conflict when, in the
third bar, the Neapolitan chord of D major (in C sharp minor)
strangely disturbs the harmonic perspective. Then follows a
mysterious modulation from the minor of the relative (E) to the
flat submediant (C major)—all this in a piece in C sharp minor!
But this C major proves to be only a kind of 'Neapolitan'
preparation for B minor: which leads to the subdominant
(F sharp minor), followed by a long dominant pedal which
takes us back to the tonic and a recapitulation. The tension is
expressed melodically as well as harmonically, in the interval
of the diminished third (a 'Neapolitan' C natural to A sharp):
this produces acute dissonances of minor ninth and major
seventh with the accompanying figuration (Ex. 23). In the
pseudo-recapitulation this passage is screwed up a tone.

Ex. 23. Beethoven: Sonata in C♯ minor opus 27 No. 2. (first movement)

The interlude that forms the second movement is in the
major, D flat standing for C sharp. The theme is a transformed
version of the prelude's motive; but whereas the prelude is, in
its modulations, all suppressed tension, in the interlude there is
virtually no modulation and no tension at all. It is a 'dream-
minuet, wherein the illusory nature of the tranquillity is suggested by the persistent syncopations that disguise the simple
harmony. The dream is abruptly shattered by the tornado of

the last movement, a full-scale sonata presto which in ferocity
of modulatory conflict and in dynamic keyboard technique far
outstrips anything Beethoven had attempted previously. Here
the anguish that was deceptively hidden beneath the rocking
movement of the prelude, to be dreamfully soothed away in the
illusory minuet, breaks loose; and the relation to the flat
supertonic which had been the root of the prelude's tension
becomes the rhetorical climax of the storm. When this syncopated outburst on the flat supertonic reappears in D major
during the recapitulation, its violence is so extreme that the
movement explodes in a rhetorical coda of seething scales and
arpeggios. Thus in the relationship between the three movements of the sonata, form is reborn in the light of Beethoven's
spiritual autobiography; and the end of the sonata is like a
bursting of dykes, a drowning of consciousness.

This remark is specifically apt, for the work was composed
during the first of the two spiritual crises of Beethoven's life.
He was experiencing what we would now call a nervous break-
down, the causes of which were complex. They had something
to do with his relations with women, or a woman; more to do
with his maladjustment to people and the world in general;
most to do with the threat of approaching deafness, of which he
first became aware about this time. All these causes were so
subtly interlinked as to be in essence one; indeed, one might say
not perhaps that Beethoven's deafness was self-willed, but at
least that it was metaphorical as well as physical. It was a
symbol of his separation from the world; his physical deafness
complements the spiritual isolation to which he had committed
himself, even before his deafness was manifest.

However this may be, it is certain that in 1802 he retired to
the country, shut himself up in solitude, and went through a
period of terrifying mental suffering. While in the country he
wrote an extraordinary, not entirely sane document which is
now known as the Heiligenstadt Testament. It is not in fact a
will, though it makes a few bequests to his brother; it is, however, a document in which, in lamenting his condition,
Beethoven appears voluntarily to relinquish all hold on life.
Some say—on rather inadequate evidence—that Beethoven's
sanity was preserved only by the love of the Countess Giulietta
Guicciardi, to whom he had dedicated the 'Moonlight' Sonata.
But in any case he did not die. He came to admit that

henceforth he would be cut off from the world physically as well as spiritually; but that in becoming a law unto himself he would find salvation. "For you, poor Beethoven," he said, "there is no happiness to be found outside. I have no friends, must live with myself alone." But his isolation is a challenge. "Even with the frailties of my body, my spirit shall dominate. . . . I shall seize Fate by the throat; it shall never wholly subdue me." If he despises the world, it is because "it never divines that music is a greater revelation than the whole of philosophy". If he has no friends in the flesh, he has them in the spirit. If the world is beastly, malignant, and chaotic, he can create order in his art. The more ferocious are the blows of Fate, the more energetically must Beethoven's will subdue them. His art becomes the imposition of order on chaos. The Mozartian equilibrium between the artist and his world has gone. Now the artist's will must shape the world anew.

This process starts in the work which Beethoven began to conceive at Heiligenstadt, though he did not complete it until some years later. His first two symphonies contain anticipations of his later technique, while being based on classical principles. They are insignificant compared with the greatest works of Haydn and Mozart, though fascinating as the creation of a young man of revolutionary genius working within an established tradition. But the Third Symphony is a new kind of music; and we can learn something about the nature of its newness from the sketch-books in which Beethoven recorded the gradual shaping of his works.

Of no composition did he leave more copious annotations than of the 'Eroica' Symphony,* which he was well aware was a key-point in his development—and in that of European music. From these sketch-books it becomes apparent that Beethoven did not, at this period of his career, begin to conceive his symphonic allegros with themes in what one accepts as the 'normal' way. He began by notating brief figures and rhythms, planning the whole movement as a conflict and resolution of motives and tonalities. The precise form of the opening theme of the 'Eroica' emerged only at an advanced stage of the creative process. For Beethoven, at this period of his development, music is conflict, a battle with forces outside the self, before it is self-contained song.

* For a detailed analysis, see the appendix to Riezler's *Beethoven*.

The first movement opens with two hammer-blows of Fate, on the whole orchestra. Then the first theme enters, in the bass. It is not a melody, but an arpeggio of challenge; and it ends, not in triumph, but in conflict, for the bass line lands up on an ambiguous C sharp which might be D flat (Ex. 24). Out of

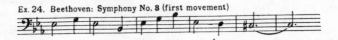

Ex. 24. Beethoven: Symphony No. 3 (first movement)

this equivocation two new motives emerge—a figure rotating around a fixed point, and a rhythmic pattern; these lead into a long dominant preparation in hemiola rhythm (a cross rhythm of 3–2 against the basic 3–4). Then there is a transitional theme built on leaping ninths, another version of the arpeggio motive, inverted and filled in with bouncing semiquavers, more dominant preparation, and then the second subject group: this is partially derived from the rhythmic motive and from the turning figure. This multiplicity of contrasted material goes to create the longest sonata exposition yet written.

The development is on a vast scale, modulating through two cycles of fifths: an upward followed by a downward cycle. Fugato —contrapuntal writing which is freely fugal in character— adds to the excitement; and the climax comes in a tremendous expansion of the hemiola rhythm in which the whole orchestra builds up a progressively accumulating dissonance (Ex. 25):

Ex. 25. Beethoven: Symphony No. 3 (first movement)

Here the orchestra is used like a gigantic percussion instrument; one sees why the piano and the symphony orchestra, rather than the string quartet or violin sonata, were Beethoven's favoured media during the middle years of his life. The screeching, percussive minor seconds of this climax also introduce the most remote possible modulation—to E minor, which stands for F flat minor, the flat supertonic. And then, in this already enormous movement, Beethoven gives us a new theme, which is contrasted in mood, though derived from the turning figure and the motive in triple rhythm. (The sketch-books tell us that Beethoven decided very early on that there should at this point be a new theme, and a modulation to the remoteness of E minor.) The music slips down to the tonic minor, varied scraps of the initial themes reappear, until softly and tentatively the horns re-enter with the arpeggio motive: only too soon, so that they clash with the harmony of the strings! (Even as progressive a musician as the young Wagner used to 'correct' this passage in performance.) In the recapitulation the ambiguous C sharp of the exposition behaves this time as though it were D flat; but apart from the altered modulations produced by this stroke the recapitulation is orthodox. No straight recapitulation could, however, be an adequate resolution of this cataclysmic upheaval; so Beethoven expands the recapitulation into a coda which is itself nearly as long as the exposition. Here the arpeggio theme is transformed so that the tension in its chromatic tail disappears (Ex. 26). It becomes jubilant major

Ex. 26. Beethoven: Symphony No. 8 (first movement)

etc.

arpeggio; and the excitement is enhanced because the themes are combined in double counterpoint. Conflict becomes triumphant apotheosis.

Both the slow movement and the scherzo are built on themes which have hidden affinities with the challenging arpeggio motive. In the *Marcia Funebre* Beethoven deals, in the relatively static form of rondo, with the Hero's death; in the dynamic scherzo with his resurgence. He was not thinking of a literal birth and death; he meant that for him life was the process of Becoming, so that being alive was a series of spiritual deaths and rebirths. The goal of the work thus proves to be the last movement, which is built on the 'monistic' principle of the chaconne: variations on a bass which remains constant. The chaconne theme is the simplest and boldest possible version of the E flat arpeggio with which the symphony had opened; the battle won, the theme can now exult in its strength. It is significant that this theme had first been used by Beethoven in his ballet, *Prometheus*, and again in the 'Eroica' Variations, opus 35.

Now Prometheus challenged the gods and, with the gift of fire, offered man the potentiality to control his own destiny. The Hero about whom Beethoven wrote his symphony is not, of course, the God-King of eighteenth-century autocracy, but the man of strife who is the architect of a new world. Napoleon seemed such a man; though Beethoven contemptuously tore up his dedication when Napoleon proved to be only the architect of a new tyranny. In any case, the real Hero of the symphony is Beethoven himself, as Prometheus; and the battle he fought is not Napoleon's, but the more terrible one he fought alone at Heilingenstadt. He was right in thinking that the battles for his and Europe's salvation were closely related. Haydn and the Enlightenment had seen the alternation of Light and Darkness, Order and Chaos, as primarily a social evolution in which the individual played his part. For Beethoven the alternation of Life and Death has become primarily subjective: because social regeneration can spring only from what used to be called 'a change of heart'.

Immediately after he had finished the 'Eroica', Beethoven started work on a Symphony in C minor, now known as No. 5. He put it aside in order to write the Fourth; but in the Beethovenian cycle the Fifth is the natural successor to the Third, for it develops still further the technique of thematic transformation. The Fifth is the state of Becoming in music, as Bach's last chorale prelude is the state of Being. The movements are not four more or less closely related pieces. They are evolving facets of experience which grow, or are willed, to an inevitable end. The 'form' is the process of evolution, like life itself.

The assertion of the Will in the 'Eroica' had called for a gigantic expansion in the dimensions of the classical symphony. In the Fifth, Beethoven concentrates, and thereby intensifies, his power.* In its aggressive metrical patterns and contrasts of tonality the first movement is the most vehement conflict piece that had ever been written. But Beethoven's intention was not merely to fight a hostile world and an obdurate destiny, but also to subdue them. And in fact each movement is dominated by the same thematic contour, which is transformed during the course of the symphony. In the first movement it takes this

* For a detailed analysis, see Rudolf Reti, *The Thematic Process in Music*.

shape—the rising minor sixth and seventh, with their expression of yearning: followed by the falling and rising third: followed by the minor triad (Ex. 27). The music continually seeks the stability of this arpeggio phrase, with its implied tonic and dominant; and is repeatedly frustrated by the interjections of the rhythmic Fate motive.

In the slow movement each of these three elements reappears, slightly modified, in the passive key of the flat submediant. This

Ex. 27

more lyrical version of the theme is a dream of serenity, which is destroyed by the Fate rhythm (associated with a tonally disruptive diminished seventh), and then transformed into a battle-cry in C *major*. Rondo form is here used to express unresolved fluctuations between submission to dream and challenge to reality. In the scherzo the 'basic' theme is even more clearly evident; until, through the strange melodic wanderings over the dissonant timpani note in the coda, the latent theme emerges in the last movement, born afresh. Now the last phase of the theme appears first, translated into jubilant major arpeggio; the rising *major* sixth and seventh follow (Ex. 28). The fateful rhythm which pervades the figuration is

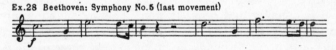

Ex. 28 Beethoven: Symphony No. 5 (last movement)

no longer threatening, but an expression of power; even the direct reminiscence of the scherzo's battle resolves tension into arpeggio. One might almost say that the form of the symphony is the search for the shape which the implicit theme takes in the last movement. At the end even themes are unnecessary; the blaze of C major is enough, for we hear it as though for the first time. A new world and a new sound are born. This is literally true, for Beethoven's orchestra has no precedent: no one before had used trombones in the way Beethoven exploits them at their first entry in the major apotheosis, while piccolo and double bassoon are added purely as noise, to extend the sonorous resources.

In the Fifth Symphony Beethoven has imposed unity on chaos, integrating highly disparate modes of experience. This is reflected both within the single movements, and in the relationship between the movements. The first three movements are not fully intelligible except in relation to the last; and in all his mature music Beethoven seeks, under the pressure of experience, for new relationships between his basic principles of sonata, variation, and rondo—to which he later added fugue. This interrelation exists too between groups of works; we may regard the Third and Fourth, and the Fifth and Sixth Symphonies as complementary.

Beethoven is a composer of strife, and strife between wildly contrasting kinds of experience may sometimes be not tragic, but comic. We are apt to forget that Beethoven's music is often funny; and we have some excuse for forgetting, since his humour is a disruptive force, like his passion. Both his humour and his self-assertion are dramatic, a threat to complacency. We are told that after Beethoven had held his audience spellbound with the rhetoric or pathos of his improvisation he was liable to round on them with a burst of raucous, scarifying laughter, calling them dolts or blockheads. The humour in his music is often similar in effect. Perhaps humour is not the word, and we may rather find in Beethoven's music an exaggerated form of the intense levity which we discovered in Haydn and Mozart, but which disappears in the age of romanticism.

Intense levity we may certainly find in the Fourth Symphony. It opens in archaistic fashion with a slow introduction, solemn, veiled in tonality and orchestration. This heroic sublimity is then abruptly debunked by a burst of Beethoven's raucous mirth—a tootling, footling allegro theme like those of the *buffo* overture or the early rococo symphony. During the development, however, the most weird things happen to this frivolous tune; and the recapitulation is approached by a mysterious passage of enharmonic modulation,* in which a pianissimo pedal note on the timpani gradually changes its significance from A sharp to the tonic B flat. This is a musical pun, and puns are supposed to be funny. But the effect of the passage as a whole is far from comic; it is dramatic and, still more, strange. And its strangeness was already implicit in the mysterious equivocations of the slow introduction: so that, as things turn

* ENHARMONIC MODULATION depends on the fact that, in the equal tempered scale, two notes with different names and functions may have the same pitch. Thus the tonic note in B flat is identical in pitch with A sharp, which might be the leading note in B major or minor, or the major third of the tonic chord of F sharp.

out, it is not the sublime but the debunker who is debunked. Things are not what they seem. There are no clear-cut barriers between the varieties of human experience. The solemn may be absurd, the absurd sinister; the simple mysterious, the mystery an illumination.

Before he had finished the Fifth, Beethoven had already started work on a sixth symphony; in this case he deliberately planned it as a companion-piece. The Fifth is a work about Experience: suffering, frustration, conflict lead to rebirth. The Sixth is its polar opposite, dealing with the state of Innocence.. It is 'pastoral' not because it depicts the external sights and sounds of Nature (though it does that to some extent), but because it expresses a peasant simplicity which is the opposite of Beethoven's tormented self-consciousness. Haydn accepted Nature as the background to human life, and—in *The Seasons*— indicated that the 'laws' of Nature were to some extent a guide to human conduct. Mozart rejected Nature in favour of human beings. Beethoven, more romantically Rousseau-like, used Nature as a refuge from people, saying that only when alone with meadows, woods, and hills did his spirit feel entirely free. As his deafness increased, he became more and more devoted to solitary country walks.

We shall note later than an ambivalence between a peasant-like innocence and the artist's self-consciousness is the impulse behind Schubert's most representative music; and in Beethoven's own last works we shall see him attaining, in a reborn technique, an innocence which is the ripest fruit of experience. The innocence of the 'Pastoral' Symphony is distinct from either of these. One might almost say that it is a deliberate study in innocence by a sophisticated consciousness: Beethoven depicts the state in which he is not, because he cannot understand Experience unless he also knows what Innocence is. So the work is in essence a paradox: a sonata with the minimum of conflict! Tonic and dominant are musical symbols of stability and simplicity, and all the main subjects of the Sixth are pervaded by tonic and dominant arpeggios. An extraordinary proportion of the work is based harmonically on static tonic or dominant chords as a pedal; in the last movement the 'bagpipe' chord of the open ninth compresses tonic and dominant into one chord (Ex. 29). The only section of the symphony to be more richly harmonized is the 'Storm': and this is an

objective presentation of conflict, in the archaic fashion of the
operatic storm (scurrying scales and diminished sevenths),
instead of the subjective drama of sonata style. The peasant

Ex.29 Beethoven: Symphony No.6 (last movement)

consciousness has its storms in the outside world, without being
racked by inner conflict; the only characteristically Beethovenian feature here is the transformation of the theme when
the storm is over.

The treatment of the development section in the first movement is especially interesting. Here, of course, the conflict and
drama ought to occur. In fact, there is no conflict. Beethoven
avoids it by making his modulations simply an effect of colour.
One rhythmic motive and one major triad are repeated
innumerable times in a cycle of descending thirds, with
changing instrumental colours. The effect is significantly like
many of Schubert's submissive modulations to the submediant;
modulation is made to express not strife, but a relapse into
sensuous enjoyment; Beethoven suns himself, like a cat, in these
warmly floating triads. As a whole, the symphony contains
many anticipations in scoring and harmony of Schubert and
even Wagner: consider the romantic use of horn and woodwind
in the telescoping of tonic and dominant seventh in the last
movement (bars 57–64); or the climacteric use of the chord of
the ninth (bar 227).

Though its simplification of technique was a part of Beethoven's evolution, the Sixth Symphony is in some ways a
'sport' in his creative career. In the Seventh he carries on from
the point where the Fifth left off. Conflicts are seething beneath
the surface—Beethoven's modulations have never been more
ruthlessly abrupt, and the whole work is obsessed by the same
contrast between tonic and flat submediant as occurs in the
Sixth, only it is no longer submissive, but a dramatic event.
These conflicts are now, however, obliterated by the fierce
assertion of metre; the wilder the passion, the more vehement is
Beethoven's desire to control it, come what may. Thus the

first movement has only one basic rhythm and one theme; at least if there is a second subject it serves no function as contrast. Even the frenzy of the last movement is strictly controlled. The coda owes its shattering power to the fact that the whirling scales in which it explodes reveal themselves—if only to our subconscious minds—as the fulfilment of the solemn rising scales of the introduction to the first movement. There is still law and order in Beethoven's wild music, though he has become a law unto himself. "Power," he said, "is the morality of those who stand out from the rest, and it is *mine*." That demoniacally obsessive rhythm, those savage transitions, pauses, and silences, the sheer physical impact of the orchestration with its fanatically barking horns—have we perhaps heard these things so often that we have ceased to hear them at all? If we listen afresh, we shall surely find this one of the most terrifying pieces of music ever written, far more scarifying, after a hundred and forty years, than Stravinsky's *Rite of Spring* after forty. If it is 'joyful', it can only be the bloodcurdling joy of battle. No wonder that Weber, on first hearing the extraordinary revolving ostinato that introduces the coda to the first movement, said that Beethoven was now ripe for the madhouse. Weber was no old fogy. He was a younger man than Beethoven, clever, sensitive, one of the most progressive musicians of his day.

The Seventh Symphony relies for its impact largely on metre, tonality, and scoring; melody is comparatively unimportant in all the movements. Indeed, almost the only works in Beethoven's middle period in which cantabile melody is the essence of the music are the Violin Concerto and the slow movements of the third and fourth piano concertos, which preserve the classical relationship between concerto style and opera. In the 'Emperor' Concerto, however, Beethoven associates the exhibitionism of the display concerto with the emotional exhibitionism of his middle years. It seems that in a sense Weber was right: Beethoven could have done nothing further along the lines of the 'Emperor' Concerto and the Seventh Symphony without going mad. In any case, he wrote no more concertos; and the Seventh Symphony and its comic but scarcely less volcanic complement the Eighth are followed by a significant gap in his creative output. For about five years he composed very little music. When creative fecundity returned, he was already producing music radically different from his previous works.

How are these differences manifested in terms of musical
technique? What do they signify in philosophical terms?

Before we attempt to answer these questions we must look
at two works which Beethoven composed during his fallow
years. The E minor Piano Sonata, opus 90, resembles the
middle-period piano sonatas in being highly dramatic; it differs
from them in being concentrated rather than expansive, and in
using themes which combine trenchancy with a *song-like
lyricism*. This sonata movement is followed by one other movement—a rondo in the major, on one of the loveliest song-tunes
ever written. Conflict still exists in the modulatory episodes; but
dissolves away in the lyricism. Now Beethoven himself said
that the first movement of this sonata dealt with the conflicts
and passions of human love—love between man and woman:
and that the second and last movement dealt with their consummation and resolution. Into this rondo Beethoven introduced streams of trills, written out as semiquavers; and we shall
see in a moment that trills came to have a peculiar significance
for Beethoven in his last years.

Shortly after writing this sonata, Beethoven returned to the
violin and piano duo. During his 'middle' period his opus 47
had been his only attempt to apply the shock tactics of his piano
and orchestral music to the relatively inapposite medium of the
violin sonata. Now, in these transitional years, he creates in his
opus 96 a first movement in which the mysterious drama of the
modulations is absorbed into the radiant lyricism of violin
melody; a slow movement which is a hymn-like aria typical of
Beethoven's final years; and a rondo which is a subtly dramatic
metamorphosis of the innocence of popular song. In all the
movements trills play a significant part. Both opus 90 and opus
96 seem to attain the peace of earthly love; and perhaps their
trills suggest that, for Beethoven at least, earthly love was a
necessary step towards heavenly.

With the 'Hammerklavier' Sonata, opus 106, we cross the
threshold into Beethoven reborn world. The first movement in
many ways carries on from the Seventh and Eighth Symphonies.
It is one of the most titanic 'of Beethoven's conflict pieces,
based on assertive metre and modulation. These qualities are,
however, modified by several features. The second subject is
extremely cantabile in character, and is accompanied by extended trills; there is a considerable amount of fugato writing

in the development; and these passages tend to employ a hollow, wide-spaced texture very different from the massive, percussive keyboard style which Beethoven exploits in the opening of this sonata, and consistently throughout a middle-period work such as the F minor opus 57. The Scherzo is also a development from dynamic, middle-aged Beethoven, differing from earlier works mainly in being more elliptical; not even in the Eighth Symphony does Beethoven indulge in punning as terse as the conclusion of this movement.

With the slow movement, however, we approach a new conception. Here we have a sublime song movement in Italian aria style, even with quasi-vocal coloratura. Although the piece is in sonata form, it does not sound like a sonata movement. The second subject does not serve as a dramatic contrast, but is an unbroken lyrical evolution from the first; and the subtle modulations that occur (for instance, the Neapolitan G major within F sharp—really G flat—minor) are harmonic 'colourings' rather than incidents in a tonal argument (Ex. 30). The

Ex.30 Beethoven: Piano Sonata opus 106 (slow movement)

brief development section is also a climax to the expanding lyricism; and the recapitulation is so long and so floridly decorated that it sounds like, and is, a further lyrical growth of the themes. Rhetorical passion dissolves into melody.

Then follows a strange interlude like a recitative, out of which the last movement strives to emerge. Gradually it gathers momentum until it burst into a stupendous fugue: the lyrical evolution of the adagio leads into the principle of Unity itself. But it is a fugue such as never was before or since—a titanic assertion of power. Unity is attained, but after how wild and terrible a struggle. If in the Fifth Symphony Beethoven is in conflict with the forces that threaten the fulfilment of personality, with Fate or Providence or a hostile society, here he is in conflict with himself. He strains to make the ultimate assertion: I will *not* be divided; I *will* be whole. The screaming trills which

dominate the theme and therefore the contrapuntal texture
would seem to express the anguished determination to achieve
unity of being; and in the serene D major episode which
succeeds the most prodigious of all the climaxes he is afforded a
brief visionary glimpse of the peace which this grinding movement is seeking (Ex. 31). Here the parts move mainly by step,

Ex.31 Beethoven· Sonata opus 106 (last movement)

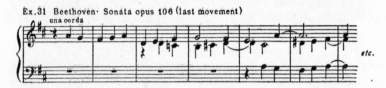

and the texture is as luminous as in the main fugue it is opaque.
The grinding quality of the music is expressed in the struggle
with the medium itself: which is why attempts to orchestrate
this work—or the comparable *Grosse Fuge* for string quartet—
are misguided. The fugue is almost unplayable because it is
an experience that is almost unattainable. Even Beethoven does
not fully attain it here. The vocal-seeming D major episode is
soon routed by the trills of the first fugue-subject; the movement
ends in wild disintegration, only partially redeemed by a final
assertion of the will. So the sonata ends at the point where it
started; and the cycle begins afresh.

What Beethoven strives after in opus 106 he achieves in his
last three sonatas, especially the last of all, opus 111. Here the
first movement is a profound fusion of the contradictory
principles of sonata and fugue. There is one theme, tense in its
harmonic implications, which acquires a more relaxed and
cantabile quality when freely transformed in inversion for the
second subject (in the flat submediant again). This theme is
treated now in fugato, now in sonata style. The two principles
are resolved in the coda that provides a transition into the
second and last movement. The reconciliation of sonata conflict
and fugal unity flows into the oneness of the arietta with
variations. The adagio of opus 106, though it no longer sounds
like a dramatic conflict, is still a sonata movement; in this
arietta the tonal conflict of the first movement is stilled in
heaven. The texture is almost purely diatonic—it even suggests
a Palestrina-like modality; and the theme, having been conceived during the turmoil of the first movement, with the

introduction's fierce descending diminished seventh translated
into a serene fourth, is not again transformed (Ex. 32). Rather
are the variations the continuous flowering of melody, resembling not so much the eighteenth-century notion of variation as

Ex.32 Beethoven: Sonata opus 111 (last movement)

Adagio molto

the sixteenth-century principle of divisions on a ground—a
technique whereby a melody is progressively decorated by
being divided into smaller note values. Finally, the divisions
become so rapid and so ecstatic that there is nothing left except
dissolving trills. The searing trills of opus 106 have found their
rest in the unity of being which is sometimes called Paradise.
Something similar happens at the end of the greatest of all
works in variation form—the Diabelli Variations, opus 120.

Now just as Haydn and Mozart had used symphonic
techniques within their liturgical counterpoint, so they—and
Beethoven himself—had all used fugal techniques in their
sonata movements long before this. But Haydn's counterpoint
is symphonic and Mozart's (even in the last movement of the
'Jupiter') is operatic; while Beethoven's fugato in the coda to the
finale of the Fifth Symphony is simply a rhetorical means of
increasing the excitement. None of them had attempted the
identity of opposites which Beethoven seeks in his final works.
For here he combines the dualistic idea of key conflict with the
apparently irreconcilable idea of melodic growth and fugal
unity: principles which we have seen to be apposite to earlier,
more unified societies. In so doing, Beethoven has once more
recreated form itself. It is worth noting that during his
unproductive period preparatory to the last phase, Beethoven
made a detailed study of the music of Bach, especially of the
Art of Fugue; and that he devoted a good deal of attention to
Palestrina also.

Similarly, Beethoven had used the technique of division-
variation in earlier works. The variations that form the slow
movement of the 'Appassionata' Sonata, for instance, are a set
of divisions which are completely static: the theme is not transformed and the movement is entirely without modulation or
conflict of any kind. The difference between this movement

and the late variation movements lies in the fact that in the late works song melody has become the core of the music. The tune of the slow movement of opus 57 is not significant in itself, and is not intended to be; the point of the movement is to serve as a static contrast to the dynamism of the two allegros. Indeed, it is a dream, like the interlude in the 'Moonlight' Sonata: an illusion of peace which is brutally shattered by the ferociously metrical assertion of the finale's diminished sevenths (Ex. 33):

Ex. 33 Beethoven: Sonata opus 57 (transition from slow movement to finale)

But the song melodies that are the basis of the variations in the 'Archduke' Trio, or still more in the piano sonatas, opus 109 and 111, are all Beethoven knows in earth or heaven, and all he needs to know. The divisions into which they flower are not a dream, but a vision. And—particularly in opus 111—the rebirth of Song is also an escape from metre: a liberation from the shackles of Time.

In orchestral music Beethoven never reached this point. The Ninth Symphony* occupies a transitional position similar to the 'Hammerklavier' Sonata. It is a vast expansion of the technique of thematic transformation which Beethoven explored in the Fifth, in that all the themes of the work are interrelated and coalesce in the song theme of the finale: the point of the 'retrospective' introduction to the last movement is precisely to reveal these interrelations before song melody suggests the physical introduction of the human voice. The technique of division appears in the adagio; the finale is a gigantic fusion of variation and rondo.

But it is in the *Missa Solemnis* that 'late' Beethoven attains his most monumental expression. The work is symphonic in that, like the Ninth Symphony, it is thematically generative; but this style is now fused with a contrapuntal technique that is, like Bach's, basically vocal and, in the Incarnatus and Sanctus, almost as strictly modal as Palestrina. The Benedictus is pure

* For a detailed analysis, see Rudolf Reti, *The Thematic Process in Music.*

song melody, soaring into ecstatic trills, like the Arietta of opus
111. So there is no real distinction between the God Beethoven
worships in his Mass and the God he discovers in his last
instrumental works; indeed he once said: "The relationship of
men towards art is religion." In the Credo, dogma is reduced
to a minimum; Christ for him is spirit incarnate, and therefore
himself in the moments of *raptus* for which he lived and (spiritually) died. He would not, of course, have said blasphemously
that he lived and died (several times) to save mankind; but
when he called the Agnus Dei "a prayer for inner and outward
peace" he had certainly come to feel that the peace he had
himself created in the Benedictus was the only resolution of
conflict within the soul or without. He seems to regard the
trumpery hurly-burly of the world, which so oddly surges up in
the Agnus, from an immense, almost godlike height.

Yet monumentality—godlike or human—is not the most
representative quality of Beethoven's music in his last years.
The string quartet is the quintessential medium of his 'late'
phase, as the piano was of his youth, and the symphony
orchestra of his middle period. Previously, he had devoted
comparatively little attention to the quartet, which, as a
concourse of equal-voiced instruments, did not naturally lend
itself to his dynamic style. When, in the opus 18 series, he composes a Quartet in C minor to some extent inspired by Mozart's
G minor Quintet, he does all he can to imbue Mozart's taut
tragedy with rhetorical melodrama; while in the only quartets
of his middle period, the three of opus 59 and opus 74, he
inflates the quartet into a pseudo-symphonic style. The linear
nature of quartet writing prompts him to create themes rather
more lyrical than his symphonic motives; but the first movement
of opus 59, no. 1, is not only symphonic in its dimensions; even
the texture acquires a symphonic richness and solidity. Though
superbly written for the instruments, in that all the effects
come off, this is hardly a true quartet style.

An authentic string quartet idiom appears for the first time
in the F minor Quartet, opus 95. The first movement is symphonic in that, as Tovey said, an immense drama is packed into
a few minutes; but its extreme concentration relates it to a movement such as the scherzo of the 'Hammerklavier' Sonata. The
second movement is a cross between lyrical song and fugue.
The flow of the lines purges the chromatic harmony of subjec-

tive emotion, much as it does in the polyphony of Bach (Ex. 34).
This is probably the earliest instance of Beethoven's creative
're-thinking' of Bach's style. Already the texture has acquired
that luminosity typical of the slow movements of Beethoven's
last years.

Ex.34 Beethoven: Quartet opus 95 (slow movement)

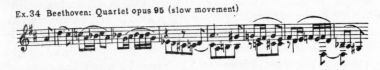

The cycle of 'late' quartets begins with opus 127 and ends
with opus 135. Perhaps the most comprehensive, and certainly
the most complicated, of the works of Beethoven's last period is
the C sharp minor Quartet, opus 131, which Beethoven himself
believed to be his greatest work. The first movement is pure
monism, pure fugue, completely thematic to its smallest detail.
The texture of the music is as smoothly vocal as a fugue of Bach
or even a Renaissance polyphonist; yet the augmented second
in the theme imbues the harmony with an acute inner tension
(Ex. 35). Only in the last movement shall we become fully

Ex.35 Beethoven: Quartet opus 131 (first movement)

Adagio

aware of the fierce spiritual turmoil which has gone to create
this painful serenity.

Then there is an abrupt transition to a scherzo in sonata
form, but with only one subject. This is in the apparently remote
key of D major. Again, the significance of this modulation, in
relation to the fugue, will be revealed to us in the final allegro.
Only then shall we understand why the scherzo theme, for all
its contrasting emotional temperature, should have a hidden
affinity with the theme of the fugue. After the scherzo, an odd
recitative passage leads into the great central piece, an aria
with variations in A major (again the flat sub-mediant, the key
of relaxation which Beethoven favours for so many of his late
slow movements). Like the Arietta of opus 111, this is the
flowering of melody: lyrical generation creates divisions, fugato,
and finally 'a halo of trills', to use Tovey's profoundly appropriate metaphor.

Then follows a strict scherzo, the theme of which is again obscurely related to the Fugue subject. If this is a dance movement, with a Ländler-like trio, it never suggests the earthiness of Beethoven's middle years, nor even Schubert's nostalgia for a sensuous beauty that has passed. The texture is now ethereal, other-worldly. The last movement is prefaced by an arioso passage balancing that between the D major Scherzosonata and the variations. Here the original fugue theme stirs as it were, in its chrysalis, striving to emerge as aria. When, however, the last movement finally bursts upon us we find that we face directly the passions that had been resolved into fugue and lyrical variation. For this is a dramatic sonata movement on a theme which is a freely inverted version of the fugue subject. The harmonic tension of the augmented second has, in this transformed version, become much more obtrusive (Ex. 36); while the development involves a modulation first

Ex.36 Beethoven: Quartet opus 131 (last movement)

to the relative minor of the flat supertonic, then to the flat supertonic itself—the key of the sonata-scherzo that had followed the fugue. In the recapitulation and coda occurs a fight between unifying, stabilizing fugato and sudden eruptions of flat supertonic scales. Fugal unity achieves its victory, though in a singularly melancholy, drooping inversion of the theme, rounded off by a desperate assertion of the tonic major. After this the work can, by implication, start again. Next time we hear the opening fugue we are not surprised that its vocal-seeming calm, its unified diminutions, augmentations, and stretti, should be none the less instinct with suffering.

Just as the quartet forms a cycle of human experience, so it is a kind of microcosm of European musical history. The drama of the sonata principle is resolved back into its elements: first into operatic aria and recitative—with no longer any direct suggestion of the theatre—out of which the interior drama of sonata had grown; then into the rediscovered unity of song variation and fugue. A similar process is evident in other works, such as the A flat Piano Sonata, opus 110. Most subtly of all, perhaps, we find it in the last quartet, opus 135—a work which

seems superficially not only shorter, but also more conventional
in structure than the other late quartets.

The first movement is a terse example of Beethoven's
technique of thematic generation: the basic material of the
quartet germinates as we listen. The scherzo is Beethoven's
middle-period rhetoric restated in epigrams; its tonal shocks are
rarefied in the tenuous texture—as is a long passage built on an
obsessive revolving 'cam' comparable with the notorious
ostinato in the Seventh Symphony. To the slow movement,
which is a cross between aria and variation, in the flat submediant once more, Beethoven appended the significant
direction *'cantante e tranquillo'*. There is virtually no modulation.
Melody dissolves into figuration. In the introduction to the
finale the theme 'created' in the first movement is stated in
unison, and then in a reversion to operatic recitative. The
allegro finale itself is halfway between sonata and fugue; and
the texture grows increasingly rarefied until the theme has shed
both sonata and operatic drama and become as simple as a
folk-song. But this is not, like the 'Pastoral' Symphony, a study
in innocence: it is the innocence that is born of experience.
Beethoven has gone back beyond sonata to opera; beyond opera
to religious polyphony; beyond polyphony to song melody
which is an end in itself; beyond song to the source of melody in
the undivided human consciousness.

In his last works Beethoven has given up the struggle with
the external world so typical of the middle-period symphonies,
because he has fought and won a more important battle in
his own spirit. He had wished to conquer himself in order to
conquer life: "even with the frailties of my body my spirit
shall dominate". But now he says: "O God, give me strength
to conquer myself, for nothing must bind me to this life." This
is the profoundest sense in which his deafness is both a physical
fact and a spiritual allegory. While Beethoven lay dying a
thunderstorm was raging. Just before the end, he raised himself
from the pillows and shook his fist defiantly at the heavens.
Then he fell back; on his face there was an expression of infinite
beatitude. His death, like his life, is a parable which complements his music.

Against the theme which is stated in unison at the beginning
of the finale to his last quartet, Beethoven wrote the words:
"Muss es sein? Es Muss sein." (Must it be? It must be.) This

musical motive has been derived from the thematic discovery of the first movement. The first half of it—the question—is tense, with a diminished fourth (Ex. 37); the second half—the answer —is relaxed, with a perfect fourth (Ex. 38). From this, the angelically childlike song of the coda is evolved. Now Beethoven said that the words he wrote against the theme had

Ex.37 Beethoven: Quartet opus 135 (last movement)

Ex.38 Beethoven: Quartet opus 135 (last movement)

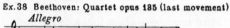
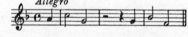

reference to a request by his housekeeper for more money. Possibly they did: the explanation is typical of the Beethoven who would rend his audience's awe-struck silence with harsh mirth. But the words are also metaphysical. The question summarizes Beethoven's years of revolt against destiny; the answer summarizes his new-found humility. In his last work question and answer have become one. Like Blake, Beethoven knew that 'without contraries there is no progression'.

With the exception of Bruckner, Beethoven was the only composer born after Bach who had, or, rather, came to have, a profoundly religious mind. A movement like the 'Song of Thanksgiving on Recovery from Sickness' (from the A minor Quartet) is an altogether new kind of religious music, however much its modality may link it with techniques that were obsolete in Beethoven's day. Haydn's religion was ethical humanism, and Mozart's was love of life balanced by an acceptance of death. But Beethoven in his last works found, like Kant, that "we live in an invisible church, God's kingdom is in ourselves". Unlike Palestrina or Bach, he had no accepted creed to help him. He had to win his joy and his peace—his unified being, his glimpse of Paradise—out of "air which is now thoroughly small and dry, smaller and drier than the will.... Consequently I rejoice, having to construct something Upon which to rejoice."

And that we have paraphrased T. S. Eliot's *Ash Wednesday* is no accident. It is well known that Mr. Eliot wrote his cycle of poems, *Four Quartets*, with the impact of Beethoven's late quartets in mind. He would not claim to be a Beethoven; but in his smaller and more self-conscious way he has been trying—and in circumstances that seem now even more 'unpropitious' than they were in Beethoven's day—to deal with precisely the kind of experience with which Beethoven was preoccupied. We should perhaps leave a great poet with the last word; for the conclusion of *Little Gidding* comes about as close to describing in words what Beethoven's last quartets are about as is humanly possible:

> We shall not cease from exploration
> And the end of all our exploring
> Will be to arrive where we started
> And know the place for the first time.
> Through the unknown, remembered gate
> When the last of earth left to discover
> Is that which was the beginning;
> At the source of the longest river
> The voice of the hidden waterfall
> And the children in the apple-tree
> Not known, because not looked for
> But heard, half-heard, in the stillness
> Between two waves of the sea.
> Quick now, here now, always—
> A condition of complete simplicity
> (Costing not less than everything)
> And all shall be well and
> All manner of thing shall be well
> When the tongues of flame are in-folded
> Into the crowned knot of fire
> And the fire and the rose are one.

5

SCHUBERT

WE HAVE seen that Haydn, Mozart, and Beethoven were all revolutionary composers in the sense that they reacted against certain elements in the society in which they lived. Mozart's reaction was more conscious than Haydn's, and Beethoven's was more conscious than Mozart's. Yet Beethoven no less than his predecessors still believed in civilization; at least until the last years of his life he thought that although change was necessary it was feasible, and that the future was worth living for. Not all his calculated will to be misunderstood can alter the fact that he achieved as great a material success as any composer has a right to expect. He was an international celebrity who, on his own admission, had seven or eight publishers—blackguards though they might be one and all— vying with one another for permission to publish his works. He was able proudly to follow through his destiny.

With Schubert [1797–1828] one approaches the typically romantic view of the world. When he was born, in 1797, Mozart had been dead six years, and Beethoven was approaching the first crisis of his career. By Schubert's time, the corruption within Viennese society could be disguised neither by the tawdry frivolity of a degenerating aristocracy, nor by the industry, piety, and cosy sentimentality of the middle class, to which Schubert's parents belonged. Both aristocratic triviality and the bourgeois mentality represented by the newspaper cartoon Biedermeier—an anticipatory 'little man' or 'man in the street'—were an escape from fear. Schubert had no use for either, except in so far as he absorbed Italian opera from the the one and urban popular music from the other. He rather sought his salvation in a communion of kindred spirits. Popular legend used to interpret the 'bohemian' behaviour of the Schubert circle as the irresponsible gaiety of the artist's life. In fact, it grew from a deepening despair. The members of the Schubertiad were poets, dramatists, painters, all university men and mostly brilliant, cultivated, worldly-wise. Schubert would not have been their companion had he been no more than the unthinking song-bird of romantic myth. So far from being irresponsible, Schubert and his friends were acutely conscious of political oppression in Austria, even to the point of revolutionary fervour. At the same time, they felt powerless to change their own and their country's destiny. Corruption had gone too far. All they could hope to do was to find in friendship a society which, being based not on autocratic power, but on human feeling, kept alive, instead of stifling, the spirit. They were an intellectual minority, awaiting their doom, if not calmly, at least with their eyes wide open.

One might almost say that Schubert is a composer of Friendship as Bach had been a composer of the Church and Handel a composer of the State. We shall see later that although Schubert wrote music for the Church, he no longer believed in an institution which he equated with political oppression: so that his music is never liturgical in spirit. He also wrote operas, though he no longer believed in the State which heroic opera had been designed to celebrate: so that his operas remained unperformed or were unsuccessful. All his greatest music he wrote for himself and his friends; yet by writing this music he was no longer able to keep himself alive. Beethoven may have felt bitter that his greatest material success was *The Battle of Vittoria*, while his last quartets left the public bemused, if not hostile; none the less, he made a substantial income by composing, by and large, the kind of music he wanted to compose. Schubert, on the other hand, as a freelance musician, had to produce entertainment music for a degenerate aristocracy and a sentimental bourgeoisie whose tastes he could no longer fully share. While he enjoyed writing his innumerable waltzes, marches, and polkas, he would have preferred to spend some of the time composing symphonies and sonatas; and while it would be going too far to say that there is a split between Schubert's 'occasional' and his 'serious' music, it is not extravagant to say that they are beginning to differ in kind as well as, like Mozart's, in degree.

So there is throughout Schubert's personality and music a strange equivocation. As a man he was, like Beethoven, conscious of political oppression in Austria; unlike Beethoven, he did not think it was possible or perhaps even desirable to do anything about it. As a musician, he revered Beethoven with self-obliterating fanaticism; yet he deplored what he called Beethoven's "eccentricity, which drives a man to distraction, instead of resolving him in love". And so his own quintessential music seems to be created simultaneously out of conflict with the world as it was (the Beethovenian aspect of his work) and out of a utopian yearning for Viennese civilization as he imagines it had once been (the early Mozartian, lyrical, and vocal aspect of his work). Hence his music's combination of strength with melancholy. From one point of view, like Beethoven, he heroically protests; from another he seeks in his music to resolve his frustration in love, to create a world in which ideals are not corrupted by people's malice or stupidity. "Often I feel I do not belong to this world at all," he once said. He becomes his own Wanderer. Communing with solitude, he discovers a world of the imagination which can soothe and satisfy as real life cannot.

We have observed that the essential characteristic of Mozart's mature music is its equilibrium between lyrical melody and tonal drama: which is the musical epitome of a precariously balanced civilization. We have seen too that through the course of his life Beethoven achieved out of tonal drama a rebirth of the lyrical and contrapuntal principle: which is also a re-creation of a religious view of life. Schubert, with his romantic sense of separation, has not the Mozartian equilibrium; lyricism and tonal drama are not miraculously at one, but have to win through to a reconcilation. On the other hand, there is nothing in Schubert's work comparable with Beethoven's conquest of serenity. The innocence that Beethoven attained was the fruit of experience; the innocence that Schubert seeks is, like that of the 'Pastoral' Symphony, the expression of a pre-self-conscious state. We shall see that his most representative music springs from an ambivalence between the anguish of the conscious mind and a nostalgic reversion to the simple acceptance of childhood.

It is significant that whereas Beethoven discovered song melody through the course of a spiritually tormented life, Schubert was, as the saying is, 'born' with a gift of unpremeditated song. He is essentially a lyrical composer; and of the classical masters only Mozart seems to have had no problems in accommodating song melody to sonata drama. We must say

'seems' because we have Mozart's own admission that the
critical works in his career, the 'Haydn' quartets, cost him a
great deal of trouble. Certainly, Schubert's first efforts as a
sonata composer were not convincing; and he achieved maturity
as a song composer at an age when his symphonies and sonatas
had not advanced beyond prettiness and pastiche.

The importance of solo song in Schubert's day was not
fortuitous; for the Lied was domestic and intimate, an art of
friendship. History books used to refer to Schubert as 'The
Father of Song'. Although the description is nonsensical—in so
far as great solo songs have been created from the troubadours
to Dowland, from Dowland to Mozart himself—it is not as
silly as it seems: for Schubert's *kind* of song is a creation of his
age. A song of Dowland is passionate, but never dramatic; the
passion is absorbed into the flow of line. A song of Bach or
Handel is dramatic, but never subjective. Even Mozart, who
was still essentially an opera composer though his notion of
opera differs from Handel's, in his songs objectifies his experience in 'characters'. Thus his little song, '*Als Luise die Briefe ihres
ungetreuen Liebhabers verbrannte*', summarizes an operatic situation
in a couple of pages; we experience Luise's feelings through the
glass of Mozart's creativity. Even the lovely setting of Goethe's
Das Veilchen incorporates into its tender lyricism something of
operatic rhetoric and of the interior drama of sonata style:
consider the development-like minor opening of the middle
section, and the diminished sevenths of the recitative climax.
Abendempfindung is perhaps the only song of Mozart which
approaches the introspective lyricism of the Lied; and it is still
partially Italianate in line.

Now, Schubert was brought up on Italianate opera: on
reminiscences of the high baroque; on Gluck; on his beloved
Mozart; on Rossini [1792–1868], whose fashionably glittering
re-creation of bel canto was all the rage in Vienna. The earliest
works of his adolescence were operatic scenas in recitative and
arioso. Like their prototypes, the ballads of Zumsteeg [1760–
1802], they deal, in the German language, with subjects usually
taken from German folk-myth, rather than from the myths of
classical antiquity. Musically, however, they simply transfer
Italian opera to the drawing-room, with the piano taking the
place of the orchestra. The young Schubert even set a scene
from Goethe's *Faust* in this style; the music is interesting in both

its strength and its weaknesses. The vocal line is powerful and the setting of the words sensitive; the harmony and modulations are bold. But the young composer shows no capacity to organize his audacities; and in the drawing-room he cannot rely on the adventitious support of dramatic action. After his youth, he composed no more of these scenas. To the model of the Rossinian aria, however, he returned intermittently throughout his life. *Der Hirt auf dem Felsen*—in which sophisticated Rossinian coloratura merges into the Austrian rusticity of the yodelling song—is a composition of Schubert's maturity. One of his last compositions was a series of settings of poems by the old-style Italian opera librettist, Metastasio.

While the operatic element remained potent in south German song, there was another tradition in the north. The prototype of this we can examine in the beautiful religious songs of C. P. E. Bach. These were meant to be sung in the home rather than in church, to the accompaniment of a chamber organ. They may be grouped into three main types: songs based on the style of the Lutheran chorale; songs in cantata aria style; and songs in the rococo manner, with tunes of a more popular flavour. Of these types the two former were developed from the techniques of his father, though Carl Philipp emphasizes the 'pathetic' effect of chromaticism and of appoggiaturas so strongly that the music seems more subjective than liturgical. The third type, in being related to folk-song, forged a link between Sensibility and the Bourgeois.

Such domesticated religious songs provided a model which was finally secularized by composers such as Reichart and Zelter; in whose songs, of course, the piano takes the place of the chamber organ. Musically, their work seems pallid compared with C. P. E. Bach's pathos; but their historical interest is considerable, for they rendered Sensibility homely. Their declamation is supple; their harmony and piano writing gently illustrative of the text. J. S. Bach had developed illustrative figurations in his instrumental parts for symbolical as well as for musical reasons. The early composers of Lieder used them for their naturalistic appeal; for their music is a portrayal of everyday life.

The intimate character of these Lieder is thus inseparable from their relation to their texts; the growth of a new school of song parallels the growth of a school of lyric poetry. All the

members of Schubert's circle wrote verse; Mahyrofer was a poet
of romantic melancholy who may claim a modest distinction
in his own right. The supreme figure of Goethe dominated the
literary scene, and most song composers set his lyrical poems.
A collection of folk poems published under the title of *Des
Knaben Wunderhorn* also made a deep appeal to romantic
sensibility, as an escape from introspective perplexities; so did
the philosophical abstraction of Schiller, and the 'gothick'
medievalism of Sir Walter Scott. The lyric poets were all
romantically subjective: Novalis dealing with frustrated love,
consumption, and heavenly aspirations, Rückert, Rellstab, and
Heine with the ego in love and torment.

All this ruminative poetry found an ideal partner in the early
nineteenth-century piano. For Schubert the piano, as opposed
to the harpsichord, was an evocative instrument. It could be
warmly cantabile, while at the same time it could efface itself
to create a poetically 'orchestral' background. Song for him is a
union between lyric poetry, the human voice, and the piano.
Each element is equally important. The words must be heard,
but the voice must sing, not speak; the piano must both support
the singer and underline the meaning of the text. Schubert once
said that when Vogl and he performed his songs, singer and
pianist were as one. Such a performance is essentially intimate;
Schubert gave only one public concert in his life. He wrote his
songs for himself and his friends to sing and play. If they were
published, they could be performed by other people in their
homes also; but they were not addressed to the outside world.

In his adolescence, Schubert composed two kinds of song:
domesticated operatic scenas of the type we have already
discussed; and simple strophic songs in folk style, on the model
of Zelter [1758–1832]. His first songs of genius fuse these two
manners. Two of the most justly celebrated songs—*Gretchen
am Spinnrade* and *Erlkönig*—were written in his teens. Both have
lyrical melodies of great beauty; both use figuration in the
piano part suggested by the poem (the spinning wheel and the
galloping horse); both develop this figuration as a purely
musical means of organization, as J. S. Bach had done; both
extract a tremendous dramatic urgency from the interplay of
vocal line and piano figuration.

One cannot imagine these songs being improved if Schubert
had composed them at a more mature age. None the less, his

art deepens and develops; during the next decade he learns to imbue his song writing with the melodic flexibility, harmonic richness, and symphonic breadth of his later instrumental works. Thus his setting of Goethe's *Prometheus* is a through composed song* which derives from the quasi-operatic scenas of his youth; only whereas they were diffuse, this is concentrated. The declamatory line now has lyrical power; and the audacious modulations—the sequence of diminished sevenths and the extraordinary chromatic climax—become progressive stages in a structure related to both melody and tonality, rather than unco-ordinated, if fascinating, incidents. The association of this massively potent song with the Promethean legend is significant; the Beethovenian aspect of Schubert here finds its apex in song writing.

Prometheus is a declamatory song which has become lyrical and symphonic. *Die Junge Nonne* is a lyrical and meditative song which has become dramatic. It tells a story and paints a scene: but does so by means of a self-contained melody and a piano figuration suggested by the poem. The girl who is singing has retired to a convent as a consequence—it is implied, if not stated—of frustrated love. Outside, a storm is raging. She welcomes her heavenly bridegroom, instead of an earthly lover; and the tolling of the convent bell gradually transforms the storm's conflict into ecstasy. The melody has the girl's simplicity; while the storm figuration of the piano part— oscillating enharmonically between the tonic minor and the minor of the flat supertonic—suggests the suppressed agitation of her soul. The change from agitation to ecstasy is effected through the alternation of minor and major—a relationship of peculiar significance in all Schubert's mature music.

This song is thus lyrical in character. Yet its lyricism includes passionate drama; and this drama is a projection of Schubert's own situation. It is not a religious song. The nun, like Schubert, is voluntarily separated from a pain-inflicting world. Having lost her real lover, she idealizes him into a dream-lover who is free of the imperfections of mortality. She seeks a new Eden. The contrast with Mozart is interesting. His Luise is a being other than Mozart, though we experience her sufferings through

---

* THROUGH COMPOSED SONG: a song in which the words are set to music continuously, as compared with a STROPHIC SONG, in which the same music is used for each verse.

Mozart's personality; Schubert's young nun is one of many masks for Schubert himself. Mozart's song is operatic and objective; Schubert's is domestic and self-revelatory.

Schubert's use of the mask reaches its culmination in the two Müller cycles which are his supreme achievement as a songwriter. Müller was born in the same year as Schubert, and died a few months earlier. He was an intellectual and a soldier, and in both capacities a misfit. His cycle of poems about the miller tell a story, set in the Austrian countryside, of a young man's disappointed love. The girl is stolen from him by a mysterious Green Huntsman; left alone, he contemplates suicide. As poetry, Müller's verses are undistinguished. He expresses a stock romantic myth in conventional romantic gestures. Yet this myth has deep roots in the human mind. Whether or no Schubert had a soul-destroying love affair of the kind described here, there is no doubt that this is how he—as well as Müller—saw himself as a lover. He cannot compete with the Huntsman's buoyant vitality. It has even been suggested that there may be another strand to the allegory: the Huntsman is Beethoven, the puny hero Schubert, and the girl Recognition and Success.

The *Winterreise* songs form a sequel. The girl has gone before the cycle opens. Winter has followed spring, and the pilgrim trudges down a solitary road. He lulls himself with a dream of spring renewed, but has to awaken to a cold and hostile world. A signpost points the way he must go; at the end of the path is the setting sun. His life's sun sinks, following the suns of love and hope. As he walks on his lonely road the only human figure to be seen is the hurdy-gurdy man who grinds out a wheezy tune to which no one listens. The brook, the trees, the raven, the weather-vane, the hurdy-gurdy man to whose one tune the pilgrim sings his story become projections of the unconscious. If in the Miller songs Schubert wrote out of his own frustrated life and love, in the *Winterreise* songs he was thinking of his illness and death. He called the cycle "a bunch of terrifying songs", and said that he thought more highly of them than of anything he had created. Almost immediately after their completion, his health broke down finally. Terrifying is the right word: not because they are grisly, but because of their complete absence of emotional indulgence. "Human-kind cannot bear Very much reality": but this Wanderer can, to the point of madness or death. The two cycles are the apotheosis of the personal life in lyrical song, as is Wagner's *Tristan* in a new kind of opera.

Musically, for the Miller songs Schubert returns to the lyric types of his youth, as befits the simplicity of the miller, and the rustic setting which appealed to him with so deep a nostalgia. But the folk-song-like tune is subtly enriched, partly through the intrusion within the strophic pattern of arioso elements (or lyrical declamation); partly through the symphonic treatment of the piano part and the structure of the cycle as a whole. Thus the cycle opens with the miller singing at his work, in unaffected innocence, unseared by experience. The brook is murmuring in the background, and in the next song rambles at its own sweet will. As the miller's story unfolds, the sounds of brook and birds become an emotional commentary in the piano part. At the end, only the brook is left, oblivious of human suffering. The songs that deal with the brook itself and with the miller in his Eden are in the simple strophic form, unmodified. When the vocal line becomes more distressed and declamatory, the piano parts tend to become more symphonic: consider the use of the ostinato figure in *Pause*.

This tendency is developed much further in the *Winterreise* songs, in which the vocal lines are relatively tortuous. Lyricism acquires elements of arioso and recitative in order to express the intensest feeling. The falling leaves of *Letze Hoffnung* suggest a distraught rhythm that disrupts the bar-line; *Der Greise Kopf* is built on an immense ascent up a thirteenth which falls like a breaking wave, to express the anguish that destroys the body as well as the soul (Ex. 39). The wandering line of *Die Krähe*,

Ex.39 Schubert:

with voice and piano in unison, accompanied by inexorably flowing triplets, marvellously evokes a mental and spiritual desolation; and all the introspective lamenting is finally projected into the figure of the solitary beggar, in the whine of whose hurdy-gurdy rest the sorrows of the world. This is the conclusion not only of a song cycle, but of a cycle of experience. Schubert has passed beyond the romantic individualism which was his original impetus, and has reached the tragic apotheosis. The Pilgrim is himself; but the beggar with whom he becomes identified, who sings his song and whose song he sings, is other than himself. His suffering is absorbed into that of humanity.

The same is true of Schubert's 'swan-songs', the Heine settings. In *Die Stadt*, that strange anticipation of the static harmonic technique of impressionism, the traveller's sorrow merges into the desolation of the silent town; in *Am Meer* personal grief is swallowed in the eternal lament and consolation of the sea. Finally, in *Der Doppelgänger*, the *alter ego* meets the Self and "mocks those torments I went through years ago". Schubert stands apart from his suffering; the intense declamation of his new lyric style is controlled by a passacaglia-like austerity of form. Even the piercing enharmonic modulation at the climax does not break the remorseless repetition of the Dies Irae motive in the bare, skeletonic piano texture (Ex. 40):

Ex.40 Schubert: 'Der Doppelgänger'

There is one song in the *Winterreise* cycle which epitomizes the Schubertian paradox. In *Frühlingstraum* the sensuously harmonized, folk-like melody, yearning up to the major sixth and drooping down to the fourth, is his dream of spring, his nostalgia for a lost innocence (Ex. 41). The Raven of experience shatters

Ex.41 Schubert: 'Frühlingstraum'

the dream in acute dissonances and in rapid sequential modulations ending in the minor (Ex. 42). The slow section that follows hovers ambiguously between major and minor, questioning whether the dream be revelation or deceit (Ex. 43). The final answer is the stark minor triad; innocence once lost is lost for ever. Perhaps this is why the major melody in this song is even more melancholy than the minor section: the heart remembers spring, but cannot reawaken it.

Ex.42 Schubert: 'Fruhlingstraum'

da war es kalt und finst - er es schrieen die Rab-en vom Dach

Ex.43 Schubert: 'Fruhlingstraum'

Wer mal-te die Blät-ter da? Ihr lacht wohl ü - ber den Träumer

If this equivocation between innocence and experience is the core of Schubert's music, we can understand why he should have taken longer to attain maturity in instrumental terms than in song. As an instinctive song-writer, he created melodies which were self-contained, rather than material for development. Similarly, his romantic harmonic and modulatory sense lent itself to rhapsodic effects that were convincing in a song but disruptive in a symphony. Yet he could ignore his melodic and harmonic gifts only by denying his creativity. So at first, in instrumental music, he had to be content with pastiche of the masters he revered and feared. Playing down the tense equilibrium of Haydn and Mozart and the subversive violence of Beethoven, he accepted the hedonistic style that was so popular in Vienna. Gradually he learned how to make his own kind of melody and harmony symphonic.

Many movements in Schubert's early symphonies and quartets, being modelled upon particular movements of Haydn, Mozart, and Beethoven, are inspired by art rather than by life. Their fundamental weakness is not, however, the parasitic nature of the material, but the tug-of-war between the dramatic, classical nature of this material and the lyrical, romantic nature of Schubert's temperament. His second subjects tend to be too long and cantabile; in enjoying them, Schubert forgets the dramatic structure of his symphony. Even when the themes are short, they are usually self-contained tunes, so that there is nothing to be done with them except to repeat them in sequences. Schubert's expositions then anticipate the only technique he can use to extend the music during the development section. Even when—as in the approach to the recapitulation of the first movement of the First Symphony—he lights on an impressive idea, the effect is no more than a romantic incident. To repeat the material of the slow introduction in the tempo of the allegro leads one to expect a grand apotheosis. In fact, nothing happens except a literal repeat, bathetic after so exciting a preparation.

Schubert's passive luxuriance in flatwards-tending modulations is another source of trouble to him. Frequently he will introduce his second subjects not in the dominant, but in the flatter subdominant; to compensate for this he has to append a long codetta insisting on the dominant. These threefold expositions are partially responsible for the inconclusive nature of his developments: and for his reliance on mechanical sequences to effect a recovery.

In the Fourth Symphony, which he himself termed 'Tragic', Schubert courageously attempts to advance beyond rococo pastiche and to measure up to the Beethovenian ideal. The slow introduction suggests not only Beethoven, but the Mozart of the 'Dissonance' Quartet and Cherubini. Its sweeping phrases, romantic modulations, and acute dissonances are powerful, as is the opening theme of the allegro. If this boldly leaping arpeggiated theme reminds us of Beethoven's opus 18 Quartet in the same key and to a lesser degree of Mozart's G minor Symphony and Quintet, it also has character of its own. It grows into a contrasting, consoling theme in the flat submediant —a key-relationship which is to play so important a part in Schubert's later music. This theme is abruptly cut short by a descent to E major, standing for F flat—a further descent to the flat submediant at once sensuous and dramatic. This is a magnificent opening which Schubert is unable to sustain. Drama is frittered away in sequential modulations; and none of the other movements even attempts a Beethovenian grandeur.

Having failed to create a Beethovenian symphony, Schubert

seems, in his Fifth and Sixth, to take a contrary path. The Fifth is as unpretentious as early Mozart; and though he calls the Sixth a 'Grand' symphony, the heroic manner survives for no more than a few bars of the introduction. The first allegro theme is song-like and unsymphonic. It lasts eight bars; but is spun out by sequences and appendices to seventy-four, before we arrive at the dominant. The second subject is also Rossinian. On such material the development can be no more than a charming amble; and without any dramatic argument there is no way of bringing the music to a stop except a *più mosso* coda to work up the excitement in a synthetic theatricality. The movement is not unsuccessful since it is without pretension. But it did rather seem that, as a composer of symphonies and quartets, Schubert had lost heart.

A way out was perhaps suggested by the E major Quartet of 1816; for this work shows how Rossinian vivacity can be imbued with the dramatic urgency of the Viennese sonata. When, after a period of four years, Schubert composed another work for string quartet he had entered a world that was neither Rossinian nor Beethovenian, but his own. In the Quartettsatz in C minor the melodies are no longer Italianate; their yearning lyricism marks the emergence of the solitary Schubert of the last years. The fluttering ostinato accompaniment suggests some demoniacal night-ride such as he depicts in the piano parts of his songs; and the contrast between this feverish C minor and the sweetly submissive flat submediant in which the second subject appears is the impetus behind the music's structure.

In the two succeeding years Schubert achieved a comparable maturity as a symphonist. In the E major and the 'Unfinished' B minor he is no longer writing classical pastiche nor emulating Beethoven; he has created his own type of autobiographical symphony, for "my compositions are the product of my mind and spring from my sorrow; only those that were born of grief give the greatest delight to the outside world". Songs such as *Die liebe Farbe*, *Suleika*, and *Der Doppelgänger* suggest that B minor had a peculiar evocative significance for Schubert. Not only the poetic theme, but also many of the musical motives of the songs appear in the symphony. The unharmonized opening theme, with its rising third and falling fourth, is a melodic seed from which song generates. The strings hum as the theme slowly comes to life on oboe and clarinet—an effect which

Bruckner was later gigantically to expand. The music comes to rest on a sustained D which changes its meaning from a third to a fifth: so that the second subject appears in the flat submediant again, without preparatory modulation. It is a song tune with a folk-like simplicity, though its persistently drooping fourths are full of regret. It flows to silence: which is savagely sundered by a C minor arpeggio.

The development creates a tremendous battle out of the lyrical material of the opening eight bars. The first-group song themes try to re-establish their identity, but are repeatedly shattered by the surging arpeggio. The consolatory second subject does not reappear until, after a terrific martial climax on the Neapolitan chord to B minor, the music dies back to its source. Song melody has achieved its victory: so the andante that follows can be lyricism unperturbed. It is in rondo form, but unlike Schubert's earlier, cheerfully fragmentary rondos in that all the richly exquisite lyricism grows out of the rising third of the opening. The movement is in E major—the key of the nostalgic heaven of the Wanderer in *Der Lindenbaum, Des Baches Wiegenlied*, and many other songs; and in its unity and its unfettered songfulness is a vision of bliss. But the heaven of Schubert's Pilgrim is not the mystical state of pure Being for which Beethoven sought in his last works. It is the recovery of Eden, of the innocence of direct response to Nature. For this reason it is in essence sensuous: as is the mellifluous woodwind scoring in this most poetic of all symphonic movements.

These three crucial works in Schubert's development—the Quartettsatz in C minor, the E major and B minor Symphonies— were all left unfinished. Various explanations have been offered. May not the basic reason be very simple? Schubert had finally solved his most difficult technical and imaginative problem. He had resolved drama into song; and in the andante of the B minor had followed this resolution with the bliss of Eden. He could not rest permanently in a recovered Eden; but at this stage in his career he could not see how he could continue without descent to bathos. He found an answer only in the last three quartets and the C major Quintet, composed during the last four years of his life.

In some ways, the A minor Quartet is the most representative of all Schubert's instrumental works. It opens with one of his most nostalgic song themes, oscillating around the mediant: a relationship very common in Schubert's tunes and partially responsible, no doubt, for his fondness for mediant modulations. This song melody is surrounded by a pianissimo haze of floating quavers: a romantic, orchestral sonority which suggests the withdrawal of the lonely singer from the hurly-burly of life (Ex. 44). The world of dream appears in the andante, which is

Ex.44 Schubert: Quartet in A minor (first movement)

based on a song from *Rosamunde*; but its pastoral innocence is threatened by upsurgings of feverish energy. The minuet adapts Schubert's earlier setting of Schiller's *Schöne Welt, wo bist du*: 'O lovely world, where are you? Return once more, O fair and flowered age of Nature.' The key is minor, the mood as desolate as that of the *Winterreise*. Innocent happiness appears in the major interlude of the trio; but the theme is again dreamily nostalgic, the happiness retrospective. Throughout, yearning for the 'fair and flowered age of Nature' alternates with despair of ever attaining it. Even the last movement, though it seems to be gay, is mysterious beneath its exuberance; continual alternations of major and minor recall the *Frühlingstraum* rondo.

The A minor Quartet is pervaded by the consciousness of death, but soothes in its lyricism. In the posthumous D minor, the poetic idea is contained in the andante, a series of variations on Schubert's early song, *Der Tod und das Mädchen* ('Death and the Maiden'). Although the maiden's song flowers from its elegiac opening into a blissful major conclusion, the mood of the quartet is more fevered than that of the A minor. Perhaps because he is more death-haunted, Schubert organizes his material more tautly. All the movements are dominated by a grim rhythmic motive which, in the final sonata-rondo, gathers itself into a Dance of Death in tarantella style. The music is fiercer than anything in the *Winterreise* cycle: but equally unflinching.*

The last quartet, in G, is the biggest and most powerful of all.

* It is worth noting that Vienna, in the decade following Schubert's death, produced perhaps the first two distinguished composers to devote all their energies to the creation of 'functional' music for entertainment—the waltz kings Lanner [1801-1843] and the elder Strauss [1804-1849].

Schubert's first quartets had been domestic music for amateurs. This quartet is extremely difficult to play, and extracts from the four instruments an almost orchestral sonority. The alternation of major and minor, which we have seen to be both a poetic idea and a sensuous effect in Schubert's music, here becomes dramatic and structural. It is stated at the massive opening (Ex. 45), is the source of the development's conflict, and is stated in inverse order at the beginning of the recapitulation. The

Ex.45 Schubert: Quartet in G (first movement)

andante expresses the alternation of innocence and experience in one of Schubert's typical modifications of rondo form. A sweetly lyrical melody, with nostalgically yearning sixths, is repeatedly interrupted by a feverish agitato figure. This both disrupts the flow of melody with its frantic tremolandos and splinters the music's tonal stability with its weird enharmonic modulations. An obsessively reiterated figure strives to preserve a tonal centre against these destructive forces (Ex. 46); in the

Ex.46 Schubert: Quartet in G (slow movement)

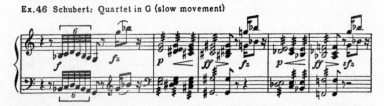

coda the terrifying Reality is resolved in a major apotheosis of the Dream. The innocence attained, if attained it is, is retrospective, and therefore melancholy. In music such as this one might almost say that Schubert has become a 'modern' composer: not merely because his technique is advanced, but also because the experience which the technique serves is centred in moral isolation, rather than in the solidarities of belief.

The last movement of the G major Quartet is again a wild tarantella, with kaleidoscopic modulations and abrupt oppositions of major and minor. Though it is less frenzied than the finale of the D minor Quartet, there is something obsessional in its driving vitality; and in that respect it points the way to the C major Symphony—the Grand Symphony which Schubert had aspired to create throughout his working life. Aiming at epic grandeur in the manner of Beethoven's Ninth, this symphony turns out to be as unlike Beethoven as it is unlike the lyrical 'Unfinished'.

The slow introduction with which it opens is a classical precedent reborn in the spirit of romanticism. The solo horn theme is one of the earliest horn-calls through the forest of German romanticism. But the tune itself is in a sombre march rhythm, like a chorale or a pilgrim's song; and the marching pilgrim is the solitary Wanderer of the *Winterreise*, for the symphony is an epic statement of what the *Winterreise* songs say in intimate terms. Despite its classic grandeur, the theme is romantically irregular in rhythm, and wavers in tonality between C major and A minor. It leads by way of a gigantic crescendo into the first allegro theme, in an energetic motor rhythm. The second subject opens in the minor of the mediant— not the flat submediant in this powerfully assertive work. It is derived from the rising third of the introduction, as is much of the material of the whole symphony. The development is short, after so vast an exposition; but there is an enormous coda in which the chorale returns accompanied by a multiplicity of subsidiary marching and stamping rhythms. Song melody proves triumphant after metrical violence and tonal drama have done their worst; but the song is not itself transformed, so this glorious conclusion has no resemblance to Beethoven's symphonic finales.

The slow movement is a Schubertian rondo which alternates a wry oboe theme in the Wanderer's march rhythm with a cantabile melody is Schubert's passive flat submediant. This march rhythm may have derived from Schubert's obsession with the allegretto of Beethoven's Seventh Symphony; the significance it came to have for him is certainly un-Beethovenian. The Wanderer in *Der Wegweiser* trudges on because he cannot escape his destiny; even in the symphony the appeasing hymn melody, with its sensuous scoring, is a dream of peace which the march obliterates. In both song and symphonic movement the music peters out through sheer inanition. In the scherzo, which is a combination of scherzo and trio with conflict sonata, Schubert attempts to emulate Beethoven and to "seize Fate by the throat". Yet we rather feel that Fate seizes him—in this cataclysmic eruption as much as in the implacable monotony of the Wanderer rhythm; and that the nostalgic trio reflects once more his desire to escape.

The motor rhythm of the last movement again recalls the last movement of Beethoven's Seventh, and the paean of triumph at the end of the Ninth, from which Schubert quotes the 'joy' theme. But Beethoven's finale to the Seventh is a battle-piece in which the Morality of Power subdues all opposition; and the finale of the Ninth is a song theme created from chaos during the growth of a vast symphonic structure. Beethoven is a man in possession; Schubert, in the last movement of the C major, is a man possessed. Although Schubert increasingly seeks for interrelations between his themes and employs a motivic technique throughout a large-scale work, he does not create themes through metamorphosis, as Beethoven does. For all its romantic trappings—for instance, the 'impressionistic' scoring and harmony of the approach to the recapitulation— this finale is closer to the classical tradition than the mature works of Beethoven.

And so even after he has evolved his own kind of lyrical-romantic or epic symphony, Schubert retains something of the reverence with which, in his youth, he had regarded his classical heritage. As a piano composer, he had always been less awed by tradition. The piano was his own instrument: domestic, intimate, improvisatory. His first piano sonatas reveal the fluency of the improviser's melodic gift and the luxuriance of his harmony more spontaneously than do the early symphonies and quartets. The E major Sonata of 1816 is not a successful solution of the problem of the lyrical sonata; but the typical features of Schubert's later work are all present—the song tunes that proliferate in motives capable of development; the keyboard figurations derived from song accompaniments; the sonorous spacing of the keyboard texture; the sensuously wandering modulations, usually tending flatwards.

The youthful phase of Schubert's piano sonatas concludes with his first entirely successful song sonata—the exquisite A major of 1819: a work on a modestly Mozartian scale which is essentially Schubertian in spirit. The first song melody is smilingly innocent; the presence of the Wanderer rhythm in the second subject suggests, however, that the possession of such innocence is precarious. In the little coda the chromatic alteration and the warm spacing of the piano writing emphasize the retrospective quality of the happiness (Ex. 47). Already this is a young man's dream of youth.

Ex. 47 Schubert: Piano Sonata in A opus 120 (1st movement)

Schubert did not compose another sonata for four years; he then produced three works utterly different in character from the A major. This work epitomizes Schubert the lyrical song-writer in terms of the piano sonata. The two tragic A minor sonatas (opus 42 and 143) and the unfinished C major are the apotheosis of Schubert the dramatic song-writer. They have one quality—their economy—in common with the A major. But it is now an economy of tension, observable as much in the elliptical ambiguities between major and minor tonality as in the stark, austere keyboard writing, as compared with the earlier luxuriance. In all these qualities—and in the quasi-orchestral use of pianistic tone-colour—the sonatas might be studies for the *Winterreise* cycle.

The next sonata, the D major, opus 53, is again different in mood. Unique among Schubert's sonatas in being written for a professional virtuoso, it is appropriately opulent in lyricism, harmony, and keyboard technique. The bareness of the A minor sonatas and the richness of opus 53 meet in the style of the last four sonatas, which are the culmination of Schubert's work as a piano composer. The radiant G major, opus 78, resolves tragedy in love; the posthumous A major at last exorcises the daemon of Beethoven by reconciling his grandeur with Schubertian lyricism. But Schubert's most profound (and un-Beethovenian) fusion of song melody with drama is the first movement of the posthumous B flat Sonata. The serenely singing first theme oscillates between the tonic and Schubert's submissive flat submediant. It appears to soothe: no Beethovenian aggression here, but rather regression to childhood's single-minded simplicity. Yet the most mysterious drama is attained in the modulatory equivocations of the long, quiet approach to the recapitulation. The movement's 'heavenly length' is inherent both in the nature of the themes and in Schubert's conception of the dramatic.

Much the same is true of the slow movement. We are lulled to bliss by the seductive melody's barcarolle rhythm, until the softest enharmonic modulations seem to open the ground beneath our feet (Ex. 48). We are unsure whether the dream comforts, or breaks the heart. Even more poignant than this sudden enharmonic transition is the final appearance of the

Ex. 48 Schubert: Piano Sonata in B♭ (op. post) Slow movement

barcarolle melody in the major. The effect is visionary: yet profoundly sad, because the happiness is subject to mutability. In a letter to his father, written in 1825, Schubert said, speaking of a mutual acquaintance: "He probably still keeps crawling to the Cross; and he will certainly have imagined himself to be ill another seventy-seven times and to have been on the point of death nine times, as if death were the worst thing that could happen to us mortals. If he could only take a look at these divine mountains and lakes, whose aspect threatens to stifle and devour us, he would not be so attached to this petty existence as not to think it a piece of great good fortune to be confided once more to the incomprehensible power of the earth to make new life." Haydn, we saw, regarded man and Nature as partners in a humanitarian scheme; Mozart considered Nature as insignificant in comparison with man; Beethoven used Nature as a means towards his own salvation. But Schubert has no humanitarian morality, no mystical salvation; he has only the moments of ecstasy given him by his exquisitely tuned senses, which are pitifully subject to Time. For this reason he is scared of death, as he is awed by mountains and lakes because they are impervious to human feeling. He can but conquer fear in his pantheistic acceptance of his pettiness.

The letter quoted above is an extraordinary document to come from an ostensible Catholic. In fact, Schubert merely paid lip-service to his Church. He wrote masses in his youth, because they were a legitimate source of income. But he cut out the words, "I believe in one Catholic and apostolic Church"; and his was never a religious nature, either in the doctrinal or the Beethovenian sense. His early masses sound like the operas of Pergolesi [1710–1736] or, occasionally, Mozart; they even have *buffo* finales. This is the traditional, Austrian, theatrical side of Schubert's Catholicism. The other side is fervent, ecstatic, Marianic, and has nothing to do with the Church. It becomes personal—indeed, sensuous—experience; and finds its expression in songs—notably the Novalis settings, the Scott *Ave Maria*, and the four-part setting of *Psalm 23* for two sopranos and two altos—and in the unfinished oratorio, *Lazarus*, which Schubert composed partly as a palliative for his operatic failures.

When in the last years of his life Schubert turned to the Church again, he no longer pretended to make his masses liturgical. They become choral and symphonic poems of a subjectively romantic nature. The A flat Mass contains some of Schubert's boldest harmonic and modulatory flights. The tonality is the 'romantic' key of A flat. But the Gloria is in E (the flat submediant again), the Gratias in A, the Credo in C, the Sanctus and Hosanna in F: the main key does not return until the Benedictus. The only compromise with tradition is the big fugal Gloria; even this Schubert shortened in a later version. He makes little attempt to emulate convention and none to approach the new contrapuntal spirituality of Beethoven's *Missa Solemnis*. He is content to be a romantic harmonist; and in being himself becomes almost a mystic of the senses, as he is in the barcarolle of the B flat Piano Sonata, and as Wagner was to be in *Parsifal*.

The E flat Mass of the last year of Schubert's life is more stable in tonality and stronger in line: less subject to the sensory flux. But it has no more in common with traditional church music: or at least the liturgical elements in it play much the same part in relation to secular Experience as folk-simplicity does in his songs and instrumental works. For instance, in the Domine Deus the Gregorian-like melody with its solemn trombones symbolizes a Faith which is shattered by the agitated figurations of the strings and the weird modulations of the chorus. There is a similar equivocation in the Agnus Dei—a chromatic, harmonically founded contrapuntal movement with a double theme, one part identical with the subject of Bach's C sharp minor Fugue from Book I of the *Forty-eight*, the other with Schubert's own *Doppelgänger*. The marriage of Schubert's *alter ego* with religious assurance seems unlikely: perhaps we may say that it is not consummated.

Powerful as is this equivocal music, one would not expect to find Schubert's most representative achievements in his liturgical works. The single work which most comprehensively embraces every facet of his genius is probably his last chamber work, the String Quintet in C. We see at once how the second 'cello gives Schubert the sonority his harmony demands. The first subject group combines lyricism with the dynamic manner of the big C major Symphony, with bounding dotted rhythms; the second subject is one of the most acutely nostalgic of his song-tunes. The wild conflict between these two moods has already been anticipated in the dissonant cadential harmony of the opening phrase.

In the slow movement we are in the E major bliss of Schubert's Eden, harmonized at first in warmly sustained diatonicism, then in melting, regretful sevenths and ninths. This song melody is followed by a 'middle section' which jumps abruptly from the blissful E major to the 'Neapolitan' flat supertonic, F minor. In panting, almost hysterical rhythms, accompanied by sinister triplet figures, a more operatic theme flows through a range of enharmonic modulations that sunder tonality no less than the mature work of Wagner. When the E major song returns, the triplets have become delicate demisemiquavers. At the end, the threat of F minor again obtrudes; but this time leads not to the fever of Experience, but to a simple cadence to the tonic. The effect is psychologically very odd. The childlike coda is warmly secure, though we know that terror is but a little way beneath the surface.

The mysterious, if not the terrible, crops up again in the enharmony of the scherzo's trio. The scherzo itself returns to the dynamic exuberance of the C major Symphony, with startling modulations. With the rondo finale Schubert seems to forget the tempests of his joys and sorrows in recalling the café music of his early days. Yet the movement begins oddly in C minor, and goes through several keys before establishing the major; and the more jaunty the figurations grow, the more enigmatic grow the adventures of harmony and tonality. The

strangest things of all happen when Schubert adopts the conventional Rossini device of concluding a movement by whipping
up the tempo. As the music becomes ostensibly more frivolous,
it grows also more hectic; and the final section of the coda takes
us back to the enharmonic dissonance of the first movement.
The last thing we hear is the cryptic 'Neapolitan' relationship of
D flat to C.

This strange metamorphosis of café music occurs in what is
perhaps Schubert's greatest, and certainly his most personal
work. To the end of his life he continued, for commercial
reasons, to compose occasional music alongside works of subjective experience; and the nature of this music gradually
changed. On the comparatively rare occasions when Schubert
had composed display music for the platform, he had usually
been content with the decorative techniques of fashion; such
music always involved the piano, and adapted its pianistic
style from Hummel [1778–1837]. Now, in the two piano trios
and in the 'Trout' Quintet, Schubert imbues even café music
with personal feeling; while in the G major Duo for violin and
piano he creates a virtuoso piece which is great (and characteristically mysterious) music. The big virtuoso Fantasy for piano
on the Wanderer theme is not only serious music, but also one
of Schubert's most progressive experiments: for in attempting
to evolve all the material of a four-movement work from a single
theme he anticipates Liszt's romantic re-creation of mono-
thematic principles.

These display pieces were all written on commission. There
is a comparable change in the small works intended for
domestic performance. The medium of the piano duet (symbol
of friendship) prompts Schubert to some of his most tragic
utterances, which might have been symphonies if orchestras had
been available to play them. Even the salon pieces themselves
became personal confessions. The early dances were occasional
music that both technically and imaginatively measured up to
the occasion. The last dances, the C sharp minor *Moment
Musical*, and the *Klavierstücke* of 1828 are testaments as romantically lonely as the dances and nocturnes of Chopin. Probably
Schubert himself was not conscious of the change. Publishers
and public probably felt that they, rather than Schubert's
music, had been sold.

Schubert died at the age of thirty-one—four years younger

than Mozart. He is closer to Mozart than is any other composer, but the lyrical and dramatic bases of his art are more widely separated; from the struggle to reconcile them sprang the mingling of passion and nostalgia which is his music. From this point of view, we may compare Mozart's 'Longing for Spring' in the last movement of his last concerto with any of Schubert's *Frühlingstraum*-like movements. Mozart, we saw, is graceful and apparently impersonal in his perfection: the dancing interplay of parts seems the Essence of mutability itself. Schubert's singing melodies and harmonic ambiguities are his own consciousness of mutability, romantic in spirit: so that, despite his respect for the past, his late music is inexhaustibly prophetic—especially of the sensuous individualism of Wagner. With him we therefore feel, as with Mozart we do not, a tragic sense of potentialities unfulfilled.

On the other hand, the anticipations of romanticism in all his mature music are perhaps inseparable from the sense of doom which hung over his world and himself. He composed much superficially merry music; yet from the moment he attained personality, the merriment is tinged with melancholy; and the spine-tingling beauty of his last works is related to their consciousness of death. Again, the essential Schubertian experience is sensuous. We feel this beauty with our melodic and harmonic senses; and in knowing from his music (not from the books we have read) that he himself had so little time in which to experience it, we become aware that for us too beauty is as transient as a dream. The music is still almost before we have heard it; the dream is past that was more real than the waking life.

6

BRUCKNER, BRAHMS, AND MAHLER

THE MUSIC of the Viennese classics depends, we have seen, on a balance between Tradition and Revolution: between an Age of Faith and an Age of Anxiety. Haydn was born into a faith against which he did not consciously rebel, though he unwittingly transformed it from mystical dogma to ethical humanism. Mozart reinterpreted the faith in personally emotional terms, so that it was no longer a faith that the Church could recognize. Beethoven rejected the past, but created new belief out of conflict. Schubert turned still more violently from orthodox Catholicism; but discovered nothing to take its place except a vague pantheism. Beethoven said he could have 'no friends'; Schubert used friendship, as he used music, as a bulwark against a hostile world. Yet Beethoven created a faith through his music, whereas Schubert found only moments of illumination. This is why Schubert's late music is, in its loneliness, inexpressibly sad: while Beethoven's late music is, in its profundity, inexpressibly joyful. There is no deeper experience than the joy Beethoven discovered; though conventional romanticism came to believe that only unhappiness could be profound.

The change in the attitude to belief which develops between Haydn and Schubert runs parallel to the slow deterioration of Austrian Catholicism. Schubert's dismissal of the Church was echoed by his successors as Catholicism in Austria grew increasingly remote from the realities of the nineteenth century. By the time of Francis I, the identification of the Church with oppression was unmistakable; and the Jesuitical spirit pervaded every aspect of life. The revolutionary stirrings of 1848 were soon suppressed; conditions returned to an even more reactionary conservatism. The Concordat of 1855 handed over the entire educational system to the Church.

Yet the fact that Austria preserved through the nineteenth century a fossilized feudalism alone made possible the strange phenomenon of Anton Bruckner [1824–1896]. For in Bruckner one finds again the innocence that the self-conscious mind of Schubert yearned for; he is a medieval survival in a country cut off from the creative development of Europe. He believed in his Church as unequivocally as a medieval peasant; the evils consequent upon it in nineteenth-century Austria he either failed to see, or considered as an entirely secular matter. He must be unique among nineteenth-century artists in being completely without self-consciousness: anecdotes about his *naïveté* are innumerable. A penchant for counting stars is a fixation that has a touching, cosmically medieval flavour; and his grave acceptance of the waggish intelligence that he was to be elected Emperor of Austria is more beautiful than ludicrous. He knew—maybe at a pre-conscious level of understanding— that he had the heart of the matter within him. He was kingly and saintly by nature: which was more than could be said of those officially in power.

Born in 1824, the son of a schoolmaster, Bruckner spent his boyhood remotely in the country, where village life had not substantially changed for hundreds of years. When Anton was thirteen, his father died, and the family moved to Ebelsberg, near Linz. Anton became a pupil and chorister at the neighbouring monastery of St. Florian, thereby acquiring his first taste of the musical riches of Europe and his first experience of Catholic domination, both of which he accepted with enthusiasm. Grown to manhood, he became, as professional musician, a servant of his Church, working at St. Florian and later at Linz for more than twenty years. When eventually he settled in Vienna he was a mature composer of forty-two, with several large-scale works behind him. He had to wait another twenty years for recognition; for the cultural backwater of Vienna had no more use for him than it had had, thirty years earlier, for Schubert. He felt no bitterness at this lack of recognition; it did not occur to him that he might be getting less than his due. Provincially self-taught, he knew that his technique was defective. All his life he was learning to compose better: for he wrote music to praise his God, and for God nothing less than his best could suffice. Believing in musical, as in religious, dogma, he had no ambition but to follow his revered masters. If he was not aware of the revolutionary elements in most of his predecessors, still less was he aware of the originality within himself.

Yet in matters that deeply concerned him Bruckner was hardly naïve; he had an intuitive insight that amounted to clairvoyance. At St. Florian he had acquired a firm basis in traditional harmony and counterpoint; but his acquaintance with the European classics was certainly not wide and probably not deep. When he first visited Vienna to acquire a more adequate technique he found in Simon Sechter a truly great teacher. Now, Sechter was the man from whom Schubert, in his last years, had hoped to take counterpoint lessons. From the strangely sensuous Bachian texture of the C sharp minor *Moment Musical* we can but vaguely hazard what profound technical and spiritual changes might have developed in Schubert's music, had he lived to put this scheme into effect. In Bruckner's case, the meeting with Sechter in 1855 was the first decisive event in his career. What he gained from Sechter was knowledge and love of the music of Bach, and of the late works of Beethoven. Whether Bruckner divined that Sechter would give him what he wanted, or Sechter had the insight to see what Bruckner needed, is immaterial. Bach was a religious composer who employed techniques based on contrapuntal unity. Beethoven was a *modern* religious composer who in his last works fused the dualism of sonata with the monism of fugue. Bruckner was a man of faith, like Bach; yet he lived in a world which, since Beethoven had recreated it, would never be the same. To find them, and to reconcile elements in them that seemed discordant, was to find himself. They were perhaps the only two composers from whom he could have learned.

We think of Bruckner as primarily a symphonist. Yet the symphony depends on conflict; and to Bruckner's quasi-medieval mind conflict might seem to be extraneous. We shall see later that there was a real and deep reason why Bruckner wished to write symphonies as well as liturgical music. It is none the less true that Bruckner is a symphonist of unusual character; and that some of the apparent weaknesses in his symphonic method seem more convincing when we consider them in relation to his own church music, rather than in relation to the nineteenth-century sonata. With Haydn, Mozart, Beethoven, and Schubert, church music is an appendix to their instrumental work; they recreate traditional liturgical techniques in the light of their experience in sonata and symphony. For Bruckner the opposite is true. He starts from the liturgy of the

Church; and transforms the symphony into a confession of faith.

As a natural conservative, Bruckner, beginning his career at St. Florian, accepted the liturgical styles that were handed down to him by his predecessors. His models were Haydn, of whose 'Nelson' Mass he possessed a score, and from whom he learned to conceive the liturgy symphonically: and Schubert, from whom he derived the roots of his lyricism and his harmonic sensuousness. It never occurred to him, any more than it had occurred to his masters, to wonder if his style were too theatrical. Yet the spirit of his church music is not Haydnesque, and is remote from Schubert. We saw that Schubert began in his church music by being prettily frivolous, and ended by expressing that search for a lost innocence which is the impulse behind his instrumental work. Bruckner had never lost his innocence; so he can turn rococo theatricality into a paean of praise. He achieves this not by throwing over the rococo, but by absorbing it once more into the baroque. The tarnished splendour of the monumental baroque lives again in Bruckner's church music, for he was born, as most of his contemporaries were not, with an instinctive sense of glory. Baroque grandeur involves baroque counterpoint—of the type that was handed down from the seventeenth century to Fux, and from Fux to Sechter: so that in a sense Bruckner had rediscovered Bach before Sechter revealed to him the depths of Bach's art.

The mature E minor Mass returns, beyond Bach, to the vocal principles of Palestrinian counterpoint, and even revives the traditional baroque scoring for double chorus, brass, and wood-wind. The melodic lines, despite the Schubertian sensuousness of the harmony, are frequently tinged with Gregorian modality, with which Bruckner became familiar during his association with the Cecilian movement. Yet despite this archaism, there are other features in this resplendently noble music which are neither baroque nor rococo. We may associate them with the obsessive influence exerted on Bruckner by Beethoven's Ninth Symphony and by the mature music of Wagner—especially *Tristan*, the production of which at Munich in 1865 marked the second spiritual crisis of Bruckner's life.

The tremendous impact made by the Ninth Symphony on Bruckner is significant. It is an evolutionary piece, dealing with the experience of Becoming. Yet it is a monumental work, and in that sense related to the baroque; and the slow movement attains the serenity of a reborn belief typical of Beethoven's last years. The obsession with *Tristan* is superficially more difficult to understand, though not quite so difficult if one sees *Tristan* as complementary to the sensuous abnegation of *Parsifal*. For Bruckner, Wagnerian harmony, on the Wagnerian orchestra, was simply the most beautiful sound he had ever heard. To refuse to use this sound to praise God with would have been blasphemous. It is interesting that Bruckner used to sit through Wagner's operas with his eyes shut. To the end of his days he had not the faintest idea what it was all about; had he known, he would have been revolted. Almost the most remarkable evidence of the original force of Bruckner's genius is the fact that he transforms Wagnerian harmony and orchestration into radiant spirituality—into the liturgical and baroque.

Yet these subterranean hints of the Ninth Symphony's cosmic strife and of *Tristan*'s heroic egomania must surely imply some oddity in Bruckner's religious experience. Do they suggest, perhaps, a pre-conscious uncertainty—some intuitive awareness that after all the world was no longer medieval? His 'innocent' fixations were at times not far removed from pathological neurosis. His faith saved him from the dementia that destroyed Wolf's spirit; but faith had to win its victory over the obscure terrors of the subconscious mind, and victory is not won without a fight. In Schubert's mature work the Beethovenian features and the anticipations of Wagner testify to a split in sensibility of which he was certainly aware emotionally, and possibly intellectually. Bruckner, Schubert's successor, was not so aware. He achieved sublimity; but he moves us so much because we know, as he knew in the depths of his heart, that his sublimity soared over an abyss.

It is interesting that Bruckner unconsciously carries Schubert's modulatory experiments to still more extravagant lengths. With a Schubertian fondness for Neapolitan relationships, Bruckner will write not single chords, or even progressions, but extended sections in the flat supertonic. The E flat trio to the D minor scherzo of the String Quintet, the G flat slow movement to the F minor finale, extend this Neapolitan complex to the relationship between two movements. Bruckner's fondness for mediant relationships derives partly from Schubert, partly perhaps from his knowledge of sixteenth-century polyphony,

with its 'melodically' related triads. It is worth noting that
Bruckner had an especial fondness for the work of Jacopus
Gallus [1550–1591] among early seventeenth-century polyphonists; for Gallus's work is often enigmatic, chromatically
unstable, and even, perhaps, secretly revolutionary.

The essential Brucknerian experience is contained in the
symphonies, which were naturally more personal than his
liturgical music. But it is impossible sharply to differentiate the
religious and the symphonic elements in Bruckner's work.
Both masses and symphonies are constructed on broadly the
same principles, except that the former involve voices and a
literary text, and so can afford to be relatively episodic. Now,
we have seen that all the Viennese symphonists before Bruckner
dealt in varying degrees with the experience known to philo-
sophers as Becoming. It is therefore understandable that
Haydn, Mozart, Schubert, and above all Beethoven should
manifest a prodigious spiritual and technical development
during the course of their lives: that the first and last quartets of
Haydn or Beethoven should seem to belong to distinct imaginative worlds. Bruckner significantly differs from his predecessors
in this respect. His last three symphonies reveal his genius more
richly than his previous symphonies; but they add little new to
his experience. Nor did he intend them to. There was for
Bruckner only one experience worth writing about; and though
one's comprehension of God's love and glory may deepen, love
and glory are themselves unchanging and unchangeable.

So the pattern of all Bruckner's symphonies is basically the
same. The first movement never opens directly with a theme,
but with an ostinato bass or tremolando that serves as a neutral
background. Here Bruckner's model was the opening of the
Ninth Symphony, and possibly the tremolando which Wagner
used to arouse expectation. Yet the effect, in Bruckner's music,
is quite different. In both Beethoven and Wagner expectation
leads to drama; whereas from the neutrality of Bruckner's
openings emerges the creative life of melody. The enormous
asymmetrical melody that swells from the void at the beginning
of Bruckner's Seventh Symphony has a kind of divine inevitability: and nothing in common with the assertiveness of Beethoven's middle years. Even when Bruckner's first themes have
a heroic quality (expressed in a prevalence of trumpet-like
fifths) or a dynamic quality (expressed in gigantic Beethovenian

upward leaps in dotted rhythm, like a vastly expanded Mannheim skyrocket), they temper their energy with a Schubertian
lyricism and with a prose rhythm resembling the 'endless
melody' of late Wagner. The first theme of the Ninth Symphony
embraces all these elements in its soaring splendour (Ex. 49):

Ex. 49 Bruckner: Symphony No. 9 (first movement)

Bruckner's second-group themes are very lyrical and
Schubertian. He usually introduces two, sometimes three, such
themes, treating them in double counterpoint. They thus
acquire a winging ecstasy which counteracts the nostalgia
inherent in their chromatic harmony (Ex. 50). We have seen

Ex. 50 Bruckner: Symphony No. 6 (first movement)

that Schubert is often seduced from dramatic argument by the
lyricism of his second subjects. All Bruckner's secondary themes
are in the classical sense unsymphonic. Though they are
usually built on four-bar phrases sequentially repeated, they
are characterized by their enormous span and by a sense of flow
reinforced by Bruckner's partiality for quintuplet rhythms (a
bar of four crochets divided into two crochets plus a triplet).

The themes do not need development except in so far as they are, as melody, growing all the time.

Now Bruckner's first-subject group tends to be firmly diatonic, while the second group is usually chromatic in harmonization and sometimes in linear contour. The codetta themes of his exposition usually re-establish diatonicism, and a more clearly defined metre. His two main groups of themes thus bear some relation to the classical notion of dualistic contrast; but with themes of such vast scope it is no use expecting from his development sections anything approaching the operatic cohesion of Mozart, let alone the rhetorical argument of middle-period Beethoven. Bruckner allows his themes to expand of their own volition, and builds up his climaxes over relatively static ostinatos and pedal points. Then the music breaks off and starts again, with another theme. These recurrent climaxes, being spaced over a considerable period of time, do not attempt to build up a progressive drama. None the less, the sequence of keys in which they appear gradually changes the tonal perspective, so that the succession of climaxes becomes cumulative. By the time we reach the ultimate climax we have usually arrived at the most remote tonality. Though his modulatory effects are never Beethovenian, Bruckner's command of tonality was masterly. If we listen to his symphonies without preconceived notions as to what a symphony ought to be like, we shall sense how inevitably the climax of the subsidiary climaxes becomes the goal of the movement. It is interesting to note how often Bruckner's ultimate climaxes resemble his vivid, almost visual treatment of the Et Resurrexit in his masses, especially the symphonic F minor. In these passages harmonic oppositions disappear and the music blazes for several pages on a single major triad. Climax becomes not conflict, but the glory that renders conflict superfluous.

The constructive principles of Bruckner's slow movements are not radically different from those of his opening allegros. The adagio to the Seventh, for instance, opens in C sharp minor, has important structural modulations to F sharp and A flat (the major of the sub-dominant and dominant), attains its final climax on the remote triad of C major, and ends in the major of the tonic. But whereas the first movements are in essence preludial, the adagios are self-contained song. If they are in sonata form, they recall the slow movement of the

'Hammerklavier' in that they purge sonata of interior conflict.
More commonly they are modelled on the adagio of Beethoven's Ninth or the 'Song of Thanksgiving' from the A minor
Quartet in being in a compromise between sonata and rondo:
a solemn, hymn-like first theme alternates with a celestially
floating melody, often treated in double counterpoint. The
harmony is richly chromatic and the modulations often
enharmonic, emulating *Parsifal*; the orchestration too appears
to follow Wagner, even to the point of introducing Wagner
tubas. Yet out of this humility towards his masters grows one
of the most original manners in musical history. Even the
Brucknerian orchestra, influenced by his experience as an
organist, sounds more baroque than Wagnerian in its use of
distinct groups of strings, woodwind, and brass. The incandes-
cent blaze of brass in the adagio of the Ninth, followed abruptly
by pianissimo woodwind, produces an effect of almost Byzan-
tine splendour, instinct with the awe of God as well as with His
peace. Again we may observe that Bruckner's symphonic
adagios are similar in treatment to the Benedictus and Sanctus
in his mature masses, for which his prototype was the comparable movements in Beethoven's *Missa Solemnis*. Bruckner was an
'orthodox' Catholic, unlike Beethoven; but both of them, having
profoundly religious minds, were aware of the terror within
God's majesty—as most artists of the nineteenth century
were not.

Bruckner's scherzos are usually in Ländler style, following
the Schubertian type. Their trios might even be said to intensify
Schubert's nostalgia in their chromatic part-writing and
modulations. The scherzo of the Seventh, however, employs
one of Bruckner's metrical trumpet themes, perhaps to compensate for the lack of such a theme in the first movement;
while the scherzo of the Ninth is a weird movement in which
the abyss beneath Bruckner's sublimity gapes wide open. Its
chromaticism becomes spectral, its tonality being always slightly
out of perspective (Ex. 51). Intermittently, the sensuous dream
is battered by the stark metrical assertion of percussion and

Ex. 51 Bruckner: Symphony No. 9 (Scherzo)

Vivace

brass, hammering out a peasant dance rhythm with Beethovenian ferocity.

In his finales Bruckner attempts to synthesize the previous movements, in the manner of the finale to Beethoven's Ninth. He does not, like Beethoven, re-create his themes; but their interrelation leads to an epilogic statement of a kind of Catholic 'chorale' on the brass—the Hymn which has been implicit in the whole symphony finally takes explicit form. The most impressive of Bruckner's finales is probably that to the Fifth, which has an introduction recalling the themes of the previous movements, on the analogy of Beethoven's Ninth; and then coalesces the material into a double fugue which also embraces elements of sonata style, rounded off with a chorale. The contradictory elements of fugue and sonata remain much more loosely co-ordinated than they are in Beethoven's ultimate synthesis of opposites. None the less, this is one of the very few movements by later composers which can strictly be compared with Beethoven; and again there is a parallel in Bruckner's church music—the Agnus Dei that concludes the F minor Mass.

In later symphonies Bruckner discarded the retrospective introduction to the finale, feeling perhaps that it was justified only by Beethoven's thematically 'generative' technique. His instinct, as usual, was right. Yet noble and satisfying though his chorale epilogues may be, one cannot altogether regret that he left his last symphony unfinished. What could possibly succeed the meditation of this adagio? And in this case we cannot regard such a confession of faith as divinely anachronistic: for this symphony is at once profoundly religious and profoundly modern. It is revealing to compare it, from this point of view, with the Seventh. The rhythmic energy of the Seventh's scherzo is, on the whole, rural and positive, the seductiveness of its trio is a visionary Golden Age. In the sublime song melodies of the adagio the slowly rising sextuplets of the accompanying figure can surge inevitably upwards into resurrection. But the scherzo of the Ninth, with its neutral tritonal chords and melodic figurations, its fiercely destructive rhythm, its harsh scoring, is a vision of Hell. In the following adagio there is thus a sense of strain in the vast leaps of the melodies: while the panting, broken demisemiquavers of the figuration *strive towards* resurrection. Both the enormous leaps of the themes, and the sharp, acid edge which Bruckner gives to his rich scoring, reappear in Mahler's bitter-sweet anguish; and Schoenberg [b.1874] inherited them from Mahler [1860-1911], so that they have become part of our own tormented century. In no later composer, however, does one find anything approaching the bliss of the final pages of Bruckner's adagio, when his yearning achieves resurrection in the serenity of the major triad. (The key—E major—is the same as that of Schubert's heaven.)

Many of the apparent weaknesses in Bruckner's music—his long-windedness, his inconsequentiality, his naïve literalism—prove to be motes in our eye rather than in his ear. We listen with irrelevant preconceptions; and this is not entirely our fault because it is not easy to hear Bruckner's scores as he wrote them. So great was his humility that he allowed well-meaning friends to rewrite and rescore his works in order to make them more acceptable to conventional notions of symphonic style. His themes—except perhaps in the scherzos—are spacious and not time-obsessed; and although the first movement of his Fifth is undeniably shorter without its recapitulation, it does not make better sense. Even if one never comes to recognize the logic in Bruckner's vast structures, there are still moments when one wonders, listening to these last three adagios, whether since the last works of Beethoven music has reached this point again. The climax of the adagio to the Seventh—and therefore of the whole work—is a conflictless paean of bells on a C major triad, which grows out of softly upsurging scales on the violins. It is naïve, if you like. Yet it is also an incarnation of Glory, and only a man who had seen this vision could have written the elegy with which the movement then concludes: funereal music, inspired by the death of Wagner, in which there is regret, but no shadow of fear. In his very innocence, Bruckner seems in such moments to belong to a nobler race than our own. It is no more than a sober statement of fact to say that we shall not look upon his like again.

In their lifetime, Bruckner and Brahms [1833–1897] were the unwilling leaders of rival factions: the acrimony among their disciples at times amounted to hysteria. Nowadays, we find this difficult to understand, for both composers seem to us late romantics who worked within the same tradition. Yet there is a sense in which the disputants were right. They argued about the wrong things, or at least about differences that now seem superficial; yet they must have felt, if they did not know, that beneath these superfices Bruckner and Brahms represented opposite poles of the human spirit. In Bruckner's personality such contradictions as there may be are buried as deep underground as they are in his music. Brahms's personality is in essence a contradiction; his is as much a dualistic temperament as Bruckner's was single-minded and simple-hearted.

Bruckner's early background was that of a Catholic Austrian peasant; he preserved a peasant-like innocence throughout his life. Brahms's family came from the north, of bourgeois Protestant stock; he had both the stolidity and the tenacity of his kind. When, having settled in Vienna, he came to move in exalted circles he was as arrogant and offensive as Beethoven, but for the opposite reason. Beethoven exulted in the pride of his spirit; Brahms was afraid of the passion that burned within him. The stolidity, the caution, the gruff exterior hid another Brahms whose soul was all that the northern bourgeois and Protestant was not. We can see this in his approach to his art. Like Bruckner, he reverenced the Masters. But Bruckner reverenced them in humility: feeling himself 'a pygmy' beside Beethoven, he could not think of himself as a rival. Brahms was not conspicuous for humility. He paid homage to the past because this was one means of controlling the turbulence of his spirit. His use of the past—and to some extent his interest in folk-song—was a conscious intellectual activity, rather than an instinctive gesture.

From this point of view Brahms's opus 1, the C major Piano Sonata, is a fascinating document. It begins with an act of homage to his master, Beethoven—an almost literal quotation from the heroic opening of the 'Hammerklavier' Sonata; and then builds a fierce conflict on the same tonal opposition that Beethoven exploits in the first movement of the 'Waldstein' Sonata. This is both a tribute to the past and an assertion of the combativeness of his own temperament. The effect is quite different from the opening of the 'Hammerklavier'. Beethoven's opening bars are an epic challenge: Brahms's suggest a vigorous bourgeois stolidity, partly because the pace of his harmonic movement confines him to the earth (he has at least two, sometimes four chords a bar to Beethoven's one). Similarly, Brahms's modulations suggest physical energy, whereas Beethoven's hint at mystery—at the new tonal perspectives which are to be explored in the later movements. Brahms's second movement is folk-like in spirit: Schubertian in its lyricism, Schumann-like in its poetic treatment of the piano. The scherzo also has a Schubertian, nostalgic trio; but is in the main aggressive and exuberant, with a typical use of thick thirds and sixths. This technique Brahms probably picked up from the 'Hammer-klavier', though he creates from it a quite different effect—sturdier, earthier, if not less fierce. The final rondo again has a lyrical, rather folk-song-like theme: which is developed in Beethovenian sonata style.

Though aggression and nostalgia—the two contrasting elements of Schubert's temperament—are already present in the work of the young Brahms, their relationship is different. Instead of being in conflict, they become allies: the conflict in his music is between lyricism and drama as symbols of romantic individuality, on the one hand; and, on the other hand, his innate caution and Teutonic stolidity. In order to become allies, the two elements have to change their natures. One can see this if one compares Brahms's lyricism with that of Bruckner or Schubert. The cantabile symphonic melodies of Bruckner, and to a lesser degree Schubert, tend to be long and supple; direct references to a folk-like style are usually restricted to the scherzo. Though Brahms's lyrical melodies are frequently asymmetrical, their component phrases tend to be relatively brief; he has nothing comparable with the enormous winding melodies at the beginning of Bruckner's last three symphonies. Moreover, his lyrical themes frequently introduce arpeggio formations. In Bruckner's long themes arpeggio figures tend to be absorbed into step-wise progressions planned on a vast scale: consider the opening theme of the Seventh Symphony, in which the arpeggio 'opens up' the slow growth of the melody, sending it winging to the heavens. Brahms's arpeggio formations divide the melody into harmonic segments, and so tend to root it to the earth. This we can see most immediately in his songs.

Schubert, in his mature songs, is always at once musical and psychological; his variety of song forms is apparently inexhaustible. Brahms is much less interested in the poems he sets; he regards them not as psychological experience, but as the impulse to a tune. These melodies are often of extraordinary beauty and richness; yet in their clearly defined and subtly balanced phrases

—as well as in the firm harmonic basis to even the folk-like tunes—they are often melodies that would be amenable to development in sonata. Indeed, some of the greatest songs, such as the *Sapphische Ode*, seem to demand symphonic scope for their adequate realization; certainly the grand arpeggiated contours of the phrases call for instrumental powers of sostenuto from the singer. Brahms actually used two of his loveliest songs as basic material for sonata movements in his G major and A major violin sonatas. When Schubert uses themes from his songs in instrumental works, it is almost always in movements in the more static technique of variation or rondo.

So it is that Brahms's lyricism and his dynamism temper one another. In Schubert's bitter-sweet idiom there is a tug-of-war between the two impulses: but Brahms's lyricism, with its relatively harmonic bias, curbs his exuberance, while his ferocity protects his lyricism from too painful a nostalgia. This is why the works that sum up the achievement of his youth are the piano quartets, especially the F minor. Strings are cantabile instruments; the piano, for Brahms as for middle-period Beethoven, is a percussive instrument. When Brahms brings them together he expresses all the dynamic power and lyrical passion of his romantic youth and of his love for Clara Schumann. Already, however, their interrelation creates a controlled sobriety in the realization of passion which became his ideal. We can see this again in his first large-scale work, the D minor Piano Concerto. This began life as a symphony closely modelled on Beethoven's Ninth; it turned into an extremely difficult virtuoso concerto in which there is the minimum of ostentation. The piano writing has Brahms's singular massiveness and richness, the orchestration is darkly sensuous; yet the heroic proportions of the work are never endangered by the incidental seductions of chromatic figuration or scoring.

The D minor Concerto is the climax of the romanticism of Brahms's youth. A new phase begins as his instinct towards self-discipline prompts him to renewed contrapuntal studies. Unlike most sonata composers, Brahms had always been contrapuntally minded; his opus 1 is full of polyphonic ingenuities which help to give coherence to its figuration. This was partly due to his Protestant and northern background: for even Schumann, the most romantic of his masters, was trained in the Bachian tradition. Some of the works Brahms composed at this time hardly claimed to be more than exercises in outmoded techniques; others, like the choral motets, revived archaic styles while achieving through their harmony a personal flavour. This series of works culminates in a number of piano compositions built on the static principle of variation.

The biggest and finest of these variation-sets is the 'Handel Variations' of 1861. These conclude with a fugue which, like that of Beethoven's 'Hammerklavier' Sonata, is an assertion of power. It is, however, in every sense an easier and earthier work. The fugue subject itself is harmonically conceived; except perhaps in the magnificent A flat minor Organ Fugue and a few of the late chorale preludes, Brahms's counterpoint—despite his veneration for Bach—is less Bachian, more Handelian, than that of late Beethoven. He has little of Bach's tension between line and harmony, and none of Beethoven's recalcitrance between a stable diatonicism and the direction in which the counterpoints want to move. So although in this assertion of fugal unity Brahms, like Beethoven, wins a victory over himself, he has less to conquer; the struggle has been less wild because the opposing forces have always been ready for compromise. Beethoven's triumph over the self is a prelude to a vision of Paradise. Brahms cannot take this further step. When he achieves his own resolution, it takes the form of a stoic resignation, rather than a winged joy. This we can see in the course of his development as a symphonist.

The first of the symphonies, the C minor, was conceived about the same time as the D minor Piano Concerto, though Brahms did not complete it until he was over forty. In it, his Beethovenian ambitions are so obvious that it was known, either waggishly or reverentially, as 'the Tenth'. It is a dynamic work which begins in conflict and ends in triumph with a tune comparable with the Joy theme in Beethoven's Ninth. Brahms himself deprecated any attempt to relate this tune to the Ninth Symphony: not merely because 'any jackass' could see that the tunes were similar, but because he knew, as many of his disciples did not, that in spiritual essence the tunes were not related at all. Beethoven's theme has not the Paradisal joy which flowers in his last slow movements in variation style; but it is a gateway to Paradise. Brahms's theme may be hymn-like; but it is a hymn to earthy contentment, stocky, burgomaster-like, a bourgeois modification of the folk spirit. It resolves the turbulence of Brahms's youth, as expressed in the first movement of the symphony, into sanity and power. It neither achieves nor attempts Beethoven's apochryphal resolution.

Though it seems slighter, the Second Symphony, in D, is more subtly Beethovenian. It is the most lyrical, and therefore Schubertian, of all Brahms's large-scale works; yet it also employs a technique of thematic transformation as complex as Beethoven's. The singing opening theme characteristically weaves arpeggio figures into its contour, so that it is easily susceptible of both harmonic and contrapuntal treatment. A second, transitional theme is a more fluid expansion of the first theme: and the second subject group derives from this transitional melody. Brahms's contrapuntal skill becomes the means whereby the disintegrating and reintegrating themes preserve continuity during the modulations of the development. The complex organisms that are his themes can be split into their components, without resorting to mechanical sequences to keep the music moving.

As in Beethoven's mature works, all the transformations of Brahms's symphonic themes tend towards the last movement, which is their resolution. We have seen that the last movement of the First Symphony emulates the superfices of the finale of Beethoven's Ninth without touching its essence. The last movement of the Second, however, attempts and achieves something different. Here the metamorphosis of the themes leads to a march-tune that one might possibly call jubilant. But if it is jubilant, it is also strenuous: certainly more so than the spring-like melodies of the first movement. Whereas Beethoven—even in his First Symphony, and still more from the 'Eroica' onwards—tends to free his themes of harmonic tension in the last movement, here Brahms increases their tension. Not only in the modulatory passages of the development, but even in the exuberant coda there is an undercurrent of unease; so that the exuberance becomes fierce. This fundamental change is much more obvious in the Third Symphony, in which the first movement is built on a Beethovenian arpeggio of challenge (in the major), while the last movement transforms the themes into minor conflict and turmoil. The work ends with a quiet coda in the major, wherein the arpeggio motive becomes not Beethovenian triumph, but Brahmsian resignation.

This prepares us for the elegiac power of the Fourth—and last—Symphony. The initial theme leaps aspiringly up a sixth, but then falls in descending thirds, broken by rests. The Beethovenian arpeggio of challenge now droops in fragmentary valediction; and its harmonic components lend themselves as readily to contrapuntal ingenuities as to dramatic opposition. The slow movement's phrygian opening—E minor with flat second—hints at a distant, modal world of religious consolation; but the implacable rhythm makes it seem very remote. The scherzo returns to bourgeois earthiness: which for all its ebullience cannot answer the melancholy of the first two movements. The resolution which Brahms finally achieves is monistic, but it is neither song melody nor fugue. Beethoven attains unity in song variation and in polyphony. Brahms establishes unity by the rigid repetition of a rhythmic ground and a harmonic pattern which remorselessly controls the tempests of tonal drama. Passion and suffering are subjected to the archaic formality of a passacaglia; and the contrapuntal extensions of the passacaglia theme reveal that its stern monumentality was incipient even in the sighful theme of the first allegro (Ex. 52):

Ex. 52   Brahms: Symphony No. 4 (first movement theme)

Cf: Sequences of falling thirds in the Passacaglia

This movement is truly noble because Brahms accepts suffering without rhetoric or emotional excess. But it is not joyful. It ends unflinchingly in the tonic minor; its spirit is stoical, not religious.

The harmonic and metrical unity of the passacaglia is perhaps the supreme expression of Brahms's abnegation and agnosticism. He had earlier given us a more explicit though less intense statement of it in the *German Requiem*: which he deliberately set not in hieratic Latin, but in the German language, and from which he excluded all metaphysical elements. There is no emphasis here on Christ the redeemer; since the dead are beyond hope or help, our care must be for those left living. And so the music of Brahms's last years becomes at once elegiac and consolatory. He writes a few works like the magnificent C minor Trio, opus 101, which revive his urgently Protestant and protesting fire. But in general his music is quieter, gentler, more mellow: and at the same time more melancholy. The fiery scherzos of his youth give way to the retrospective allegretto; the words *non troppo* appear with ever greater frequency in his tempo directions.

The series of small piano pieces, many of them under the unassuming title of 'Intermezzo', are an old man's distillation of the romantic Schumanesque piano writing of his youth. They are almost all in lyrical ABA song forms, rather than in sonata style; and though the texture is lucid compared with the massiveness of his early days, the sensuousness of the sound— in pieces such as the autumnally rich A major Intermezzo—is enhanced rather than diminished. Brahms's preoccupation with the tone-colour of the clarinet is also revealing. The Clarinet Quintet is perhaps his most beautiful chamber work. Although it preserves the externalities of sonata conflict, it has many features in common with baroque variation technique.* One elegiac theme dominates all the movements—even the rhapsodic coloratura of the slow movement, which is a twilit reminiscence of the gipsy ardours of his youth. The work reveals but does not transform this theme in the course of a key-scheme of classical sobriety: so that formally the quintet is much more retrospective than, say, Brahms's Second or Third Symphony. The final sighing of the theme by the clarinet, followed by the strings' repeated minor triads, are both a farewell to earthly beauty and a recognition that there is nothing else. Yet the lucidity of texture and structure safeguards the music from self-pity.

Several of the piano pieces of Brahms's last years invert classical precedent by beginning in the major and ending in the minor. Yet although their temper is so consistently elegiac, one finds nowhere else in Brahms's music so many features anticipatory of the future. The irregularity of the phrases, the cross rhythms, the counterpoints within the figuration have never been more supple; they frequently combine to create a harmonic texture which, in its linear and tonal relationships,

---

* For Bach and Handel variation was not so much permutations of a 'tune' as lyrical evolution over a constant harmonic basis, i.e. a free version of the chaconne principle.

is as audacious as the mature music of Wagner. (The extraordinary, indrawn E flat minor Intermezzo is especially interesting from this point of view.) It is not altogether surprising that Brahms's pessimism should have been paradoxically fertile; for artists of the twentieth century were nurtured in a climate of disillusion comparable with that of Brahms; and his search for salvation in discipline anticipates the twentieth century's turning from sonata to a somewhat negative use of baroque forms. Certainly Brahms's last considerable work speaks to us, as it spoke to him, with peculiar poignancy.

In the *Four Serious Songs* of 1896, Brahms chose texts from Ecclesiastes which reflect his own death-consciousness; and effects a compromise between the style of the Lied and that of the baroque cantata. The third song is a miraculously wrought structure based on the same descending third motive that appears in the Passacaglia of the E minor Symphony (Ex. 53):

Ex. 53 Brahms: O Tod, O Tod, wie bitter

Brahms's obsession with falling thirds would seem to be unmistakably associated with his obsession with death: and from this point of view we may contrast him with Bruckner. For Bruckner, death is a liberating force; the contemplation of death promotes long, soaring melodies that float in stepwise movement, with intermittent, ecstatic leaps. For Brahms, death suggests the sequence of falling thirds which roots the music harmonically, in the earth: dust returns to dust. This idea recurs throughout Brahms's music whenever he is most deeply moved. In the little B minor Intermezzo the falling thirds form suspended triads which create an effect of polytonality (Ex. 54):

Ex. 54 Brahms: Intermezzo in B minor

If in the E minor Symphony and the third of the *Four Serious Songs* the body returns to the earth, in the B minor Intermezzo it is as though the human dust were dissolving away into air and rain.

The contrast between Brahms and Bruckner suggests a similar comparison between Brahms and Bach. The vocal line and piano texture of the third of the *Serious Songs* are so permeated with progressions of thirds and their inversion into sixths that the music is almost as completely thematic as the Chorale Prelude of Bach, from an examination of which this book began. The complex lucidity of Bach's counterpoint seems, however, as inevitable as the softly breathing pulse which, in the protracted plagal cadence, stills itself to silence. Life flows into death, almost without Bach's conscious volition. The lucid complexity of Brahms's more harmonic texture has not this inevitability; it is the ultimate act of self-discipline whereby he subdues death's terrors.

We may also compare this 'cantata' of Brahms's old age with a cantata of Bach's youth, the *Actus Tragicus*, no. 106. There is plenty of evidence—in the tenor aria '*Ach Herr, lehre uns bedenken*' and still more in the strained fugato on '*Es ist der alte Bund*'— that the terrors of death were vivid to Bach. Yet for him, in youth as on his death-bed, the grave could become, through Christ the Redeemer, the promise of bliss, as the music unfolds to the seraphic obbligato of flutes and gambas. In Brahms's songs there is no attempt to justify death; there is only a reminder, in the last song, that human love justifies life, if it cannot redeem it. When the text refers to 'faith, hope and love', which are what remains when Death has done his worst, Brahms's vocal line swells and soars in this stupendous phrase (Ex. 55):

Ex. 55 Brahms: Wenn ich mit Menschen

Nun - aber blei - bet Glau-be, Hoff-nung, Lie - be, die-se drei.

It is almost as though human love had itself become winged and angelic. And so although Brahms never learned to transcend death, as did Beethoven, or to accept it, as did Schubert and Mozart, or not to care about it, as did Haydn, one can say that at the end he arrived at a point not so far distant from Haydn.

Both found that human love was the ultimate reality, but with this difference: for Haydn, human love could regenerate a world; for Brahms, it was a dying man's solace for the ineradicable follies of the past.

Yet that is not quite all. If we look again at that 'winged and angelic' vocal phrase we shall see that its huge leaps suggest the more bitter ecstasy of Mahler and the early Schoenberg, as does the theme of the adagio to Bruckner's Ninth. So, after all, Brahms comes to terms with his polar opposite. Perhaps this reminds us that if love is the only seed of creation, in the long run it does not greatly matter whether we think of it as human or divine.

We have said that when Brahms and Bruckner finally meet, both suggest Mahler [1860–1911]: whose work is an epilogue to the Viennese symphonic tradition. Like Beethoven, Mahler is a composer of strife; like Bruckner, he is a composer of exaltation; like Brahms, he is a composer of elegiac disillusion; like Schubert, he equivocates between reality and dream. But he was born later than Schubert, later even than Bruckner or Brahms; for him the dream is more elusive, his nostalgia the more deep.

The sense of separation which we have commented on in Beethoven, Schubert, and Brahms becomes, in Mahler, racial as well as spiritual. Though he worked in a rich musical tradition, he had himself no spiritual home; and his isolation was reinforced by his family's poverty. For he was not only a Jew; he was also a poor boy who made good. His life was a battle—not only, or indeed mainly, for his own music, but for other people's. His fearsome autocracy, his tyranny as opera conductor and as a director of Vienna's musical life, were entirely disinterested; he worked himself to death through a selfless devotion to his art. The ferocious hostility he aroused only exacerbated the anguish in his spirit. Beethoven could devote all his energies to his own salvation; even Schubert could spend all his time writing music, though not always the kind of music in which he was most interested. But for Mahler composition had to be a spare-time activity: though this activity was in the deepest sense the meaning of his life.

Apart from his songs and an early cantata, all Mahler's music is symphonic; and he regarded his nine symphonies as experiments in spiritual autobiography. The technique of symphonic growth and metamorphosis which Beethoven had explored in the Fifth Symphony, and vastly expanded in the Ninth, is the basis of Mahler's approach to symphony. He said that a symphony should embrace all aspects of human experience—banal and trivial as well as tragic and profound—and that it should be a complete spiritual world, with its inherent laws of birth, growth, and decay. Beethoven, however, had the classical tradition in his blood and bones. The revolutionary elements in his music affect us so powerfully because we are clearly aware of what he is revolting against; his contradictions of tonality are not fully intelligible except in reference to a norm. In Mahler this is no longer so. His harmonic thought was far more diatonic than Wagner's; yet he treats the relationship between keys with more freedom. The early *Songs of a Wayfarer* begin innocently in D minor, modulate through F sharp minor, B major, and E minor, to end distantly in F minor. The climax of the third song, prompted by the words, is an abrupt modulation to the flat supertonic; instead of drooping back to the tonic, the music stays in the new key until the end. In such tonal vagueness it is not so much Mahler's personality as a world itself that seems to be in flux. He was aware of this, as Bruckner was not; and his awareness intensifies his music's poignancy.

A certain contradictoriness—an inextricable medley of positive and negative responses—is thus the essence of Mahler's musical temperament. Consider his relation to popular music. His genius—like that of Schubert and Bruckner, but unlike that of the symphonic Beethoven—was essentially lyrical and vocal. He did not 'belong' to an Austrian peasant community; he lived and worked in the country only during the summer months, when free of his duties as conductor and opera director. But the contours of his melodies are permeated with the inflexions of Austrian song; and the childlike simplicity of some of these melodies represented an ideal of innocence to which Mahler, like Schubert, repeatedly turned. With him, however, the sense of estrangement is stronger, as his personality was the more tormented. Schubert oscillates so sensitively between reality and dream that he is sometimes doubtful which is which. Mahler often wishes he were a child, free of adult perversities and perturbations; but his nostalgia expands the folk-like phrases into periods that become yearnfully emotive, while he subjects them to enharmonic treatment even more extreme than that favoured by Bruckner.

Urban popular music, as well as rural folk-song, is involved in this relationship to his environment. Sometimes café songs are presented nostalgically, as they are in Schubert; more often they are rhythmically distorted or tonally dislocated, as though Mahler were trying to express both his yearning for such simple-minded vulgarity and also an insidious corruption within popular music itself (Ex. 56). There is a similar ambiguity

Ex. 56 Mahler: Symphony No. 1

in the military music which haunts his work as it haunted Schubert's. The fanfares and march rhythms convey a genuine delight in imperial splendour, coupled with a sinister atmosphere of nightmare (Ex. 57). The military rhythm is always

Ex. 57 Mahler: Symphony No. 9

liable to be transformed into one of Mahler's phantasmagoric funeral marches, in which the trumpets' tattoo becomes a mortuary tolling of bells. Nostalgia for past splendour may at any moment become at once an elegy, and a dark prophecy of chaos. The dissolution of the Austrian Empire was indeed to release horrors dreamt of only in the imaginations of artists of Mahler's neurotic sensitivity. Even his horn-call themes—which derive from the heroic aspects of Beethoven, Brahms, Schubert, and Bruckner—become tonally precarious, fateful in their singularity.

Hardly less equivocal is the liturgical element in Mahler's music. Bruckner was a Catholic by birth and instinct. Mahler was a Jew who embraced Catholicism as a part of his lifelong struggle for peace. Only at moments did he achieve Bruckner's singlemindedness; never did he experience the serenity of revealed faith. But the faith implicit in Catholic dogma became a symbol of the Grail he was seeking: and led him consciously to relate his music to certain aspects of Catholic polyphony. As a Viennese, he would naturally turn to the monumental baroque which Bruckner had absorbed intuitively. How he related this to his Beethovenian conception of the symphony is revealed in his two choral symphonies, the Second and the Eighth.

The first movement of the Second Symphony is a conflict piece on a vast scale, with a first theme that surges up like a strifeful Mannheim skyrocket, straining to break the bands of the harmony's solemn processional rhythm. In the fourth movement a solo voice enters: lyrical song symbolizes a vision of innocence and light, as in Schubert and Bruckner; only such simplicity of being can lead into the resurrection of the last, choral movement. The death and resurrection of the work are subjective, as they are in Beethoven's 'Eroica'; yet they are also presented with all the naïve realism of Bruckner. Mahler did not, like Bruckner, believe in a literal resurrection; but in his search for a faith he relates his symphonic struggles to the techniques of baroque polyphony. This is still more obvious in the Eighth Symphony, the first part of which is a tremendous symphonic-choral setting of the Catholic hymn, *Veni Creator*; while the second part is a setting of the final scenes of Goethe's *Faust*. Catholic dogma is transformed into a Goethean spiritual quest; while a personal testament becomes dogmatic. Bruckner makes a Catholic hymn out of a symphony: Mahler makes a symphonic battle out of Catholic polyphony.

The polyphonic element in Mahler's music reminds us that he is after all a composer with a classical heritage, even though tradition disintegrates in his work. Vienna is not what it was and the Church cannot mean for him what it meant for Bruckner; but in the midst of decay and corruption an ideal 'essence' of the Church and of the Viennese tradition were absolutes to which Mahler yearned back, or towards which he aspired.

As a starting-point, let us look at the simplest and shortest of his symphonies, the Fourth, in G. In the first movement he begins with the classical, symmetrical phrase: at once Haydnesque and folk-like (Ex. 58). This is an evocation of a vanished world. Gradually he injects into the phrase something of his

Ex. 58 Mahler: Symphony No. 4

personal quality of rhapsodic exaltation, with wide leaps and drooping suspensions (Ex. 59). He does not exactly transform the theme into an entity of different emotional significance, as

Ex. 59 Mahler: Symphony No. 4.

Beethoven would; but he increasingly sees it from the standpoint of his own self-consciousness. As the intervals and rhythms are expanded the phrase loses its polished urbanity: becomes so free in tonality and rhythm that it implies a trend away from stable diatonicism. Mahler naturally thought polyphonically; his spare texture is habitually based on two-part writing, and frequently on fourths and fifths rather than on the triad. In that respect, as in many others, he anticipates some of the early music of Schoenberg.

With this polyphonic bias, Mahler orchestrates in a manner quite different from the classical composers. His scoring becomes almost a chamber music technique, delineating the orchestral voices with the maximum precision. The Italian element evident in Mahler—as in Mozart and Schubert and most Viennese art—is here explicit; and the wheel comes full circle. For Haydn's glowing periods had clipped the free vocal phrase of seventeenth-century Italian madrigal and opera into the symmetrical, diatonic, instrumental phrase. Starting from Haydn, Mahler stretches out the phrase, loosens it, until he arrives once more at principles analogous to the baroque rhetoric of early Italian opera, and to the supple line-drawing of the Italian polyphonists. This means that his conception of symphonic form must change even more radically than does Schubert's or Bruckner's in their attempt to create a symphony based on lyricism. The full implications of this are not apparent in the Fourth; for this is deliberately a revocation of the past which ends, with the appearance of the human voice, in the dream-world of a child's heaven. A traditional folk-poem inspires a folk-like directness of melodic speech; even the exquisite lucidity of Mahler's orchestration, though in fact sophisticated, produces an effect of naïve candour.

The implications of the Mahlerian symphony are most consummately realized in his last completed work, the Ninth. The immense first movement opens with a dreamfully singing melody in D major, in which each rising phrase nostalgically droops in an appoggiatura. (Against this theme Mahler wrote, in the original score, "O vanished days of youth, O scattered loves.") Opposed to it is a ferocious, upward-surging theme in the minor; a sinister rhythmic figure that had originally been the bass of the song melody: and one of Mahler's mysterious trumpet calls in march rhythm. The impact of these wild and striving elements on the nostalgic vision of 'Viennese' serenity changes its significance each time it reappears. Its component intervals and rhythms become increasingly attenuated; it splinters up into fragments divided between the first and second violins; it proliferates in acutely dissonant counterpoints. The 'conflict' themes themselves mate in wildly contrarious polyphony: until finally they carry the song melody far from the stable props of diatonic tonality into a spare, widely spaced, glassily scored linear counterpoint. Yet the whole of this vast movement is enclosed within a dominant-tonic progression. The symbol of the stability of the classical world is strained to breaking-point; it hangs on the single thread of the final high D on piccolo and 'cello harmonic.

The second movement is a gigantic Ländler which is now not merely nostalgic, but also spectral. It is a ghost of the past, frightening as well as endearing: which again disintegrates into linear fragments. The third movement, called 'Rondo Burleske', is a wild parody or inversion of both positives of Mahler's art— folk-song and monumental polyphony. The simplicity of folk-melody and the solemnity of monumental counterpoint become savagely grotesque; though just before the end there is a visionary, serio-comic anticipation of the final adagio. This seems to suggest that for Mahler neither folk-song nor dogmatic polyphony could offer salvation; such peace as he can find must be in the meditations of his own spirit. So the last movement is a passionately subjective adagio, carrying the vast leaps of Bruckner's exaltation and the fluidity of his (and *Parsifal's*) enharmonic transitions to so extreme a point that the music literally breaks with its world-weariness. First harmony disintegrates into linear counterpoint, in the chamber-music scoring which anticipates so many developments in twentieth-century

music (Ex. 60, plate XXXIV). Then melody itself disintegrates in piteous chromatic fragmentariness; with the fading of
the melodic strands there vanishes too a world and a mode of
belief. Even the basic tonality has sunk from the first movement's D to D flat.

In the passages of linear polyphony in the Ninth Symphony,
and still more in the last movement of his symphonic song-cycle,
Das Lied von der Erde, Mahler attains a translucent texture that
seems in some ways more Eastern than European. The cycle sets
Chinese poems without superficial Orientalisms. But in the
'Farewell' appear strange linear arabesques—sometimes pentatonic, sometimes in chromatically inflected modes, sometimes
almost as non-tonal and inhuman as bird-calls: while in the
ineffably protracted suspensions on the word *'ewig'* music strains
to release itself from harmony and metre. Beethoven, we saw,
had to free himself from Time and the Will if he was to preserve
his sanity. He found his salvation, if Europe did not. In the dying
fall of Mahler's last music the madness of a world burns itself
out. The obsession with Time, which has dominated Europe
since the Renaissance, begins to dissolve into Asiatic immobil-
ity; and the process is a laceration of the spirit. Mahler lingers
on those suspended dissonances, his last hold on the life he loved
with all his richly attuned senses; while the hollow reverber-
ations of percussion sound like falling masonry, thudding
through an eternity of years. The chord on which the 'Farewell'
finally fades to nothingness is a 'verticalization' of the pentatonic scale; and of all melodic formulae the pentatonic is most
void of harmonic implications. Yet out of harmonic disintegration grows a new seed. The linear principle of twelve-note
music already is inherent in the texture of the music of Mahler's
last years.

II OPERA, RITUAL, AND MYTH

THE BIRTH OF A NEW KIND OF OPERA

W<small>E</small> have seen that during the second half of the eighteenth century the seminal force in music was sonata; and we have touched on some of the reasons why its development was associated with Austria. None the less, its impact was felt all over Europe. France of the Revolutionary era had in Gossec [1734–1829] a symphonist whose energy and audacity rivals the early Beethoven; while Italy produced in Boccherini [1743–1805] a composer of symphonies and chamber music who achieves a highly personal fusion of Italian lyricism with instrumentally dramatic fire—more sensuous and popular, less bitter-sweet than Mozart. Both Gossec and Boccherini are, at their best, great composers; yet it is none the less true that in Italy and France the central stream of music remained operatic rather than symphonic. Nor was this surprising, for these countries had seen the rise of the great autocracies of the seventeenth and eighteenth centuries; and we have already noted that baroque opera was a projection into visual and aural symbols of the rituals by which the heroic age lived. In Austria, perhaps, the revolutionary force of sonata could come into the open; in Italy the conventions of aristocracy, in art as in life, were so deeply entrenched that they were more likely to be undermined from within. And so the comic interludes that used to provide light relief between the acts of heroic operas gradually encroached on the main performance. The *opera buffa* became a 'low' parody of the heights of heroism, which now seemed stilted rather than tall by nature.

We have already commented on this popular operatic style, in relation to the development of the Austrian sonata. It is perhaps worth adding that the three leading composers of *opera buffa* all spent part of their lives in prison for political reasons. Piccinni [1728–1800] was a man of the old world who, brought up on *opera seria*, still composed fine music in the baroque tradition. He made a fortune by composing operas in the new style, was embroiled in politics vicariously through his relatives, and died in misery, bemused to the last. Paisiello [1740–1816], who also made a vast fortune out of the new opera, was an opportunist of a modern type. He wrote for whichever party happened to be in power, often using the same music, with different words, for either side; he found himself in trouble only because he was not agile enough to keep in step. Cimarosa [1749–1801] represents the third stage. Though in his art his aim was the same as Paisiello's—to entertain and to make money—he was a sincere revolutionary, martyred for the cause.

In France, the change in operatic style ran parallel to that in Italy. The grandeur of Lully was superseded by the more sensational heroics of Rameau [1683–1764]: which in turn gave way not to a deliberate cult of the Low, but to a Rousseauistic cult of Nature, simplicity, and moralistic rationality.* In his own amateurish compositions Rousseau opposed the naturalness of Italian *buffo* style to the archaic splendours of Rameau. Italian *opera buffa* had reduced recitative—always an important element in classical French opera—to a patter that was almost speech. Rousseau, in *Le Devin du Village*, took the further step and employed spoken dialogue, interspersed with descriptive musical interludes and songs: this 'musical comedy' being presented in a setting of idealized rusticity, rather than of mythological magnificence. The composers who followed his lead—Duni [1709–1775], Philidor [1726–1795], and Monsigny [1729–1817]—soon realized that partisanship between the French and Italian cause in what came to be called the *Guerre des Bouffons* was a waste of time. The sprightly symmetries of Italian *buffo* melody could be employed by French composers to good effect; but that was no reason for excluding tunes founded on French popular music, or even on simplifications of the old-fashioned aristocratic *air de cour*.

So it came about that *opera buffa* and *opéra comique* met in the Opera of Sentiment that flourished in both countries. Whereas *opera buffa* based its characters on the stock types of Italian Comedy, but transformed mythological beings into ordinary folk, *opéra comique* started with ordinary people and romanticized them. Both represented a democratic 'levelling'. In

* Jean-Jacques Rousseau [1712–1778] was, as writer and philosopher, a premonition of romanticism in that he believed in the significance of the intimate inner life, as opposed to the public life of Church or State. He was also an amateur composer and musical theorist.

opera buffa the heroic becomes commonplace, in *opéra comique* the commonplace becomes extraordinary; the new sentimental operas might deal with a low subject glamorized, or with a high subject domesticated. One of the greatest European successes of the time was Piccinni's *La Buona Figliuola* (1767), based on a permutation of Richardson's *Pamela.* This heroine of English middle-class sensibility might be you or I, for we all relish a self-righteous assumption of virtue. Perhaps we also like to think of ourselves as the rakish seducer, or as the girl whom an aristocrat might want to seduce; certainly we take pleasure in a nice cry over our misfortunes. The popular opera audiences of the later eighteenth century were not so different from the cinema audiences of to-day; their partiality for variations on the Cinderella story—the poor girl who is the potential princess—is especially interesting. But Piccinni's music must have given a richer satisfaction than the average product of Hollywood, for it manages to combine the virtues of Italian and French opera without the impoverishment of either.

This is equally true of the most representative opera composer of the French school in the second half of the century. Grétry [1742–1813]—a Belgian, born at Liège—spent his adolescence in Rome. He then went to Geneva as a fully-fledged Italianate composer; heard the operas of Monsigny and Philidor; and moved to Paris, determined to emulate their success. His triumph was not long delayed; for to offset a restricted harmonic range and a rudimentary contrapuntal technique, he had a spontaneous melodic gift and a sure instinct for theatrical effect. Most of his operas were in the fashionable vain of the *comédie larmoyante*. When he attempted a heroic theme, as in *Richard Cœur de Lion*, he simultaneously domesticated and romanticized it by concentrating on the Blondel story. When he attempted a mythological theme, as in *Zémire et Azor*, he and his librettist, Marmontel, adapted a fairy tale of the classical age in a way that became unconscious allegory. For the Beast in this version of the Beauty and the Beast legend becomes a Common Man (or animal) who—in a romantically exotic setting—proves himself worthy of the glory that was Versailles. The glory is tarnished, of course. Artistically there is little to justify the claim of Grétry's disciples that he was 'the Molière of music'; the moral intensity beneath the wit has gone, nor has the music the linear power and harmonic subtlety of Couperin and Rameau. On the other hand, his admirers' description of him as 'the French Pergolesi' was valid, for he certainly recreates the easy delights of *opera buffa* in French terms. Though it was considered impolitic to present *Zémire et Azor* at the Dauphin's marriage in 1772 (and perhaps would have been so, for reasons deeper than the obvious one), the music the Dauphin missed owes its charm partly to the fact that its fresh lucidity, heralding the dawn of a new world, is reconciled with an aristocratic past.

The overture and most of the allegro arias are Italian *buffo* music of no very distinctive character. But the duo in Act I, '*Le temps est bel*', testifies to Grétry's dictum that "La parole est un bruit où le chant est renfermé". Although he dispenses with recitative in favour of speech, his melodies recall Rameau's, and even Lully's, in their intimate relationship to the French language. Even Azor's touching air in Act III, '*Du moment qu'on aime*" is no more Italianate than the comparable if richer airs of Rameau; and takes its place beside a chanson-like ariette such as Zémire's tender '*Rose chérie*'. Orchestrally and theatrically, the loveliest moments in the opera are simplified, popularized versions of classical convention. For instance, the orchestral texture of the duo mentioned above, with its softly floating quavers on the strings, and sustained notes on the bassoon, derives from the Lullian *scène de sommeil*, while the trio in the magic mirror episode has its prototype in the supernatural scenes in Rameau.

It is irrelevant to complain that the music lacks Rameau's grandeur and intensity. Grétry dramatized a fairy tale which was not, as it seems, mere make-believe; and inserted into it sequences of songs and dances with little attempt at formal cohesion. He did this not because he was irresponsible, but because, as an ardent Encyclopaedist, he wanted his art to be immediately intelligible to as large a number of people as possible; so concerned was he about intelligibility that he even maintained that it would be a good idea to add explanatory words to Haydn's symphonies! We may doubt whether he appreciated the undercurrent of tragic power in Haydn's music. Yet there had been theatrical composers who did appreciate it, and who had created a new grand opera which combined the musical power and subtlety of the baroque with the psychological interest appropriate to a more democratic order.

Even by the time of Grétry's relaxed, popular manner the old conventions had not been entirely forgotten. In the operas of Jomelli [1714–1774] and Traetta [1727–1779] they preserved their grandeur, while absorbing the more flexible techniques of *opera buffa*, *opéra comique*, and the Italo-Austrian sonata. Significantly, the consummation of this recreated tragic opera came through one of the international figures dear to an age of rationality and enlightenment.

Christoph Willibald Gluck [1714–1798] was born in Bohemia, of peasant ancestry. His cultural heritage was thus German; but since in 1736 he went to Italy to study with Sammartini, his training was entirely Italian. In 1745 he visited London, where he was much impressed by the music of Handel; on his way through France he became familiar with the operas of Rameau and the new *opéra comique*. During the next sixteen years he divided his time between Vienna and Paris, with intermittent excursions to other European cities, producing operas in both Italian and French.

In the early part of his career Gluck wrote a stream of Italian operas, all in the heroic manner. It is unreasonable to suppose that these works contain no evidence of his later genius: but certain that they can lay no claim to the lyrical power and harmonic imaginativeness of Handel or Alessandro Scarlatti. Nor is there much to be said for Gluck's direct attempts to emulate the *opéra comique*, for his talents tended no more to a homely charm than to the *buffo* humour which he cannily avoided. His instinct in turning to France was, however, sound, since in Rousseauistic philosophy he found not so much a moral principle as an emotional attitude which could regenerate old forms. It is significant that his first creation of genius should have been not an Italian opera, nor even a French opera, but a French ballet; and the ancestry of the ballet in France went back beyond the heroic opera and tragedy to the court ritual of the Renaissance.

In Gluck's day there was a movement for reform in the ballet comparable with that which he was to initiate in opera. In heroic French opera, ballet had been as intrinsic a part of the ritual as poetry and music. With the decline of the heroic, ballet had degenerated into the *divertissement de danses*—pretty, but unrelated to the action, as rococo ornament is unrelated to structure. The protagonists of the new ballet, notably Noverre and Angiolini, found their impetus in the operas of Rameau, wherein ballet became not decorative, nor even purely formal, but dramatic action in pantomime. When Noverre decided to create a ballet-pantomime based on the Don Juan legend, he had lighted on a theme which, as an expression of a clash between the individual and social convention, went home to his society with peculiar force. He had also found a subject which had to be treated with dramatic immediacy, or not at all.

That Gluck, in composing a ballet, did not have to think about the human voice was a tremendous asset. Unburdened with operatic convention, Gluck creates a symphonic score which in dramatic urgency can stand beside the music which Haydn and Mozart were to compose twenty years later. Certainly no symphonic music written in the 1760s approaches Gluck's prelude or the fight scene in concentrated ferocity: or the awesome graveyard scene in imaginative orchestration. The exigencies of dance gesture prompt Gluck's vigorous instrumental style, with its wide leaps and prancing rhythms; here the ceremonial dancing of heroic opera becomes dramatic action (Ex. 61). It is obvious that Mozart was familiar with

Ex. 61 *Allegro risoluto*

Gluck's score when he wrote his own *Don Giovanni*, which also centres around the key of D minor. Though Mozart's musical-dramatic sense is subtler and more highly organized, he nowhere displays a more vivid awareness of theatrical effect than does Gluck in the terrifying single note crescendo at the appearance of the Commandant.

Gluck found himself in creating dramatic-symphonic music for the dance. In the following year (1762) he produced the first of his so-called 'reform' operas, *Orfeo*. Superficially, this differs but little from the many other Italian operas he had produced in Vienna. It is based on a classical myth; it is a singers' opera rooted in Italian *bel canto*. True, it combines its Italian aria and arioso with dance pantomime from the French ballet, and with big homophonic choruses of the type so magnificently developed by Rameau; but there was nothing new about that, since both Rameau as a Frenchman and Traetta as an Italian had effected a fusion of French and Italian techniques. The only technical innovations which Gluck makes are negative: he avoids vocal ostentation, and dispenses with the *da capo* aria and with the harpsichord continuo. He is thus able to achieve greater dramatic continuity; the music stops less frequently to accommodate the reflective aria, while the recitative, being accompanied by strings, can be absorbed more readily into the symphonic texture.

Although *Orfeo* appears to be an Italian opera, this amounts to a victory for the French cause. From the time of Lully onwards the French had regarded opera as a tragedy in music. Monteverdi's notion of opera had been much the same; but by the eighteenth century opera had become, for the Italians, a theatrical concert. There was no reason why opera should not be virtuoso music for star singers; indeed, the baroque essentially involves display. But with the decline of autocratic culture, the display ceased to serve an imaginative purpose; opera began to lose its moral and ritualistic significance when display became an end in itself. In *Orfeo* Gluck re-created the heroic ideal. He did not—indeed, he could not—merely revive it, for the moral values he was trying to portray could not be the same as those of the baroque age. The way in which they differed from the past is expressed precisely in his more symphonic conception of the heroic. He looks back to Rameau and Traetta; he looks forward not so much to Mozart as to Beethoven.

In purely musical inventiveness Gluck is inferior to a great master such as Rameau, or even to a minor composer of genius such as Traetta. But it is erroneous to accuse him of defective technique. He had the kind of technique he needed: more counterpoint (even as much as Handel's cook), more opulent lyricism, would have been not only superfluous, but wrong. In *Orfeo* his vocal writing is very simple, compared with that of Rameau or of Alessandro Scarlatti; but it is wonderfully sensitive to dramatic propriety, and where necessary is content to be subservient to the drama of the choral and orchestral writing. In the scene of the Furies both the orchestral music—with its scurrying scales and hectic repeated notes—and the choral invocations have their precedent in Rameau and even in Lully.

In Gluck, however, the spirit is quite new; the music acquires—
largely through its remorseless rhythmic impetus—an urgent
terror and awful simplicity which suggests Beethoven in his
revolutionary mood (Ex. 62). Again, the scene in the Elysian

Ex. 62 Gluck: *Orfeo*. Furies' Chorus
Chorus at three octaves

f With string tremolandos

Fields derives from the pastoral convention of heroic opera; yet
its melodic directness, its simple homophonic texture and lucent
scoring create a new world of feeling—the vision of order and
light which the eighteenth century associated with Hellenism.
Even Gluck's preservation of the castrato* is given dramatic
relevance. In baroque opera the male soprano voice was considered god-like and super- rather than sub-human, natural male
voices being employed only for low characters; Gluck associates
the silvery tones of the male contralto with Orpheus in *his*
non-human aspect—not as god-king, but as the spirit of
music.

Throughout, the conventions of heroism are becoming themselves the symbols of change; and that change is inseparable
from Gluck's insight into the human heart. It is significant that,
as compared with the extravagant intrigue of baroque opera,
there is virtually no action in *Orfeo*: the drama takes place in
the minds of the two chief characters. Gluck prefaced his
second 'reform' opera, *Alceste*, with a manifesto in which he
explained that he had resolved to divest opera of "all those
abuses introduced into it whether by the mistaken vanity of
singers or by the too great complaisance of composers. . . . I have
striven to restrict music to its true office of serving poetry by
means of expression and by following the situations of the story
without interrupting the action or stifling it in a superfluity of
ornaments." He goes on to point out, quite justly, that he was
aided in his endeavours by a librettist, Calzabigi, who had
substituted for "florid descriptions, unnatural paragons, and
sententious cold morality, heartfelt language, strong passions,
interesting situations, and endlessly varied spectacles". Between
them, they have proved that "simplicity, truth, and naturalness are the great principles of beauty".

* CASTRATO: the artificial male soprano or alto. See *Castrati* Part II.

The last of these remarks is a valid comment on this wonderful opera; but Gluck did not really mean, any more than did Wagner, that he wanted music to be subservient to poetry. He meant that he wanted the music to evolve as a coherent dramatic structure related to the text: so we find that musically *Alceste* does not depart radically from the style of *Orfeo*, but carries further Gluck's symphonic orientation of the heroic. Thus Gluck accepts from Rameau the conventional association of key-relationships with human emotions: modulations sharpwards imply an increase of animation, flatwards modulations a depressive influence, and so on. But these relationships now become part of a symphonic argument; the classical equilibrium which we commented on in the mature work of Haydn and Mozart is already evident in the moving scene between Alceste, the High Priest, and the chorus, with its pathetic, symphonically developed motive on the oboe. Greek myth is no longer a vehicle for the rituals of autocracy, usually based on a fight between personal passion and duty to the State: it is a means of exploring the passions of men and women who, while not being themselves heroic, were becoming increasingly conscious of their humanity.

Gluck deliberately set himself a different human situation to deal with in each opera. In *Paride ed Elena* Calzabigi makes Helen an honest woman and Paris the wicked seducer, so that the legend becomes an ennobled version of the Pamela story that appealed so deeply to eighteenth-century moralistic piety. Gluck significantly says that he has not scrupled to make the music banal and trivial where the dramatic sense demanded it. "He who is concerned with truthfulness must model himself to his subject, and the noblest beauties of harmony and melody become serious faults if they are misplaced." He gives the Greeks a rather bare, uncouth music, the Trojans a more Latin and sensual style, and symphonically objectifies the tension between his two principal characters in this racial differentiation. Again there is almost no action outside the minds of the lovers.

Although these two operas were extremely successful when produced in Vienna, Gluck seems to have felt that this centre of *buffo* frivolity was no suitable place for the fruition of his talents. Despite its Italianate elements, *Alceste* had already indicated that Gluck's art was in some ways the fulfilment of

French philosophical and theatrical ideals. He sought for 'truthfulness and simplicity', and in that sense was a Rousseau-like Child of Nature as well as a '*Paysan du Danube*'. It is not therefore surprising that, having obtained an opera commission from Paris, he should have experienced a triumph with *Iphigénie en Aulide*. This was followed immediately by French versions of *Orfeo* and *Alceste*; then he paid the French tradition the compliment of resetting one of the opera-books that Quinault had written for Lully. The comparison of the two *Armide*s is interesting, if by no means always to Gluck's advantage. The change in stress is significant. For Lully, the central character is Renaud, a man torn between passion and duty. For Gluck, the central character is Armide, a woman conscious of her power. He even adds a scene at the end in which Armide, left alone, frustrated in her love, determines to destroy the world she has created, and herself with it. In this subtly psychological conclusion, the heroic conventions become subjective experience. Armide's monologue is woven into a little wailing orchestral figure sequentially repeated, with almost romantic melancholy; the final cataclysm attains, within its apparently limited convention, a Wagnerian violence. The sudden change from the tempestuous D minor scales and arpeggios to the unison Fs, and the re-establishment of a solemn D major when the dust of ruin has blown away, is a stroke of the highest imaginative genius (Ex. 63):

Ex. 63 Gluck: *Armide*

For his next opera Gluck turned from the sensuality of *Armide* to the wild passion of Euripides. Guillard's admirable libretto on *Iphigénie en Tauride* chooses a subject which Goethe himself had adapted, and the highest praise one can give to

Gluck's opera is to say that it stands with Goethe's poem as the climax of the eighteenth-century re-creation of the Greek ideal: the Apollonian discipline which enables man to bear the most appalling suffering; the cult of friendship as an act of faith. *Armide* harks back to Lully, while being prophetic of romanticism. *Iphigénie en Tauride* looks back to Rameau—even the famous 'pathological' recitative of Orestes in Act III, with its simple yet extraordinary orchestral interjections, has antecedents in Rameau's *récitative accompagnée*.* At the same time it looks forward to Beethoven's *Fidelio* (the dungeon music in Act II), to Berlioz (the gruesome dance of the Eumenides, with its weird scoring for trombones), and even to Wagner (it opens with a storm which is both operatic and subjective, and a human situation parallel to that at the beginning of *Die Walküre*). Heroism has died to be reborn. Man is no longer a king pretending to be a god; but he becomes godlike in challenging the gods, in resisting whatever Fate has in store for him. This is a Beethovenian step towards Wagner's attempt at self-metamorphosis into God Himself.

Iphigénie en Tauride was not Gluck's last opera. In *Echo et Narcisse* he returns to the tradition of pastoral mythology, now imbued with his own interest in the workings of the human mind. There is nothing odd about this, for we have noted that Gluck never wished to destroy the classical ideal—only to render it once more morally valid. The notorious contest between Gluck as composer of 'reform' operas and Piccinni as upholder of the Italian cause proved only that the opposition was unreal: Gluck could not but respect Piccinni's melodic gifts, while Piccinni knew that he would have been a more effective and a better composer had he had a modicum of Gluck's dramatic integrity. Throughout his career Gluck interspersed his reformatory operas with returns to the old-fashioned *opera seria*, complete with display arias. Though the new elements in Gluck's operas were those which most powerfully expressed his genius, we should guard against thinking that because his operas were different from the baroque ideal they were necessarily better. They were better for him, and perhaps better for us, since we can never again enter into the ritual of the heroic

---

* RÉCITATIVE ACCOMPAGNÉE : recitative in lyrical or arioso style, accompanied by the orchestra instead of by continuo instruments. Such arioso was reserved for dramatic highlights or supernatural occurrences.

age; yet *opera seria* remained for many years the highest
ambition even of as progressive a musician as Mozart. His very
last, unfinished work was an *opera seria*, *La Clemenza di Tito*,
commissioned to celebrate the Coronation of Leopold II—in the
old monarch-glorifying style, modified only by a prevalence of
Mozartian ensemble numbers. It may be true that by that date
(1791) the commission went against the grain; yet Mozart
undertook it, and incorporated into it some extraordinarily
beautiful music.

As a boy, Mozart—a no less international figure than Gluck
—tried himself out in all the current operatic manners. His
training was Italian, not only because he learned his technique
from such men as J. C. Bach and Martini, but because he
had singing lessons from Manzuoli and the castrato Ceccarelli.
His first opera, *La Finta Semplice*, written at the age of twelve,
was a stock *buffo* piece on a text of Goldoni, with the conventional *commedia* characters and a musical style modelled directly
on Piccinni and Pergolesi. In the same year he composed
Bastien et Bastienne, which although in the German language was
a French opera based on Rousseau's *Devin du Village*. But these
exercises in the fashionable *opera buffa* and *opéra comique* were
literally mere child's play. The ventures to which Mozart
devoted his youthful energies were all heroic; and *Mitridate* and
Lucio Silla fail not because of inadequate integrity and devotion
on Mozart's part, but simply because he was not old enough
to attempt grandeur without seeming pretentious. Yet *Lucio
Silla* is an important step in his development, significantly
associated with the passionate *Sturm und Drang* violin sonatas
which he composed in the 1770s.

Certainly he was not pleased to have to return, in *La Finta
Giardinera* (commissioned by Munich) and in *Il Re Pastore*, to
the stock *buffo* and *galant* types; he complained that "some
people think one remains twelve all one's life". When at the
(for him) mature age of twenty-five he received a commission
to compose a big *opera seria* for Munich, he considered it the
most important event of his career. To the end of his days he
regarded *Idomeneo* as one of his supreme achievements, and
strove repeatedly to get it performed. Only our inherited mis-
trust of baroque ideals can prevent us from seeing that he was
right.

Idomeneo is the only opera in which Mozart was directly

influenced by Gluck. Like Gluck, he combines Italianate aria and recitative with choruses and orchestral interludes derived from French sources; while the orchestrally accompanied recitative he models directly on Gluck's *Alceste*. He too tends to replace the static *da capo* aria with arias in elliptical sonata style; his symphonic treatment of operatic techniques gives to the grand manner a psychological intensity. Events, for Mozart as for Gluck, are less important than their effects on the characters. Though its old-fashioned libretto makes *Idomeneo* less stageworthy than Gluck's masterpieces, it is the only opera by Mozart to achieve the note of classical tragedy. The tremendous outbursts of Electra have Gluck's dramatic perspicuity, with superb lyrical panache; the overture has Gluck's nobility, with Mozart's symphonic control, in a richly contrapuntal texture, over the boldest modulatory excursions. In the great quartet in the last act Mozart achieves something which Gluck never attempted. Here the two lovers, resigned in their mutual confidence, the furious Electra and the despairing Idomeneo, sing together, expressing the emotions which are peculiar to each of them, yet related because provoked by a single situation. This is the first great Mozartian ensemble number, in which the sonata composer's search for unity in diversity is projected into operatic terms: the psychological tension is paralleled in the modulatory drama, controlled by the classical symmetry of the form and the cantabile power of the contrasted voices. Mozart had virtually no precedent for this musical-psychological organization. Heroic opera dealt with absolutes rather than with the interplay of character, and Alessandro Scarlatti and Rameau are the only baroque composers who even attempted to exploit the musical and dramatic significance of the ensemble.*

Mozart's justifiable pride in *Idomeneo* did not, however, carry him far with the progressive Emperor Joseph II, who opposed

---

* There are, however, a few impressive examples of the 'psychological' ensemble in Handel's later oratorios, which are operas without stage action, wherein the heroic theme has become national and humanitarian rather than aristocratic. The quartet in *Jephtha* presents Isis's sacrifice simultaneously from her own and her lover's point of view, from her father's, and from the official or public point of view. Neither a composer of the old aristocratic world nor a composer of profound religious conviction, like Bach, would have allowed himself to suggest such a dubiety of intention as is contained in Iphis's and Hamor's unaccompanied cadenzas. Church, State, and Father may be willing to resign Iphis, in the general interest, to God's will; but the lovers' acceptance of the inevitable is rueful, to say the least.

the *opera seria* in much the same spirit as he opposed the Papacy.
The forces of reaction, in any field, were to be discouraged; a
local operatic art should be developed as a complement to the
Italian *opera buffa* and the French *opéra comique*. The first national
Singspiel theatre was opened in Vienna in 1778; it turned out
to be rather different from what the Emperor had intended.
Singspiel was supposed to be a popular art distinct from international Italian opera. Yet in a city as impregnated with
Italian culture as was Vienna, it was inevitable that elements
both of *opera seria* and of *opera buffa* should crop up, if in a cruder
form; and that the German *Jezter* should be closely related to the
Commedia characters.* The simple dance-songs of *opéra comique*
also crept in; and all these international features acquired, in
the decaying world of Vienna, a dream-like fantasticality. The
fairy poetry of Wieland—the main literary impulse—was
submerged in knockabout farce and music-hall numbers.
Joseph II had intended that *Singspiel* should be a national
gesture, and in that sense implicitly if not explicitly political
and revolutionary. It became what we would call an escape art:
and of a more obvious type than the sentimental opera as
practised in Italy and France.

It was for this theatre that Mozart wrote his next opera,
Die Entführung aus dem Serail. Coming to it fresh from the musical
riches of *Idomeneo*, Mozart could hardly be content to produce a
gallimaufry of music-hall turns. Parts of *Die Entführung* are in
full-flown Italianate style, performable only by great virtuoso
singers. Other parts—notably the character of Osmin—are
pathological studies of deep insight. Other parts again are
unaffectedly popular in manner. This confusion of genres
weakens the opera's theatrical effect; while each element is in
itself brilliant, the relationship between them is ill-defined.
When Mozart turned to opera again he had discovered that all
the conventional modes of his time—even the *Singspiel*—could
be converted to his imaginative ends.

Although *Die Entführung* is not a successful opera, it was for
Mozart a step in the right direction. *Idomeneo* may be Mozart's

---

* The essence of the Italian comedy was improvisation on a number of mytho-
ogical characters and situations. Its origins were medieval; its heyday, in Italy
and France, was the seventeenth and early eighteenth centuries. Many of
Watteau's paintings and Couperin's pieces '*dans le goût burlesque*', give some notion
of the beauty, pathos, and wit that the improvisation of the greatest of the *Commedia*
actors must have given to the conventional framework.

supreme tragic work; but as a man of the Enlightenment, seeking an ever greater humanity, Mozart was not to find his deepest utterance in heroic tragedy. Increasingly he found himself drawn towards an inextricable mingling of tragic and comic. In this, his art is Shakespearean; and when he said in a letter, "I deem nothing human alien to me", he expressed an attitude similar to Prospero's "This thing of darkness I acknowledge mine". He was thus able to take over the fashionable conventions of his day, for the reasons that made them fashionable: and at the same time to reveal the human impulses behind fashion, which only genius could interpret. He could do this partly, of course, because of the fruition of his talents; but also because he found in Da Ponte a librettist who had, if not genius to match his, at least genius enough to see what he wanted.

Superficially, *Figaro* is a direct descendant from *opera buffa*. The characters are founded on the *Commedia* types: Susanna is Pergolesi's Servina and also Columbine, Figaro is Harlequin, Bartolo is Pantalone, and Cherubino is Lelio and also an adolescent Don Juan. (The convention of soprano playing boy is itself a survival from the castrato soprano, and Cherubino's descendant is the principal boy of pantomime.) But Beaumarchais's play, before Da Ponte adapted it, was already a far cry from the *Commedia*. In so far as it dealt with a conflict between a 'common man' and a decaying aristocracy, it was of revolutionary significance, and Mozart was well aware of this. At the same time, *Figaro* is not anti-aristocratic. It implies an ideal aristocracy in which all classes of people—both socially and psychologically speaking—are given their due. Figaro and Susanna are commonplace common people: yet sympathetic, lovable, important (because like you and I). The Count is a villain; yet he is also a profound pathological study: his arias of rage are no longer an operatic convention, but a revelation of the heart, in which we feel for as much as against him. And the countess, though an aristocrat, is not a villainess at all, but, in the solitude of her introspection, a tragic figure.

The stock types have become real people; and the musical-dramatic structure is the interplay of their personalities. We find therefore—even in comparison with *Die Entführung*—that the set arias are fewer, and more closely wedded to the dramatic action. Opera becomes, for Mozart, dramatic conversation in music; and the ensemble numbers, especially the act finales, become the core of the work. Here Mozart attains a complexity of organization, both musical and psychological, which is approached by no other composer. We have seen how deeply this conception influenced his most representative, and perhaps his greatest instrumental works, the piano concertos.

Profoundly as it enriches convention, *Figaro* is still an opera in the *buffo* tradition. In *Don Giovanni* the Don himself is a stock figure from popular mythology, Leporello is the conventional comic servant, and Zerlina the serving-maid soubrette; yet in all the characters Mozart develops further the revolutionary elements inherent in his work. The basic theme of heroic opera and tragedy had been the conflict between Love and Duty (to the State). To minds nurtured in the early eighteenth century, the Don Juan legend was thus the story of a villain-rogue who destroyed civilization in championing an individualistic, self-justificatory love. For the romantics, on the other hand, the Don became a hero who died tragically because his passions flared beyond the limits imposed by social and religious convention. Mozart's attitude—as we would expect from our knowledge of his instrumental music—is balanced almost equally between these two extremes. His Don is at once villain and hero: a villain because if everyone behaved as he does, civilization would be impossible; a hero because if civilization has grown moribund, it is in need of assault and renovation. For Mozart, Don Juan is thus a Faust-figure; and his attitude to him is somewhere between Marlowe's and Goethe's attitudes to their Fausts. Goethe's Faust is himself, and his challenge to the gods is man's highest endeavour; Marlowe's Faust is himself, yet for the sin of pride he is justly tugged to Hell. But for Mozart the descent to Hell is tragic and comic at the same time. He could urbanely approve of Don Giovanni's fate in so far as he passionately believed in civilization; yet he could not suppress a lurking suspicion that this civilization was not worth saving. To omit the *buffo* epilogue after the descent to Hell is romantically to falsify Mozart. Its so-called 'cynicism' is both subtle and profound: for it tells us that though the Don's fate has been frightening and in a sense tragic, none the less civilization is saved (hurray): while managing to suggest that its bustling gaiety must in the nature of things be ephemeral.

This abrupt transition to *buffo* merriment from one of the most solemnly terrifying moments in music—the appearance of the Commendatore (with sepulchra trombones) and the demoniacal ride to Hell—is typical of Mozart's interfusion of contradictory realms of experience. Similarly lifelike in its apparent paradox is the through-composed duel scene: which passes from Leporello's peevish commentary on Don Giovanni's escapades to the reality of the Don's struggle with Donna Anna, while Leporello's asides become not only comic, but scared; from there to the appearance of the Commendatore, with dramatic tremolandos that almost suggest *The Flying Dutchman*; and from there to the old man's death in the duel, when the shooting-upward scales dissolve in pathetically drooping chromaticism (Ex. 64). The varieties of human experience

Ex. 64 Mozart: *Don Giovanni*

which we observed in *Figaro*—ranging from the extrovert charm of Figaro to the adolescent troubles of Cherubino, from the Countess's tragic loneliness to the grim lunacy of the Count— are still more sharply delineated in *Don Giovanni*; even at the most awesome penultimate moment—the appearance of the statue—Leporello is still cracking his sad, jittery jokes. These imply a "recognition of other modes of experience which are possible" such as we commented on in the distinctive poise of Mozart's instrumental music.

It is interesting that until the catastrophe Mozart's attention is concentrated not so much on the Don as on the women he seeks to seduce, and on Leporello as the eternal underdog. The Don has no theme, and no real arias—only set numbers like the Champagne song or the Serenade. He is protean, like experience itself. For Mozart (but not for Beethoven) the assertion of the ego is less significant than its infinitely varied effects. He lives in a changing world: but is fascinated more by the people who are changed than by the force which is changing them. Again, this is why he was essentially an opera composer, as Beethoven was not.

The *buffo* conclusion to *Don Giovanni* is a reassertion of the artifices of convention which has been (wrongly) accused of cynicism. The libretto of *Cos fan tutte*—possibly da Ponte's masterpiece—is also usually described as both artificial and cynical. Yet its main point is to contrast the artifices of convention with life as it is: while it is the essence of Mozart's genius to admit that human creatures are frail and yet, in their fallibility, worthy of love. The aristocratic modes of behaviour which these young people would like to respect may be charming, elegant, even noble: only they do not square with human nature. Mozart does not suggest that in a better—more 'democratic'—world, social conventions would necessarily be more adequate. Indeed, the explicitly revolutionary *Figaro* and *Don Giovanni* had implied that some fundamental human values belonged more to the old world than to the new; and in *Così fan tutte* he seems to admit that a society ideally compassionate and civilized could never be more than a creation of the human imagination. It is significant that the style of *Così fan tutte* tends to dispense with realistic *buffo* elements in favour of a golden, Italianate limpidity comparable with that of Mozart's last instrumental works, such as the B flat Piano Concerto. Its simplicity, tenderness, strength, and grace are not 'unreal', for they are a distillation of Mozart's knowledge of himself and of other people. But such compassion, and such disinterested detachment, presuppose genius of Mozartian or Shakespearean stature.

It was therefore logical enough that Mozart should have created his next—and last completed—opera in allegorical terms. In making his most comprehensive imaginative statement he no longer even attempted to 'imitate' reality. At the height of his powers he returned—at the invitation of Schikaneder, an actor-impresario who was, like Mozart, a Freemason—to the local tradition of *Singspiel*. In *Die Zauberflöte* he produced a work that can, if the audience wishes, be taken as the usual medley of music-hall turns and fairy-tale whimsey—an 'escapist' musical comedy. At another level, it can be taken as a Masonic allegory about universal brotherhood, ethical humanism, and the triumph of Light. Though Schikaneder took care to avoid overt offence to the Church, his text is anti-Catholic; and it appealed to the interests which most deeply engaged Mozart during the last years of his life. He even managed to instil into it his own death-consciousness, which was no accredited part of Masonic creed.

There are three main strands to Schikaneder's allegory. First there are the Masonic beings who represent Progress and Enlightenment. Tamino is the Emperor Joseph II, Pamina the Austrian people, and Sarastro Ignaz von Born, a Masonic prophet, half rational, half mystical. Then there is the realm of the Queen of Night—what seemed to Masonic enlightenment the effete Catholic world of sorcery, superstition, and seduction. The Queen is Maria Theresa, Monostatos (semi-comic creature of lust and vengeance) is the clergy, and in particular the Jesuits. Finally, there is the world inhabited by those incapable of the heights of humanism: Papageno being, in his innocence, a kind of comic Parsifal.

This, however, is only the external allegory, which is less important than the internal or psychological allegory. The fight between light and darkness goes on inside as well as outside the mind; and this is expressed not only in incidents such as the encounter with the Snake, but in a strange intermingling of good and bad forces which parallels Mozart's attitude to his characters in his more realistic operas. The sinister Queen of Night has three ladies-in-waiting eager to perform charitable acts; on the other hand, the High Priest of Light entrusts Pamina to the lustful slave of the temple. The Prince and the Bird Catcher depart together on their search for the ideal: the peasant simplicity for which Schubert yearned is the first step in the quest for serenity.

This medley of fantasticality and pseudo-philosophy prompts a heterogeneous assortment of musical styles, which miraculously become one. We have sophisticated Italian arioso, which sometimes, as in Pamina's G minor aria, achieves a withdrawn intensity almost reminiscent of Bach. We have dazzling coloratura pieces like the Queen of Night's scalp-prickling D minor aria. We have doggerel rhymes and street tunes like Papageno's songs. Alongside all these there is music like the trio for Pamina, Tamino, and Sarastro in Act III, or the Men in Armour episode in the Trial Scene. Here we find a Bachian austerity of counterpoint, and a new type of chorale-like melody, usually in the Masonic key of E flat, and with Masonic scoring for woodwind and trombones (Ex. 65). This music is at once innocently simple and mysteriously solemn; and although Mozart may have found hints for this in Bach, Handel, and Gluck, it suggests more readily and more profoundly the hymn-like melodies that first appear in Beethoven's music about the time of the Fifth Symphony. In this respect it is significant that the opera deals, in its allegorical terms, with the *growth* of character. Pamina and

Ex. 65   Mozart: *Die Zauberflöte*

Tamino are real people as well as symbols; and at the end of the opera they are not the same people as they were at the beginning. Mozart does not seek Beethoven's mystical salvation; he creates a humanistic serenity that almost becomes divine.

Die Zauberflöte was the only Mozart opera of which Beethoven approved; and interestingly enough it was Schikaneder who first offered Beethoven a commission to compose an opera. Beethoven was to produce an opera in competition with Cherubini, who was working for a rival impresario, Baron Braun. He did not fulfil this commission, but deserted to Braun's camp, partly for financial reasons, partly because he was offered a libretto that appealed to him. Bouilly's *Leonora* was a pain-and-torment and rescue libretto: a typically realistic, revolutionary modification of heroic convention. The brave girl disguised as a boy enters the dungeon as gaoler's assistant to help her wrongfully imprisoned husband. After sundry improbable adventures provoked by the infatuation of the gaoler's daughter for the new assistant, the old-style *deus ex machina* of baroque opera* is replaced by a realistic Minister of State who brings a last-minute reprieve, with a phalanx of trumpets symbolizing an earthly Day of Judgement.

Beethoven took this task very seriously. He studied the operas of Cherubini with care, finding in the Italian's fusion of classical form, symphonic grandeur, and traditional vocal technique a basis for an idiom appropriate to his own designs. He even took lessons in vocal composition from Salieri. Yet though he reworked the opera several times, he remained dissatisfied. The reason is not far to seek: even if the libretto

---

* There is no resolution of conflict, no 'Becoming', in baroque operas. At the end the god-king descends from the heavens to put to rights the chaos created by human perversity. Unruly passions must be liquidated in the best ordered of all possible worlds.

had shown a subtler insight into human nature, Beethoven was not the man to be inspired by vocal characterization through lyricism, let alone by the complex interaction of character such as we find in Mozart. Unlike Mozart, he had next to no interest in other human beings; but abstract moral qualities, black and white and all the various shades of grey, interested him profoundly, because they were what he had experienced within his own mind and senses, and expressed in his instrumental music. The subjective nature of Beethoven's music was against opera composition; for opera—notwithstanding Wagner, as we shall see—of its nature implies objectification.

Nevertheless, *Fidelio* contains some magnificent music: which all occurs when abstract human qualities fire Beethoven's imagination. The love affair of Marcellina is conventional Italianate grand opera, not especially well composed; but Leonora's music, which grows from nobility of nature, fidelity, hope, justice—all the Beethovenian virtues—is tremendously impressive. With the scene in the dungeon, Beethoven reaches tragic heights. Here is no longer an episode in a stagey story: imprisonment and freedom becomes one of Beethoven's universal themes, most of all when the prisoners themselves are actively involved. The prisoners become humanity, and their music not operatic, but a choral symphony. Their hymns anticipate both the Joy theme of the Ninth Symphony and the impractical, because superhuman, vocal writing of that work and of the *Missa Solemnis*. The story has it that Cherubini, as a tactful hint, sent Beethoven a text-book of Italian vocal technique. This choral music is Beethoven's answer, which came from the depths of his being: for he certainly would not have wished consciously to rebuff the man whom he considered the greatest living composer—at least until his own maturity.

It is unlikely that Beethoven's interest in *Die Zauberflöte* went as far as conscious imitation; but it has been pointed out that Beethoven conceived his story as a realistic counterpart to Mozart's allegory. In both operas, a pair of lovers win through an ordeal, in Mozart symbolically, realistically in Beethoven. Human fortitude brings the victory of Light: which Beethoven expresses in the F major duet when the lovers are at last freed from the dungeon's gloom. In so far as it leads on to *Fidelio*, *Die Zauberflöte* was the end of the eighteenth century, and of the Mozartian 'equilibrium'. The odd thing is that Beethoven

should have wished to follow up *Fidelio* himself; he even angled
for a post as opera-house composer on a yearly salary, producing
one big opera a year, plus several divertimenti. The management of the opera house was, in this case, wiser than he. They
fobbed him off with a commission for a mass.

In fact, one has no need to look further than the *Leonora*
overtures to see how inessential opera was for Beethoven.
Between Mozart's operas and his instrumental works there was
always an intimate relationship; but all the drama Beethoven
deeply feels is embodied in these instrumental sonata movements. Moreover, the third *Leonora* overture is more dramatic
than the second because it is more symphonic; the Day of
Judgement trumpet-call now merely initiates the development,
instead of being the piece's 'theatrical' climax. The *Leonora*
overtures are sonata movements about the triumph of the individual spirit, as the *Coriolan* overture is about self-will and the
Egmont overture about revolution. All this was expressed at one
level in the stock revolutionary operas which became the nineteenth century's restatement of the heroic. But at a deeper level
this revolution had already been effected in the instrumental
music of Beethoven's middle years: and from there he had gone
on to a point where no external revolution could follow him.

Though the moralistic opera *Fidelio* may have been in one
sense a descendant from *Die Zauberflöte*, it is not musically in the
Mozartian tradition. Perhaps no one after Mozart achieved the
ideal balance between music and drama; but at least one can say
that the elements that were in his operas inextricably mated
became, in the work of Rossini and Weber, the source of creative
operatic development during the nineteenth century.

We have seen that in the 1820s Rossini was the most popular
composer not only in his own country, but also in Italianate
Vienna. This is easy to understand; for he was a direct successor
to the *buffo* composers of the eighteenth century, while possessing
incomparably more wit, vivacity, and fire than the average.
One must not expect from Rossini the disturbing under-
currents of passion and melancholy that occur in Mozart's
ostensibly similar operas. He does not attempt Mozart's close
interplay of character-drawing and music; his art is at a further
remove from life. Writing for a larger theatre and a more
superficial audience, he expatiates on his jokes, theatrically
'presenting' his characters instead of allowing them to create

themselves: it is significant that Rossini's characters habitually, Mozart's only exceptionally, address the audience rather than one another. This fundamental difference in approach is indicated in Rossini's abandonment of the psychologically dramatic sonata aria and his partiality for the non-evolutionary rondo aria—in which a symmetrical tune is stated twice, followed by a somewhat perfunctory 'middle' phrase and a third repetition of the original clause, usually embellished: the whole being rounded off by a rhythmic coda to work up the applause. The notorious 'Rossini crescendo' is another instance of this desire to achieve the maximum effect with the minimum effot.

Yet Rossini is not superficial in a derogatory sense. Indeed, the accusation of rococo affectation levelled at him by critics from Wagner onwards is singularly inappropriate: for, being no longer willing to trust to the taste of his singers, he merely wrote out in his scores virtuoso arabesques that in earlier operas —even Mozart's and Gluck's—would have been improvised. Nor can an eye or ear for effect be considered a liability in an opera composer. The thin orchestral and harmonic texture which (except perhaps in his two French operas) he habitually adopted was a legitimate convention which concentrated attention on the singers: only Mozart could write music which is theatrically lucid while being both vocally and orchestrally elaborate. Even in Rossini's stock *buffo* operas, such as *La Cenerentola* (again the poor girl who makes good), the virtuosity of the vocal writing, the bubbling zest of the rhythms, the lucent simplicity of the scoring are enough to express a personal view of life. In *The Barber of Seville*, where for once he has a convincing libretto based, like *Figaro*, on Beaumarchais, the *buffo* figures again become flesh and blood. Admittedly, *The Barber* is farce to *Figaro's* tragi-comedy. But it is not mere make-believe. The 'human comedy' does not always hide a Mozartian poignancy beneath the absurd façade. The slip on the banana skin—the affront to human dignity—is a joke rooted deep in our tangled natures; and Rossini's buffoonery sometimes strikes home more disturbingly, more dangerously, than we like to think. The Rossini crescendo in the slander song from *The Barber* is frightening as well as funny; we cannot always dispel the suspicion that our hearts may be as hard as Rossini suggests.

Rossini was not only a survival from the eighteenth century.

His fame was international; and while the operas he composed for Italy and Vienna adhered to tradition, the two operas he composed for Paris were startlingly prophetic. His last funny opera, *Le Comte Ory,* is a descendant from eighteenth-century *opéra comique,* revivified with Italian musicality; it is also the ancestor of nineteenth-century French light opera. The effervescence of Offenbach and the elegance of Messager are here combined with a harmonic subtlety that suggests Bizet, and a loveliness of line-drawing and of orchestral sonority that reminds us of the lighter works of Berlioz. According to Berlioz, the trio '*A la faveur de cette nuit obscure*' was the composer's masterpiece, and worthy of Mozart.

If *Le Comte Ory* is the progenitor of French light opera, Rossini's next work, *Guillaume Tell,* contains the seed of the new grand manner in France and indirectly in Germany also. He had composed, earlier in his career, a few serious operas, if not *opera seria,* some of which (notably *Otello*) contain impressive music. But *Guillaume Tell* was a new kind of music: a heroic opera which found its epic theme not in a mythological glorification of monarchy nor in a conflict between love and duty, but in historical events and national aspiration. Musically, it reconciled Rossini's Italian vocal training with the massive, homophonic choral style which Spontini and Méhul had evolved from Gluck: with the character-drawing more typical of *opera buffa*: and with an expressive use of orchestral harmony and colour. Many of the revolutionary features in the early work of Wagner are already evident in *Guillaume Tell,* along with a supple beauty of vocal line which Wagner could never emulate. An aria such as '*Sombres Forêts*' from Act II is not, as Stendhal said, "the art so popular in Germany of expressing the sentiments of the characters by oboes, 'cellos, and clarinets; it is the far rarer art of expressing by means of instruments that portion of their sentiments which the characters themselves could not convey to us". In the face of music such as this, one can understand why so many composers—even such unlikely men as Beethoven and Wagner himself in his early days—should have had so high a regard for Rossini's musicianship.

Rossini was probably right in thinking that the second act of *Guillaume Tell* was his finest work. Yet he had to force himself to create such music, which was opposed to his eupeptic temperament; and the opera as a whole is unequal. That did not affect its prodigious success; though perhaps it influenced Rossini's decision to retire immediately from the theatre, at the height of his fame, and at the early age of thirty-seven. The reasons for this renunciation are complex. The familiar charge that Rossini was congenitally lazy can hardly be substantiated of a man who had been in the habit of producing half a dozen or so operas a year. That he had made enough money to live on in comfort for the rest of his days was a relevant factor, though it could not of itself have stifled so spontaneous a creativity. The most probable explanation is that Rossini knew that the future development of opera would be opposed to his own temperament and to the traditions which he respected. In *Guillaume Tell*, indeed, he had himself anticipatorily experienced these new impulses; he could not bear to see them eventually destroy the music he held most dear.

So although he lived for another forty years, he composed henceforth only works—mostly little piano pieces and songs—designed to amuse his friends at his celebrated evening parties. To these 'sins of my old age' he adopted a somewhat ironically condescending attitude. Yet though the songs and duets of the *Soirées Musicales* are often witty, they are also often of a melting lyrical beauty which, in the 1860s, seemed to belong to a forgotten art. Nor do they ignore the chromatic and enharmonic developments associated with Wagner: only the audacities of the exquisitely lucid piano parts are a background to the emotion concentrated in the vocal lines.

Rossini himself said that he composed his last large-scale work in order that the true art of vocal writing should not be finally lost. The whimsically titled *Petite Messe Solennelle* is a full-length operatic mass for soloists and chorus, with an elaborate piano part in the style of the *Soirées Musicales*, and harmonium to support the voices. The superbly vivacious fugal movements are an extension of the *buffo* finale, with only a slight infusion of ecclesiastical learning. The solo arias and ensembles are operatic music, not merely of charm and elegance, but of unexpected profundity. This reaches its climax in the final Agnus Dei, a passionate contralto solo with suavely homophonic choral interludes. When soloist and chorus ultimately sing together—in the strangest enharmonic modulations—Rossini achieves a pathos and even a tragic power which are paralleled only in the greatest moments of Verdi (Ex. 66). At the end of the

mass Rossini appends a little address to *le bon Dieu*: "La voilà
terminée cette pauvre petite messe. Est-ce bien de la musique
sacrée que je viens de faire ou bien de la sacrée musique?*

Ex. 66   Rossini: *Petite Messe Solènnelle* (Agnus Dei)

J'étais né pour l'opéra buffa, tu le sais bien. Un peu de
science, un peu de cœur, tout est là. Sois donc béni, et accorde
moi le Paradis." It would be a hard deity indeed who could
resist so winning an appeal, let alone such moving music.
Rossini's use of the familiar *tu* in addressing his god suggests,
perhaps, how eighteenth-century self-confidence is changing
into nineteenth-century independence: just as this music effects
a transition from *buffo* jauntiness to the romantic pathos of the
Agnus Dei.

So Rossini, trained in the eighteenth century, contemplates
ironically the premonitions of the future that flicker beneath his
urbane art. His younger contemporary Weber [1786–1826]
resembles him in being essentially an opera composer; and both
followed Mozart who, as Rossini pointed out, was "lucky enough

---

* Rossini's pun is untranslatable. *La musique sacrée* means sacred music; *la
sacrée musique* means damned (i.e. shocking, awful) music.

to go to Italy at a time when they still knew how to sing". But Weber started not only from Italian opera, but also from the German *Singspiel*. His romanticism became a part of his awareness of nationality—a force which ultimately destroyed the classical tradition.

Being German, Weber (unlike Rossini) wrote a certain amount of instrumental music in sonata style. He was, however, justified in claiming that there was no kinship between his music and Beethoven's. Subjective conflict is extraneous to his temperament. When he composes concerted chamber music he adopts a coloured, theatrical version of the style of the salon, with virtuoso keyboard writing suggested by rococo vocal ornament, and with 'picturesque' alternations of instrumental sonority. This rococo manner is used by Beethoven very rarely, and then with a slightly parodistic flavour, as in the slow movement of the G major Sonata from opus 31. Weber's biggest instrumental work, the *Konzertstück* for piano and orchestra, is a brilliant piece of melodrama which seems to imply visual illustration on a stage—quite unlike the subtly 'interior' operatic drama of Mozart's piano concertos.

Even when Weber actually writes in sonata form, the conventional exposition and development are not much more than a gesture. In the A flat Piano Sonata, for instance, the resonant spacing of the protracted tonic chord at the beginning is an orchestral effect; while the second subject is rococo virtuosity. The development is sensational, with marvellously pianistic aplomb; but it is not a dramatic argument in Beethoven's sense; and the movement has to be wound up by a Rossini-like curtain-coda that plays the applause. Similarly, in the last movement Mozartian chromaticism is no longer pathetic, but an effect of colour. The first movement of the D minor Sonata opens 'allegro feroce' in operatic melodrama. The second subject is again operatic aria, and no attempt is made to relate the two. Indeed, the effect of the music depends upon its arbitrary succession of moods: which can thus be rounded off by the brilliantly extrovert virtuosity of the rondo finale. Only in the last, E minor Sonata does Weber attempt dramatic continuity, using a single rhetorically operatic theme, and basing the development on a non-melodic figuration that appears in the codetta.

All the themes in Weber's sonatas are Italianate and operatic;

yet they could never be confused with Mozart's. Rossini's
melodies are still in the Mozartian tradition, though they are
normally less chromatic, and have more rhythmic vigour, if
less rhythmic finesse. Weber's melodies use the same vocal
formulae as do Mozart's and Rossini's, but render these formulae
more obvious in their emotional appeal—as did Beethoven in
his youth. One reason for this is that they introduce a greater
proportion of wide leaps, especially upward leaps of sixth,
seventh, and even ninth. Another reason is that their rhythmic
structure is almost always regularly periodic. If this divests
them of Mozartian subtlety, it gives them a powerful drive.
Chromaticism in Weber is usually decorative: perhaps this is
another way of saying that his pathos tends to be a theatrical
gesture. The big leaps in his melodies are again often associated
with his rhetorical approach to harmony; the leaping gesture
produces, or is accompanied by, the emotive dissonance. A
theme such as this from the D minor Piano Sonata—with its
leaping sixths from strong to weak beat—is exactly comparable,
both in its contour and in its four-bar periodicity, with one of
the most famous of all Weber's operatic tunes (Ex. 67):

Ex 67 Weber· Piano Sonata in D minor (first movement)

as is the harmonic texture of this passage from the E minor
Sonata with this operatic use of the chord of the ninth (Ex.68):

Ex. 68. Weber: *Sonata in E minor* (first movement)

We can see already how Weber's musical style entails the exaggerated gestures of nineteenth-century operatic acting: gestures which would be utterly inappropriate to Mozart.

As an opera composer, Weber aimed to make his Italianate rhetoric serve a national purpose. *Der Freischütz* starts from the *Singspiel*, even preserving spoken dialogue; but the escape art of musical comedy now becomes the central experience of romanticism. Characteristically, the romantic sensibility seeks to 'get it both ways'. German folk-myth suggests German folk-song. This modifies the Italianism of the melodies and creates a style of rustic simplicity that serves as a refuge from introspection. On the other hand, folk-myth provokes the horrors of the Wolf's Glen, offering the thrills which everyday life denies us. Both complementary kinds of escape find expression in Weber's theatrical sense, his rhetorical harmony, and above all in his feeling for orchestral colour—which as we have seen pervades even his chamber works and piano music. Schubert had hinted at a dream-world of rustic tranquillity; in the *Freischütz* overture this becomes vividly immediate, and one of the creative forces in nineteenth-century music. Weber's extroversion—he was a magnificent virtuoso pianist and conductor—is one reason for the forcefulness of his impact. At a time when music was turning increasingly 'inward', he developed techniques which later composers were to use for a radically different purpose. The *Freischütz* overture is a typical modification of the sonata principle. The slow introduction 'poeticizes' the ceremonial grandeur of the old operatic overture; the sonata allegro is an exciting tussle between Bad forces (the Zamiel theme and the agitato rhythm) and Good (the Agathe theme, which begins in the relative major). The working-out excites expectation, rather than resolving this opposition. When the piece ends with a grandiose coda in which the Agathe theme is stated in the tonic major, instead of the agitato section's tonic minor, we know that virtue will triumph over evil; but the overture itself has not told us how this will happen. That is as it should be: for Weber's sonata-overture is not psychological drama in Beethoven's sense. It is designed, with theatrical acumen, to lead into the externalized presentation of conflict on the stage.

Weber's choice of subject for his next opera is no less historically significant; for *Euryanthe* deals with medieval chivalry from a romantic standpoint, and undoubtedly influenced Wagner's early choice of theme. In *Euryanthe* Weber attempts to elevate the *Singspiel* to nobility: to create a German opera worthy to be placed beside the Grand Manner of France. The grander the music gets, the more Italianate, and the less German, is the style. With *Oberon*, which resembles a *Singspiel* in so far as it is based on a poem of Wieland, the fairy-tale opera becomes an expression of romantic faith. Gluckian music drama comes to terms with the new Teutonic, rustic manner and with the new orchestral technique. There are aspects of *Oberon* which derive from Cherubini and Méhul, from Spontini and Rossini; yet Weber remains a composer of extraordinary originality in that he invests the theatrical 'property' with poetic evocativeness, almost always by orchestral rather than vocal means. The solo horn and the muted strings of the opening to the overture to *Oberon* are an exhibition of orchestral genius which is to be valued for itself. None the less, it is testimony to the potency of Weber's magic that his outward-turning theatricality should contain in embryo the dream-life of the romantic spirit.

Formally, Weber is sometimes credited with an anticipation of Wagner's continuous symphonic texture. It is true that, although he does not use leitmotives, he sometimes associates particular characters with specific key-centres: and that even when he adheres most obviously to the old-fashioned division into aria and arioso, he plans the structural sequences of his scenes with care. That his operas are no longer theatrically tenable is due not so much to his dangerous instinct for the immediate 'effect' as to his intractable libretti. Schubert's operatic ventures failed for a similar reason; and one might say that Beethoven's *Fidelio* suffers from a disparity between the conventionally operatic elements in the libretto and those which inspired Beethoven's moralistic-symphonic imagination.

This trouble over libretti is not fortuitous. Baroque opera books may seem to us idiotic, yet the philosophical bases of Metastasian convention were intelligible to both composer and audience; the glorification of the god-king and the fight between love and duty was a consistent theme which entailed consistent stylizations. Mozart found the themes which were precisely relevant to what he wanted to say in musical terms and, with the help of Da Ponte, effected a perfect balance between the world of operatic artifice and real life. This was never possible again—not even in Italy, where opera remained the central tradition. In France, the supreme opera composer, Berlioz, did not even establish a valid relationship to the public; in Germany Wagner achieved such a relationship only after herculean labours and by a prodigious exhibition of will-power. The fashionable operatic traditions in France and Germany became essentially escape-art. On the comic side, Rossinian frivolity turned into the effervescent 'musical comedy' of Offenbach [1819–1880]; while the simple, domestic aspect of Weber's German fairyland blossomed into the charming light operas of Lortzing [1801–1851] and Nicolai [1810–1849]: works which displayed a quiet musicianship without resorting to Italianate glamour. On the tragic side, the romantic horrors of Weber's Germany were taken up in the operas of Marschner [1795–1861] and Spohr [1784–1859]: works which preserved Italian lyricism in a harmonically and orchestrally more sensational setting; while the cult of the sensational as an end in itself reached a climax in French grand opera after Rossini. Opera composers had relinquished the heroic view of life because they had ceased to believe in it; but having lost their awareness of purpose, they found it difficult to establish a convincing relation between reality and convention. Both Marschner and Lortzing express only a partial truth, for life is neither as nasty as the one nor as nice as the other. The hedonistic Rossini evades less, and has a harder reality at the core of his art.

'Unprincipled' is the adjective habitually applied to Giacomo Meyerbeer [1791–1864] who—after the retirement of Rossini and the early death of Weber—became perhaps the most prodigiously successful composer in history. A cosmopolitan rather than international figure, he was a wealthy and cultivated German Jew who settled in Paris, determined to exploit the craving for a forsaken grandeur that seethed beneath the complacence of the revolutionized bourgeoisie. In the absence of an aristocracy of spirit such as could be recovered only by a mind as rare as Berlioz's, this grandeur was bound to be flashy: a rhetorical attitudinizing which found complementary expression in the plays of Hugo. Yet Meyerbeer was not artistically insincere. His command of Italianate vocal line was as powerful as Weber's and more supple: perhaps more impressive, musically, than the attempts of the young Verdi or Wagner to emulate him. His monumental use of the French choral 'tableau' was aesthetically thrilling and dramatically justified, if without the nationalistic fervour of its model—the magnificent final scene of *Guillaume Tell*. His exploitation of German orchestral technique was dramatically vivid, never merely noisy or an end in itself; and his powers of musical construction were far above those of the average operatic hack in any of the three countries to which he vicariously belonged.

It is therefore unjust that his name should have become synonymous with the meretricious, in so far as his musical technique was not only brilliant, but honestly devoted to his dramatic intentions. The trouble lies, of course, in the dubiety of those intentions—or rather of those of his librettist, the efficient Scribe. For the high solemnity of Scribe's politico-historical manner is an attitude, not a belief. Meyerbeer brings to Scribe's grandiosity his excellent musicianship and a sense of theatrical effect for which only a fool would reproach him. But like Scribe he lacked two qualities: a sense of purpose, and a sense of humour. With the former, like Wagner, he could have dispensed with the latter. With the latter, like Rossini (except in *Guillaume Tell*), he could have managed without the former. To have possessed both, like Mozart, would have been asking too much of the age of romanticism. Berlioz, who alone relived the heroic world, was alone in preserving the 'intense levity' of the classical equilibrium—at least until Verdi, in extreme old age, rediscovered it when the fire of romanticism was spent.

So the problem of the valid musical convention in opera is again inseparable from the creation, not necessarily of the good, but of the morally and socially valid libretto. As we consider the careers of the three greatest operatic composers of the nineteenth century, we shall see that Verdi paid ever-increasing attention to the nature of his libretti until he found his ideal partner in Boito; and that Berlioz and Wagner themselves created the only feasible literary foundations for their musical forms.

WAGNER

Behind the sonata epoch there are two great creative impulses: the idea of Revolution, and the escape to Dream. We have observed the former in Beethoven, and both impulses in Schubert. With him, the tendency to substitute a world of the imagination for reality is no more than tentative, for he was trained in the classical tradition. It grows stronger, however, as commercialized industry produces a world to which sensitive spirits feel increasingly inimical; and the situation is epitomized in the career of Richard Wagner, who called himself 'an outlaw for life'.

Unlike his predecessors of the classical age, Wagner [1813–1883] was born to sophistication and self-consciousness. His parents, though not affluent, belonged to cultivated society; he received a university education, read widely and—in his egocentric, emotional way—thought much. But his intellectual awareness was from the start an awareness of self. He was an outlaw because he was right, and the world wrong. Beethoven too wanted to change the world, but gave up the attempt when he discovered a deeper truth. Wagner—like Carlyle, a middle-class prophet haranguing a materialistic world—never gave up, even in the face of obstacles that would have cowed a lesser man. His courage really was—like the creatures of his imagination—superhuman, and his ultimate triumph one of the supreme achievements of the human mind. That we have to admit, however obnoxious we may find some aspects of his personality: and even if we think his victory hollow compared with Beethoven's.

Although in his youth Wagner was engaged in political activity, there is a significant difference between his interest in revolutionary movements and Beethoven's. The latter was interested in revolution as a means towards a better world. Wagner was interested in it in a purely negative sense, in so far as the corruptions of society hampered the free expression of his own desires and the fulfilment of his artistic ambitions. He was the Way and the Life; and if contemporary society refused to see that, it could only be because of the machinations of evil-doers and anti-Wagnerians, for whom the Jews could serve as a scapegoat. (Meyerbeer was a Jew, and internationally famous, as Wagner at this time was not.) If Jews are wicked, the Aryan Folk must be good; but Wagner extolled them not for themselves, but as a kind of allegorical representative of himself as Aryan Hero. "A nation of high-souled dreamers and deep-brained thinkers", he called the German people; and that is exactly how he would have described himself.

Now Weber, we saw, in his brilliantly externalized music, created many of the techniques whereby Wagner was to evoke the world of his inner life; yet he never discovered the theme implicit in his technique. It is testimony to the powerful 'inwardness' of Wagner's genius—as compared with Weber's outwardness—that he should have discovered his quintessential theme long before he had evolved a personal technique. When he was nineteen, he started an opera called *Die Hochsteit*, which is about a woman who kills a man who threatens her honour; knowing that she passionately loves him, she then dies of grief by his grave. This myth, in which the love-murderer becomes the self-murderer, lies at the heart of the Wagnerian experience. It was not until many years later that this was to be revealed in the consummatory achievements of his art. But after he had written *Rienzi*, which is a stock Franco-German-Italian opera inferior to, but in the pompous and circumstantial manner of, Meyerbeer, Wagner began to use opera as a medium for spiritual autobiography. He himself wrote libretti which present his basic theme as seen by his conscious mind. *The Flying Dutchman*, *Tannhäuser*, and *Lohengrin* are mainly about Wagner as he liked to think of himself: only in his later work, and especially in *Tristan* and *Parsifal*, do we see him as quintessentially he was.

The legend of the Flying Dutchman seemed to him to parallel his own history during the years 1839–41. He too had been driven from place to place, had been harried by indefinable longings, and was always on the point of being redeemed by a woman prepared to sacrifice all for him. Other young men have had similar experiences, without feeling the need to elevate them into a programme of universal regeneration. But Wagner is quite explicit: "My course was new", he says; "it was bidden me by my inner mood, and forced upon me by the pressing need to impart this mood to others. In order to enfranchise myself from within outwards . . . I was driven to strike out for myself, as artist, a path not yet pointed me by any outward experience."

The Dutchman suffers, is alone, and is redeemed (and implicitly deified) by Senta's love and death. Tannhäuser is also alone, fleeing from a base, materialistic, and sensual world. Again the "longed-for, dreamt-of, utterly womanly woman, the Woman of the Future" leads him from the passions of Venusberg to heaven. Even at this early date we have a relatively crude statement of the inescapable link between eroticism and renunciation; it crops up still more obviously in *Lohengrin*, in whose person Wagner becomes not only the lonely hero in an alien world, but also the god-like figure who, because he is superhuman, is bound to be misunderstood. Superficially, *Lohengrin* seems a silly story of a pompous young man who refuses to tell his name to a girl only too anxious to love him. To Wagner, "it was the type of the only absolute tragedy, of the tragic element in modern life; and that of just as great signifi- cance for the Present, as was the *Antigone* for the life of the Hellenic state. . . . Elsa is the Unconscious, the Undeliberate, into which Lohengrin's conscious, deliberate being yearns to be redeemed; but this yearning again is itself the unconscious, undeliberate necessity in Lohengrin's being, whereby he feels himself akin to Elsa. Through the capability of this 'uncon- scious consciousness', such as I myself now felt alike with Lohengrin, the nature of Woman also came to even clearer understanding in my mind. . . . This woman, who with clear foreknowledge rushes to her doom, for the sake of love's impera- tive behest—who amid the ecstasy of adoration, wills yet to lose her all, if so be she cannot all-embrace her loved one; this woman, who in contact with this Lohengrin, of all men, must founder, and in so doing must shipwreck her beloved too . . . this Elsa, the most positive expression of the purest instinct of the senses—made me a revolutionary at one blow. She was the Spirit of the Folk, for whose redeeming hand I too, as artist- man, was longing." Who would have thought it: and who, having been told, can believe it? We cannot take Wagner's interminable verbal rhapsodies seriously, any more than we can stomach his prose; but they have a kind of unholy fascination, as evidence of the completeness with which Wagner identified his own emotional turmoils with the destiny of mankind.

To turn to the music of Wagner's first two autobiographical operas, after reading his verbal expatiations on them, is a blessed relief which reveals the gulf, at this stage in his career, between his practice and his intentions. Eventually he was to fulfil his ambitions at a level deeper than consciousness; but no one would suspect this from a glance at these scores. The vocal lines in *The Flying Dutchman* are still basically Italian, and move even more squarely in four-bar periods than do those of Weber. Diminished sevenths, tremolandos, and other operatic 'properties' of Meyerbeer and Spontini reappear in much the same context; and although chromaticisms and enharmonic transitions intensify moments of emotional crises, they are no bolder than those which appear in the operas of Spohr or Marschner. The sensuous colours of the orchestra comment on the characters' passions with rather less than Weber's sensitivity. The singers no longer carry the whole burden, as they do in Rossini, but they are still the centre of the action.

Even in *The Flying Dutchman*, however, there is a sense in which Wagner was justified in claiming that he owed nothing essential to the tradition of Gluck and Weber. He always maintained that he was the heir to Beethoven, and his first works had in fact been instrumental symphonies modelled with vigour and confidence on the Beethovenian symphony of power. In *The Flying Dutchman* the structure seems to be based on the conventional division into aria and arioso, even including a direct survival from French sentimental opera like the *Romance*. Even so, the work is much more symphonic, in Beethoven's sense, than any previous opera; and this is especially true of one of the set pieces—the *Ballade*—which contains the creative essence of the opera. Here Senta's motive itself is an arpeggio challenge-theme which Wagner handles in much the same way as Beethoven handles his similar motive in the development section of a symphony. Already Wagner is beginning to project symphonic conflict into operatic terms.

The full implications of this are not evident in *The Flying Dutchman*; nor in *Tannhäuser*, though the fight between Elizabeth and Venus for the soul of the hero creates a symphonic drama which overrides the episodic effect of the set pieces. In *Lohengrin*, however, the interfusion of aria and accompanied recitative produces an almost continuous orchestral texture, and the technique of the leitmotive—the association of particular characters or places or ideas with specific musical figures—becomes an application of Beethoven's symphonic methods to opera. This aspect of the leitmotive as a principle of musical organization is much more important than its function as an aural guide-book to the action. Henceforth, Wagner's works will have 'the unity of a symphonic movement . . . that consists in a tissue of root themes pervading all the drama, themes which contrast, complete, divorce, reshape and intertwine with one another as in a symphonic movement'. It is no accident that whereas Wagner's earlier operas had been composed in the hurly-burly of a tempestuous professional life, *Lohengrin* was the result of long meditation; he wrote it (appropriately enough) in exile, after he had been hounded out of Germany for his political activities. Nor is it an accident that with *Lohengrin* Wagner discovered the first consummate form of the myth round which his life's work centred. The descent of the Grail and the ascent to Heaven in the miraculous opening may be said to symbolize the aspiration to godhead which became the essence of Wagner's life and of nineteenth-century romanticism (Ex. 69). Perhaps it is not altogether an acciden~ either that this

Ex. 69. Wagner: *Lohengrin* (Prelude to Act I)

passage should be Wagner's first transcendental moment of orchestral virtuosity. The aria-like passages, pilgrims' choruses, and other 'operatic' survivals in *Lohengrin* are often very impressive, but this orchestral prelude is more than that: it is a new sound, which tells us already that Wagner's dream will be realized not on the stage, but in the orchestra pit.

Wagner was aware that *Lohengrin* marked at once the end of a phase of his career and the beginning of something new. The precise nature of this new art was not yet revealed to him, however. After the completion of *Lohengrin*, awaiting the revelation, he wrote no music for six years. During this period, he began to plan the vast undertaking of *The Ring of the Nibelung*; and attempted to explain his attitude to art, man, Nature, and God in pamphlets that grew into tracts, tracts that grew into books, books that were swollen into elephantine tomes. It is doubtful if all the great composers of history together have written as many self-justificatory words as Wagner. We may regret that he wasted so many years writing so much nonsense. Yet the nonsense, being a pseudo-rationalization of his most irrational emotional life, was necessary to him, if not to us. Before he could create his masterpieces he had to believe in himself to the exclusion of all other positives, including the eighteenth-century values of Reason, Truth, and Nature. It was unreasonable to suppose that his own emotional life was 'the *only* modern tragedy'. It was untrue that his 'sacrifice' (like Christ's!) could provide the theme for a ritualistic union of music, poetry, and visual spectacle precisely analogous to Greek drama. It was not only unnatural, but wellnigh lunatic, to believe that because Wagner suffered from digestive troubles as a result of sensuous indulgence, the 'nobler nations' of Europe could be induced to adopt vegetarianism as a philosophic creed; and might even be willing to consider mass-migration to warmer parts of the world, where meat-eating would be less of a temptation! Yet even the lunacy is sublime. Compared with Wagner's egomania, Beethoven seems a model of respectable sobriety.

When in his youth Wagner said, "We two, the world and I, are stubborn fellows at loggerheads, and naturally whichever has the thinner skull will get it broken", he was the heir to Beethoven. But one can never imagine Beethoven saying, with the late Wagner: "I'm not made like other people. I have finer nerves. I must have brilliance and beauty and light. The world owes me what I need. I can't live on a miserable organist's post, like your master, Bach. . . . Mine is a highly susceptible, intense, voracious sensuality which must somehow or other be flattered if my mind is to accomplish the agonizing labour of calling a non-existent world into being." Wagner meant this quite literally. The world owed him what he needed because he was the world's future. It was only proper that men should give him their money and women their love (and preferably their money too) in order that Germany and Europe could fulfil their destiny. The main function of society was to help him to realize his dream. The one-time revolutionary ended by stating not only that art was a dream-image, lifting us above actuality: but that his dream was the only true reality. It is Wagner's stupendous achievement that he brought it off; the myth became fact, even if only through the agency of a young, mad king.

In *The Ring* Wagner based his poems on German folk-myth, but his identification of himself with the German race soon becomes explicit. Siegfried is Wagner as the child of Nature and the instinctive artist; the Ring itself symbolizes the prostitution of Art to Gold, or commerce. *The Ring* is thus a gigantically expanded version of the Lohengrin story; and the tendency (initiated in the earlier opera) to conceive the characters as symbols of moral and metaphysical qualities is developed to its furthest extreme. Wagner now makes no attempt to imitate human behaviour. The autobiographical element in his earlier themes is frankly accepted, so that the characters become projections of different aspects of his own mind: thus Siegfried, symbol of the instinctive life and Strength-through-Joy, is balanced by Wotan, who represents the complementary quality of sacrifice and renunciation. The other supreme opera composers—Monteverdi, Mozart, Berlioz, and Verdi—deal with men and women who are other than themselves: with dramatic action experienced through their personalities. As we have seen, Mozart's opera is essentially conversation in music. Wagner's characters never converse. They merely explain themselves; and in the deepest sense, as we shall see, their explanations are unnecessary.

Now Wagner always maintained that his music-drama was the natural successor to Beethoven's Ninth Symphony. He even suggested that this supreme work of spiritual autobiography in music anticipated his own techniques, in that in the last movement Beethoven called upon words (and ought to have used the stage) to 'illustrate' his meaning. We may think that it would be truer to say that Beethoven employed words for a fundamentally musical reason, in that the whole symphony had been the creation of a vocal melody, and if voices are introduced they may as well have words to sing. Yet Wagner's account makes sense in the light of his own experience, which was all he was interested in. For him, as for Beethoven, drama was essentially subjective, and inherent in the working out of the motives. These motives are symphonic ideas which undergo musical permutations which are mirrored in the permutations of the action: *because* the musical technique is, like Beethoven's, inherently dramatic, it must imply dramatic presentation. The literary text which the singers pronounce and the visual action which happens on the stage are thus merely one among many possible illustrations of the subjective myth which evolves in the orchestra. This is why it is possible, if undesirable, to perform extracts from Wagner's mature operas with the voice parts left out. We lose one strand of the complex symphonic texture, though often the least significant one. We lose the verbal 'illustration' of what is happening, but that may even be an asset, since what the voices say is often philosophically banal. We do not lose the rich imaginative life which is the growth of the music; and this—though Wagner was wrong in thinking that his emotional life was an explanation of the universe—is very far from being banal.

Wagner's peculiar approach to the voice, however, lands him in a fundamental inconsistency. If the voice parts are there to explain what is happening, in a style based on declamation, one would expect them to move at a pace not much slower than speech. But symphonic drama, which is the core of Wagner's music, proceeds at a pace immeasurably slower than verbal language. As a result, the singers have either to stand about doing nothing for long periods, or to repeat their phrases in a manner dramatically no less absurd than the lyrical repetitions of the conventional opera Wagner despised, or to stretch out their non-lyrical phrases into inordinately long note-values. Wagner—whose dramatic sense was so much weaker than his musical—was probably not conscious of this difficulty; and his genius sometimes managed to turn it to advantage, since all three compromises (especially the last) imbue his creatures with a certain ponderous grandeur. Their superhuman stature is thus emphasized; they remain true to Wagner's imaginative world, if not to life.

There was another and deeper problem that Wagner had to face in constructing a subjective symphony on so vast a scale: this was what he himself called 'the beautiful and convincing necessity of transition'. He could have no more set arias and recitatives; nor could he allow the stage business to prop up the musical structure, since the dramatic action illustrated the music, rather than the other way round. In fact, although he has many more themes or thematic motives than Beethoven employs in a symphony, they behave in broadly the same way. In a tonal drama planned on so gargantuan a scale, Wagner has to be content to forgo—to a more extreme degree than Beethoven—the melody of self-contained song. Melody becomes 'unending *melos*'; and Wagner used the Greek term because the word 'melody' might, to contemporary minds, have suggested Rossini. But themes built on arpeggio formations still imply stability and diatonicism; more chromatic step-wise figurations still imply instability and a sundering of tonality. The alternations between consonance and dissonance, between simple and complex modulations, extend but do not contradict established precedents. An incident that may seem to be a clumsy dramatic device—for instance, Siegfried's narration of his early life in *Götterdämmerung*—may in fact be a musical recapitulation of gigantic proportions; and in *Tristan*—Wagner's most extreme departure from tradition—the *Liebestod* begins as a recapitulation of the Love duet in Act II. Indeed, it has been demonstrated that Wagner's disposition of material and of tonal relationships was deliberately analogous to certain medieval poetical forms known as the *Bar* and *Stollen*: and is thus architecturally, if not dramatically, more formalized than the classical symphony.

One would not expect a work on so vast a scale as *The Ring*, created over a period of more than twenty years, to be consistent in style throughout; Wagner's ability to create at least an illusion of consistency is testimony to his tenacity of purpose. The first two parts of *The Ring* are certainly closer both to the Beethovenian symphony and to orthodox operatic tradition than the two later parts. In *Die Walküre*, the voice parts are still of equal importance with the orchestra, and even some of the stage business—such as Brunnhilde's imprisonment in the lake of fire—adapts conventional operatic properties to Wagner's 'metaphysical' purposes. But *Götterdämmerung* and the latter part of *Siegfried* are quintessentially Wagnerian: the change can be understood in the light of the fact that, half-way through *Siegfried*, Wagner turned aside to create *Tristan und Isolde*. We have seen that *The Ring* is in a general and indirect sense spiritual autobiography projected on to a stage. *Tristan* is quite explicitly autobiography, for it is a dramatization of the situation existing at the time between Wagner and Otto and

Mathilde Wesendonck. Wagner was driven to create it by the overwhelming intensity of his experience; and the force of his egoism now begins to destroy most of the vestiges of tradition which survived in his earlier work.

To concentrate thus directly upon himself, without symbolical or metaphysical apparatus, was for Wagner an immense advantage. The love story is legendary, but both simple and—as Wagner was reliving it—true. The text he produces may be inferior poetry, but is admirably designed as a complement to the music. Its short lines and flexible rhythms allow Wagner the freedom he needs; and his passion is so fierce that he no longer feels any diffidence about allowing the music to speak for itself. The voice parts may be dispensable (the *Liebestod* is often performed without them); but they, in common with every thematic strand in the score, certainly sing. The music glows with desire, and neither we nor Wagner care that there is little external action—or at least little that can decently be represented on a stage. We are only relieved at the absence of any attempt to symbolize the inner drama by stage dragons: which anyone with a modicum of humour, let alone theatrical sense, would have avoided like the plague.

In the music of *Tristan*, the extreme chromaticism of the lines and harmony, the continuity of the rhythms, the enharmony of the modulations are themselves a freeing of the individual spirit. The succession of harmonic tensions, reinforced by the physical impact of the orchestra, becomes an emotional orgy; and almost all overt trace of the structural principles which had characterized the classical sonata up to Beethoven's last works has disappeared. The effect of this subjective approach on the eighteenth-century key system is the same as that of the chromatic madrigal of the early years of the seventeenth century on the modal techniques of the previous period.* *Tristan* bears about the same relationship to a classical symphony as a madrigal of Gesualdo [1560–1615] bears to a motet of Palestrina. We may note that Gesualdo too was a romantic individualist and exhibitionist: though since he lived in a strong religious tradition, his egoism seemed to his contemporaries a melancholic aberration, rather than a world-shaking force. If we think of him alongside Hamlet, we shall see that the revolution he represents was in fact no less crucial than Wagner's.

* See Part II.

Although Wagner in his individualism departs far from classical tradition, this does not mean that *Tristan* has not its own principle of order. But normally Wagner no longer thinks of himself in Beethovenian terms, as a man in conflict with a hostile world. His passions have become so intense that they are themselves the universe; everything outside himself is engulfed in the surge of sound. Isolde and Mark are Mathilde and Otto Wesendonck. They are also aspects of love-hate within Tristan-Wagner himself; so the whole of the vast symphonic texture is unified by the dominance of a single psyche. We can see this in the musical unity which underlines the dramatic-symbolical unity of the leitmotives. The three 'Tristan' chords, built on overlapping fourths, with which the work opens, reappear in transmuted forms at every climacteric point in the opera. Ultimately they become the melodic basis of the *Liebestod* itself, and the harmonic basis of the final, consummatory resolution into B major (Ex. 70):

Ex. 70. Wagner:
The 'Tristan' chords

Theme of 'Liebstod'

The final cadence

Now, the opening pages of the *Tristan* prelude, in which these chords occur, have been analysed in innumerable ways according to orthodox harmonic principles: the variety is itself evidence of the music's disintegration of traditional techniques. But what anyone can agree on is that the music's overwhelming intensity derives from the fact that Wagner concentrates on the dissonant harmony at the expense of its resolution; it is always the dissonant chord that falls on the strong beat. Moreover, the effect of the passage as a whole depends on the way in which the brief, upward-yearning, chromatically falling phrase, underlined by its dissonance, is repeated several times at progressively rising intervals. This mounting excitement leads one to expect a big climax when the discord will finally be resolved on to the tonic. Instead, we get an unexpected chord (the submediant) (Ex. 71):

Ex. 71. Wagner: *Tristan and Isolde* Prelude to Act I

So we have a building up of harmonic tension, which is partially frustrated: and a tendency towards rhythmic fluidity, which is counteracted by the continuous repetition of the phrases in sequence. Wagner strains both to resolve harmonic stress and to dissolve Beethoven's metrical obsession with Time; and neither resolution nor dissolution is, in life, achieved.

Just some such combination of passionate yearning with frustration is the essential feature of Wagner's adaptation of the Tristan story; and between this and his own psychological make-up—and as we have seen the actual events of his life—there is a more than usually direct connexion. Wagner has expressed at once the ultimate triumph, and the fallacy, of humanism. He believes only in himself; his own feelings are the universe. That being so, his feelings can lead to nothing but their extinction. A yearning so fierce can be appeased only in its cessation: so the fulfilment of love is death.

This is why in Wagner's mature work passion and renunci-ation are inseparable; one might even say that for him renunci-ation is as much a sensuous experience as eroticism. In his last opera, *Parsifal*, he returns to the Grail legend which had obsessed him in his youth, and sees in it an allegory of his own quest for fulfilment. Though written several years later, it is *Tristan's* imaginative complement; nor is this at all odd, since the Grail myth, with its symbols of Sword and Chalice, is as much sexual as mystical. Nietzsche, who had welcomed the younger Wagner as a Dionysiac superman who would regener-ate a decaying world, held that *Parsifal* was a denial of the hero's birthright: that its religiosity was both spurious and offensive

from a man who had insisted, throughout his life, on the
satisfaction of every desire. Yet if Wagner had not lived in and
for his senses, renunciation would have been less important.
He did not advocate renunciation in a momentary disgust with
sensuality, but simply because the man who lives for his senses
has to submit to the irremediable renunciation of death.
Parsifal is certainly not mystical in Beethoven's sense; but for
all its metaphysical mystifications it is as profoundly felt an
experience as *Tristan*. Indeed, it is the same experience seen, as
it were, mirror-wise. Of all Wagner's works it is closest to
Tristan in technique.

Both operas are incantatory, hypnotic; both effect a curious
inversion of the ritualistic or religious approach to music. In a
Palestrina mass the personal element—the expressive harmony—grows out of the singing together of a number of vocal
lines that are in themselves 'religiously' impersonal, devoid
of harmonic stress. Wagner, in *Tristan* and *Parsifal*, starts from
the tensions of harmony, which are the passions of his nerves
and senses, and then 'spreads out' the chords into a complex
of linear motives which he called a new polyphony. The
'religion' which this polyphony celebrates is a fanatical belief
not in God, nor in Civilization, but in Richard Wagner. In the
Liebestod of *Tristan und Isolde* this new harmonically derived
polyphony attains an orgiastic ecstasy; in the melting enharmony of interlacing lines in the prelude to Act III of *Parsifal*,
it attains a mysterious sweetness (Ex. 72). At bottom, these

Ex.72. Wagner: *Parsifal* Prelude to Act III
Very slow

experiences are identical. Tristan and Isolde find that the
excruciating agony of their passion can lead only to oblivion;

Parsifal, the pure fool, redeemed in this music by the carnality
of Kundry's kiss, finds that renunciation in death leads to an
ecstasy synonymous with love.

Wagner's life's work thus culminates in a deification of the ego
which is also an admission of the ego's insufficiency. Opera
becomes a substitute for religion: for the deification of the ego
could hardly go further than the Wagner cult at Bayreuth,
where a temple is built for the performance of the Artist's
creations—instead of the music being composed to fulfil the
needs of the temple, as was Palestrina's to serve God, or Handel's
to serve the State. Wagner himself said that Bayreuth was the
fulfilment of the destiny which he had planned for himself and
humanity. And the deepest if most obvious truth, as well as the
deepest irony, is that that destiny was death.

Tristan is consistently chromatic in texture. *Parsifal* is sometimes chromatic, at other times diatonic and—especially in
the Grail music—even modal. Yet even when the component
lines are diatonic or vocal in contour, the enharmony suggests
a sensuous dissolution. The glowing orchestral polyphony is still
harmonically conceived; its voluptuousness is retrospectively
savoured, if not orgiastically enjoyed. None the less, there are
passages in *Parsifal* which have more in common with Bach than
anything in the music of such conscious Bach-addicts as Brahms
and Mendelssohn. This helps us to understand why Wagner
should have been able to create, alongside *Parsifal*, another
opera which seems to be the polar opposite not only of *Parsifal*,
but of the development of Wagner's work as a whole.

Wagner began to sketch the poem of *The Mastersingers* as
early as 1845, intending it to be a comic complement to
Tannhäuser. He composed the music between 1861 and 1867, two
years after he had finished *Tristan*. *The Mastersingers* is the only
one of Wagner's mature operas to deal with real people in
action. It thus bears some relation to the traditional notion of
opera, and its technique manifests in some ways a return to
traditional methods. It employs Wagner's symphonic leitmotive technique in its most developed form; but it also finds
room for (dramatically justified) set pieces like the *Preislied*,
and uses chromaticism mainly as an intensification of a clearly
defined diatonicism. Moreover, the harmonic-polyphonic texture of Wagner's late work assumes a form more closely related
to traditional counterpoint; chorale, fugue, passacaglia and

other Bachian techniques are obviously appropriate to the
subject and setting.

Yet this apparently objective presentation of a sturdy world
far removed from the subjective orgy of *Tristan* or the confes-
sional intimacy of *Parsifal* is not as remote from the main tenor
of Wagner's work as it seems. For Wagner himself said that
while the story unfolds before the audience in something that
looks like medieval Nuremberg, it really takes place in the minds
of Walther and Sachs: and Walther is the Artist-Hero or
Wagner-Siegfried, while Sachs is Wagner-Wotan, the man who
loves but renounces a woman (significantly called Eve). We can
see from the beautiful monologues of Sachs, in which Wagner
adopts a mellower form of Tristan's chromaticism, that *The
Mastersingers* too is a part of Wagner's religion of art. "All
poetry", says Sachs, "is but the truth of dreams made manifest."

Though Wagner called *The Mastersingers* a comedy, it has
become, as an expression of the German Soul, a national institution, almost a rite. It bears more resemblance to external
reality than the dream-world of Wagner's subconscious which,
in the orgiastic ritual of *Tristan* or the incantatory ritual of
Parsifal, takes the place of God and Civilization. But it may
be that this Nuremberg existed in fact no more than the visionary Vienna which haunted the imagination of the dying
Schubert. Those who are repelled by Wagner's egomania are
apt to consider *The Mastersingers* a uniquely 'healthy' and therefore acceptable work. Those who find *Tristan* and *Parsifal* among
the most profoundly (as well as violently) moving experiences
in art, are apt to dismiss the healthiness of *The Mastersingers* as
synthetic. The distinction may well be invalid: as dubiously
defined as are most boundaries between the conscious and the
subconscious mind.

Whatever our opinion as to the merits of *Tristan* and *Parsifal*
on the one hand and *The Mastersingers* on the other, it is
indisputable that the two former music-dramas sum up his
contribution to European history. One thinks of him as a
historical, rather than as a merely musical force: for with these
two operas Europe reaches the end of a cycle that began with
the Renaissance. So although no composer has ever had a more
powerful influence on the music that immediately followed him,
Wagner was wrong in thinking that he had created the art-
form of the future. It was because his music was an end that

Schoenberg, who inherited his chromaticism, had to start afresh. His only direct successors are consistently elegiac. From this point of view we shall see that the music of Delius is both technically and philosophically an epilogue to Wagner's peroration.

3

BERLIOZ

IF BERLIOZ [1803–1869] is still a problematical composer, he is so largely for the simple reason that he was French. He lived and worked at a time when the dominant tradition in Europe was German; and his music has been misunderstood because it has been judged by irrelevantly Teutonic criteria. It is true that even in his lifetime he was appreciated in Germany rather than in his own country; but that was because the general level of musical cultivation in France was so low. The Germans, admiring his orchestral virtuosity, could respect him for the wrong reasons: which was at least preferable to not respecting him at all. A hundred years later, we can begin to see Berlioz in perspective; and the more we do so, the clearer it becomes that he has nothing in common with German romanticism, while belonging in a profound sense to the culture of France.

We have noted that in France the revolution of sonata style was less obtrusive than in Germany: and that the conventions of French music remained basically operatic. This was partly because the aristocratic order had been, in France, so deeply entrenched; partly, perhaps, because the French, having accomplished their revolution in fact, had less need to resolve their frustrations in their art. In any case, Berlioz was born in 1803, early enough to inherit the artistic traditions of a long-established order. In Germany, most of the great artists of the Enlightenment and of romanticism came from the lower middle class, or even from the peasantry. In France, they tended still to belong to the ruling class, and to preserve aristocratic pretensions to honour and riches, as a just reward for their talents' service to the nation. Such aspirations were, in a revolutionary era, opposed to the materialistic spirit of a commercial society; and so—in the absence of an aristocracy—the artists tended to support the common people against the bourgeoisie. The people were to be the new aristocrats, who ran society in the interests of humanity and art, not for private aggrandizement. Thus the artists were *grands seigneurs* by instinct, members of the bourgeoisie by circumstance, and by sympathy something that we would call Tory Democrats.

Like the men of 1830, Berlioz intended to revolutionize; but to do so in the interests of order. His first opera, *Benvenuto Cellini*, has for theme the Artist as Hero. As a social being, the artist-hero is the opponent of all that is philistine and base. Yet while as a social being he must destroy, as an artist he must, by the nature of his calling, order and create. If he is a bandit, his banditry is purposeful. Wagner's *Tannhäuser* and *Lohengrin* had the same theme, and we saw that his banditry was purposeful in the ultimate sense that the strength of his sensations annihilated everything outside himself. But Berlioz wished to renovate a decaying world both in his own interests and in those of civilization. Like Beethoven, he had a social conscience. So we find in his music a balance between his individualism and his respect for tradition. The inward-turning aspects of his art are complemented by outward-turning elements; he creates music which expresses his inner life, and also music designed to fulfil a ceremonial and social purpose. And the one kind of music is conditioned by the other. His respect for tradition tends to objectify the expression of his inner life; his romantic individualism tends to give subtlety to his music of social purpose. This is what one might expect; for the New World depends on the strength and sensitivity of the individual spirits who live in it.

In his youth, Berlioz had two musical idols: Beethoven and Gluck. "I took over where Beethoven left off," he once said, using words similar to those frequently uttered by Wagner. In some ways, Berlioz and Wagner revered Beethoven for basically the same reason: because he embodied drama entirely in musical terms, recreating form in the interests of autobiographical expression. The aristocratic opera house was to be reborn in the democratic concert-hall; drama was to be implicit in the instrument which represented the triumph of nineteenth-century industrialism—the symphony orchestra. In his dramatic symphonies, Berlioz wished to make the drama inherent in the musical form, as it is in Beethoven's Ninth. Even when he composed for the theatre, he tried to preserve the music formally independent of, if related to, the literary and visual elements. But though Berlioz followed Beethoven thus far, he did not emulate Wagner in seeking to equate music—and life and death—with his own sensations. The fundamental difference in his approach is suggested by the manner in which he associated Beethoven with Gluck, whom Wagner dismissed as a survival of a moribund tradition.

From one point of view, Gluck might be said to have anticipated Beethoven in that he 'dramatized with the orchestra', crystallizing a dramatic situation in instrumental terms. But from another and perhaps more radical point of view, he was the heir to the vocal and operatic tradition that went back to Lully and Rameau as much as to the Italians. The line is unbroken from Lully to Rameau, from Rameau to Gluck, from Gluck to Spontini, Cherubini, Méhul, and Lesueur: and from these men to Berlioz. It is improbable that Berlioz had any intimate knowledge of Lully's operas, and his acquaintance with Rameau's scores was less than the evidence of his own later music would lead one to expect. But—apart from his fanatical devotion to Gluck—he knew the music of Cherubini [1760-1842] well; and discovered in his church music as much as in his classical operas such as the superb *Medeae*, a style which appealed to his deepest instincts. Its vocal lyricism and declamation were as gravely proportioned, and as passionate, as French heroic tragedy; its command of tonality was spacious and grand, yet instinct with a Beethovenian fire. In Spontini [1774-1851] and Méhul [1763-1817] he found a similar compromise, especially in their explicitly revolutionary operas which were the 'modern' complement to classical heroism. Here, perhaps, something of Cherubini's nobility was sacrificed in favour of a more melodramatic instrumental vehemence; in Lesueur [1760-1837], on the other hand, Berlioz found less power, but a more rarefied sensuousness, partly derived from the composer's fondness for modal melody and for exotic orchestration.

For a time Berlioz was a pupil of Lesueur at the Conservatoire. We know that he greatly admired his teacher's music. None the less, Lesueur's interest in what was then an unusual kind of melody and scoring merely confirmed Berlioz in an innate habit of mind. Paradoxically, his vehemently expressed hatred of the past—except for a few of his immediate predecessors—was an aspect of his traditionalism. He had none of the romantic reverence for Antiquity because he was conscious of being, not an imitator of, but a natural successor to, the great masters of the French tradition. We can approach Berlioz's music with understanding only when we see that he is not, as is often supposed, a completely isolated figure. His Beethovenian forcefulness is modified by his relation to the French operatic tradition; complementarily, his formal inventions all derive from the melodic rather than harmonic nature of that tradition—and of his own genius.

We can already observe this in one of Berlioz's earliest representative works, the *Symphonie Fantastique*, which was first performed in 1830—three years after the death of Beethoven. Berlioz appended to this work a literary programme purporting to describe the relationship of the music to his own (or the Artist's) biography. In so doing he was conforming to fashion and perhaps flattering his literary ability; but nothing could be further than this music from the subjectivism of Wagner. Though the musical structure may differ from that of a classical symphony, it is no less cohesive. In harmony and in key-relationships it is less advanced than Beethoven; its originality consists in the way in which a long-breathed melodic line, harking back to Gluck and classical opera, is subjected to Beethoven's technique of thematic generation and transformation. Berlioz himself pointed out that the *idée fixe* functioned on two levels: the programmatic motive itself, which recurrently obsesses the Artist's imagination: and the gradual, musical metamorphoses of the motive which are his spiritual history.

The theme of the first Allegro runs to forty odd bars (Ex. 73):

Ex.73. Berlioz: *Symphonie Fantastique* (first movement)

The initial arpeggiated phrase, with its rising sixth, suggests a Beethovenian challenge; but it is asymmetrically extended in declamatory style, always aspiring upwards but straining back to the F which droops to E natural. This aspiring phrase is balanced by a clause falling through a seventh, followed by the original sixth inverted, with a chromatic intrusion creating a change to a triplet rhythm. The cadence finally returns to the

F and E: the musical embodiment of the 'fixation' that will not allow the flexible phrases to soar. In the subsidiary themes and the development Berlioz's dramatic climaxes are attained by large-scale thematic evolution of this type, rather than by tonal contrast. In the scherzo-valse melody seems to be breaking loose from its fixation in the compulsive grace of dance movement. In the adagio *Scène aux Champs* melody learns to accept its limitations (even at the original pitch but in a different key); and from acceptance wins a luminous serenity: a Claude-like classical landscape only remotely disturbed by premonitions of storm. With the *Marche au Supplice*, however, the F–E fixation is back in a remorselessly frustrating form, reinforced by the implacably rigid rhythm; and in the last movement the complete shape of the first-movement allegro theme is parodied into a witches' sabbath; even the elaborations of the Dies Irae motive become a contrapuntal development of the work's melodic seed. Far from being romantic rhapsodizing held together only by an outmoded literary commentary, the *Symphonie Fantastique* is one of the most tautly disciplined works in early nineteenth-century music. This is only what we might expect from our knowledge of Berlioz as a man. For all the immense mane of red hair, the transports of rage, and the *grands amours*, Berlioz was, even as a young man, remarkable for an intellectual acumen rare among musicians. In this, again, he was characteristically French. He chased his beautiful Countess around Europe, equipped with phials of poison for use if she refused to love him. But he did not forget to pack the stomach-pump.

From this ostensibly autobiographical, yet fundamentally classical work of Berlioz's youth, let us turn to another earlyish work, this time composed for a ceremonial occasion. In the *Symphonie Fantastique* Berlioz was thinking of himself, but objectified his feeling in a stringently linear structure. The *Symphonie Funèbre et Triomphale* was composed in 1840, to be performed by massed military bands in the Place de la Bastille, in memory of those who lost their lives in the July Revolution of 1830. Berlioz envisaged himself conducting his vast forces with a drawn sword, and then collapsing in tears over the kettledrums. The music is not intended to be personal expression, but a vision of Napoleonic grandeur, not perhaps as it was, but as it might be. The military motive that dominates early

nineteenth-century music here becomes sublimely idealistic;
martial discipline becomes synonymous with the suppression
of the inflated ego.

Yet although march rhythms pervade this music far more
than in the restless, fluid rhythms of the allegro of the *Symphonie
Fantastique*, one need look no further than the magnificent
theme of the first movement to see that martial glory is recreated
in the light of Berlioz's sensitivity (Ex. 74):

Ex.74. Berlioz: *Symphonie Funèbre et Triomphale* (first movement)

The march rhythm does not prevent the melody from soaring in proud arches which recall the declamatory phrases of classical opera rather than the symphonic themes of the Viennese tradition; and the asymmetry of the clauses is complemented by a tonal precariousness created by chromatic intrusions in the melody, and by the dialogue between the melody and the cantabile bass. Berlioz's chromaticism, unlike Wagner's, is almost always melodic, not harmonic; it extends, rather than disrupts, the span of the theme. Even the sequences which sometimes appear in his melodies are seldom strictly reflected in the harmony. Wagner's grandeur is the apotheosis of the personal. Berlioz thinks melodically in vast phrases that acquire a more than personal grandeur. This is as true of Berlioz's ostensibly miniature works as of his most monumental: consider the longdrawn melodies of the songs *Le Spectre de la Rose*, *L'Absence*, and *Sur les Lagunes*.

Berlioz's approach to the *Symphonie Fantastique* and to the *Symphonie Funèbre* is thus, though the works seem to be diametrically opposed, basically the same. In all his mature music it is impossible to separate the inward- from the outward-tending elements. His two 'dramatic symphonies', *Roméo et Juliette* (1838) and *Harold en Italie* (1834), objectify his own experience in persons and situations outside himself. In *Roméo* he presents Shakespeare's drama in instrumental microcosm. Especially in the love scene, the soloistically treated instruments take the place of operatic voices; and the structure of the work as a whole is a curious, not entirely convincing compromise between symphonic and operatic techniques. In *Harold en Italie* Berlioz objectifies symphonic drama by writing a *concertante* part for solo viola which operatically represents himself, as symbol of the Byronic legend. Except in the last movement, the lyrical germination of the viola's song is the impetus behind the growth of the music. Even in the last movement, which is closest to orthodox sonata style, the bandit's ferocity, like Berlioz's own, is ordered and purposeful, as well as an electrically exciting noise (consider the use of the screaming, trill-like figure on the violins).

In general, however, Berlioz is least successful when he tries to emulate the sonata principle, most convincing when he allows his lyrical impulse to generate form. For all his reverence for Beethoven, his melodies are never motivic; and he was correct

in maintaining that his music was misunderstood because nineteenth-century musicians had lost the feeling for sustained lyrical
line:

"Generally speaking, my style is very bold, but it has not
the slightest tendency to subvert any of the constituent elements
of art. On the contrary, it is my endeavour to add to their
number. I have never dreamt of making music 'without
melody', as so many in France are stupid enough to say. Such
a school now exists in Germany, and I hold it in detestation. It
is easy to see that, without confining myself to a short air for the
theme of a piece, as the great masters often do, I have always
taken care that my compositions shall be rich in melody. The
value of the melodies, their distinction, novelty and charm, may
of course be disputed. It is not for me to estimate them; but to
deny their existence is absurd and unfair. But as they are often
on a large scale, an immature or unappreciative mind cannot
properly distinguish their forms; or they may be joined to other
secondary themes which may be invisible to that class of mind;
and lastly, such melodies are so unlike the little absurdities to
which the term is applied by the lower stratum of the musical
world that it finds it impossible to give the same name to both."

It is certainly difficult to think of any later music in the nineteenth century which can approach the love scene from *Roméo*
in lyrical sensitivity. Berlioz's expressiveness, like Bach's, is
always in the theme; and he disapproved of Wagner's attempt
to 'dethrone music and to reduce it to expressive accents'.
While he may have been wrong about Wagner himself, Berlioz's
instinct was right: in the hands of lesser men Wagner's leit-
motivic technique could and did become a literary and philosophical substitute for musical coherence.

Since melody—and a rhythm that is melodically rather than
metrically conceived—is the essence of Berlioz's music, we shall
not be surprised to find that his approach to harmony is un-
Wagnerian. It is hardly extravagant to say that his basic
harmonic material is closer to Gluck than to Wagner: and that
what appear to be oddities and crudities in his harmony, when
considered in vocal score, are often the result of his thinking
directly in orchestral terms—instead of, like most romantic
composers, at the piano. When his harmony is more complex,

the complexity is never a matter of Wagnerian 'added' notes or appoggiaturas; it is rather the consequence of the rhythmic flexibility and tonal ambiguity of the melodies themselves. Sometimes there is a conflict between classical harmonic convention and the direction in which the lines want to move: so that the result is odd rather than satisfying. But whenever Berlioz's imagination is working at pressure, the individuality of his melody creates the harmony: for instance, in the wonderful Sanctus of the *Requiem* a single chromatic alteration in the tenor solo transforms the radiant D flat melody into the remoteness of D major; and the music finds its way home by way of another enharmonic change and a dissolving sequence of neutral diminished sevenths (Ex. 75):

Ex. 75 Berlioz: *Requiem* (Sanctus)

The mysterious harmonic transitions created by chromatic alteration in melody and bass in the first movement of the *Symphonie Funèbre* are another example (see p. 764). Often, again, the modal features in Berlioz's melodies leave their imprint on his harmony: consider the phrygian cadence—with flattened leading note and flattened second—at the end of the Kyrie of the *Requiem*, or Marguerite's famous *Romance*, which is one of the characteristically Berliozian moments in the unequal *Damnation de Faust*.*

The freedom of Berlioz's part-writing is the fundamental reason for the originality of his harmony. The succession of apparently unrelated triads at the opening of the Agnus Dei in the *Requiem* is an harmonic effect produced by melodic

* It is significant that the romantic interpretation of the Faust legend made little appeal to Berlioz. His *Faust* contains better music than Schumann's, but is decidedly less Goethean in spirit.

means—as are most of the comparable passages in sixteenth-century music. This reference to the sixteenth century reminds us that, since Berlioz is essentially a melodist, he is also a polyphonic rather than homophonic composer. It is true that he is unconvincing when he attempts to write an orthodox fugue in the eighteenth-century tradition; but the opening of *Harold en Italie*, no less than the more recognizably polyphonic sections of the *Requiem* and *Te Deum*, is evidence that Berlioz is a master of free fugato. The Quaerens Me of the *Requiem* achieves a tender radiance almost suggestive of the vocal texture of sixteenth-century polyphony, while the fugato passage in *Harold en Italie* is chromatically taut and sinuous. In neither is the harmony 'correct' according to eighteenth-century convention; in both it is correct in so far as it is inevitable, given the nature and distinction of the component themes.

The basically polyphonic nature of Berlioz's music finds expression in the fact that he is mainly a composer for orchestra, or for voices with orchestra. Just as the root of his structures is melodic generation rather than tonal architecture, so he thought polyphonically in the orchestra, rather than harmonically at the piano: an instrument which, almost alone among nineteenth-century composers, he could not play. For all his ill-deserved reputation as a noisy composer, Berlioz's style of orchestration is a chamber-music technique. His scoring is thin, limpid, translucent, compared with Wagner's rich blurring of timbres. Again, the polyphonic texture of his scores implies objectification, as against Wagner's engulfing surge of sound. Wagner drowns you in sensation; Berlioz involves you in an imaginative act. This becomes especially noticeable in Berlioz's last works, where for the first time his music betrays some kinship with Mozart's. Until the last decade of life, Mozart had meant little to him compared with Gluck. But in his second opera, *Béatrice et Bénédict* (based on Shakespeare's *Much Ado*), the ensemble number becomes much more important than in *Benvenuto Cellini*, compared nearly thirty years earlier; and the highly personal idiom acquires an almost Mozartian lyrical lucidity. Like Mozart, too, the opera has a Mediterranean warmth in its acceptance of human frailty: and an implicit melancholy, because real life so seldom attains this union of creative understanding with critical wit.

In this connexion we may recall a most significant remark

which Berlioz made when speaking of his difficulties in composing *Les Troyens*: "Another hurdle in my path," he said, "is that
the feeling to be evoked moves me too much. . . . This is bad.
One must try to do coolly the things that are most fiery." At the opposite
pole to Wagner, he seeks always to externalize his feeling. This
is why his supreme achievements were in opera and in his own
kind of church music: for opera normally involves other people
in action, and church music involves the absorption of the ego
into something greater than itself. Berlioz displayed considerable literary skill in writing his own libretti, and it is interesting that after *Benvenuto Cellini* he chose themes which bore
no relation to his immediate personal problems. His great
Virgilian opera *Les Troyens*, finished in 1864, is the culmination
of his career. It is an idealized vision of a new heroic civilization: or rather of the old world, and the old technique born
anew. This was no puerile revolutionary utopia. Dido is a
heroic figure, but also a woman, with human passions and
frailties. In Berlioz's imaginary aristocracy, people, like Dido,
would still love, suffer, and die, as they have always done; but
human life would acquire once more the dignity and sanctity
of the heroic age.

Nothing could be more remote from Wagner's sublime
egomania than this nobly lyrical music, which preserves even
the externalities of the French classical opera in its pastoral
interludes, heroic marches, choruses, and danced pantomimes.
The relationship between Berlioz's aria and in particular his
accompanied arioso and that of Rameau, is here as intimate as it
is subtle. Since Berlioz did not betray much conscious enthusiasm for Rameau's operas, one can only assume that this
spiritual and technical kinship was intuitive. Certainly it does
not affect the profound originality of Berlioz's music. The
Royal Hunt and Storm is a traditional ballet-pantomime in
classical style, with Gluck's dramatic intensity and Rameau's
lyrical range; but only Berlioz could have created that strange
opening theme—gravely proportioned, yet at the same time
acridly melancholy in its chromaticism. Similarly, in Cassan-
dra's tremendous aria at the end of Act I of *La Prise de Troye* or
the septet in *Les Troyens à Carthage*, the grandeur comes from the
splendour of Berlioz's reborn civilization: the melancholy from
his growing sense of disparity between the ideal and the real.

Berlioz's operas, being imitations of human beings in action,

imply belief in something outside himself, and an awareness of
human potentialities. But no more than Schubert or Wagner had
he any specific religious faith; one might almost say that he
found his bible in Shakespeare and Virgil, whose tragi-comic
vitality justified life, while being reconcilable with intellectual
scepticism. He could find an emotional identity with the heyday
of Christian and of pagan humanism; while having nothing but
contempt for those vulgarized nineteenth-century 'spirits' who
had nothing better to do than to levitate tables. To the romantic
sensibility, Beethoven's last works seemed to offer freedom from
restrictions. Berlioz, with his linear approach to his art and
his understanding of the technique of thematic transformation,
was perhaps the only composer intuitively to appreciate their
formal and spiritual logic. None the less, their mysticism could
not be for him. He had to seek a world of spiritual aristocracy,
projected into classical operatic mythology; and when he composed church music that too became an objectified vision of
majesty. From this point of view we may note that the relationship between his 'liturgical' and operatic manners is exactly
comparable with the relationship between the ecclesiastical and
secular styles of Cherubini.

The earliest of Berlioz's three great liturgical works, if they
can be so called, is the *Grande Messe des Morts* of 1837. Berlioz
once said that if he were threatened with the destruction of all
his works save one, he would crave exemption for this requiem.
One can understand his choice, for no single work more
powerfully fuses the personal and the ceremonial aspects of his
genius. It embraces every facet of his complex sensibility, from
the tenuous, vocal texture of the Quid Sum Miser or the
luminous polyphony of the Quarens Me to the volcanic
eruption of the Lachrymosa, with its operatically declamatory
line and spasmodically surging rhythm: from the chromaticized
modality of the Offertorium to the weird serenity of the Agnus
Dei, with its grotesque orchestral interjections for three flutes
and bass tuba. As a whole, the work is the supreme example of
the apocalyptic side of Berlioz's imagination—not because it
(very occasionally) employs four brass bands which Berlioz
intended to be placed at each corner of the main orchestra and
chorus: but because of the incandescence of the music, as much
in the piteous, fragmentary desolation of the Quid Sum Miser
as in the blaze of the Rex Tremendae. Though this is not

religious music it has, like Berlioz's operas, the visionary gleam. Wagner's operas deal with the redemption (which means for him the fulfilment) of the self. Berlioz's requiem evokes a world redeemed; and the process is as terrible as it is beautiful, as impersonal as it is unique.

Berlioz's *Te Deum*, composed in 1849, complements the requiem. The latter transmutes intense personal feeling into impersonal ceremonial; the *Te Deum* recreates ritual ceremony into personal feeling. Even its moments of tragic terror (such as the Judex Crederis) have a classical monumentality that relate them to the splendour of *Les Troyens*. The Napoleonic legend becomes an ideal revocation of vanished glory: a vision, as opposed to Meyerbeer's delusions, of grandeur. *L'Enfance du Christ*, Berlioz's Christmas oratorio, written in 1854, achieves grandeur out of intimacy. The exquisitely strong vocal writing and linear scoring of *Le Repos de la Sainte Famille* hark back beyond Gluck and classical opera to the seventeenth-century cantata. The frequent modality of the themes (especially in the section dealing with Herod's dream) generates some of Berlioz's most piquant harmonic subtleties. He approaches the story not as a Catholic, nor as a Protestant, nor even as a Christian: but as a man whose heart warms to one of the great human myths, as it warms to Shakespeare or to Virgil. Thus it is again not religious music; and though it is often serene, it remains characteristically mysterious and, in such moments as the *Marche Nocturne*, even sinister. Its loveliness is a tribute to the strength as well as the sensitivity of Berlioz's humanistic imagination. He was justified when he reprimanded those who affected to see in *L'Enfance du Christ* a complete *volte-face* in his style:

"The prevailing characteristics of my music are passionate expression, intense ardour, rhythmical animation, and unexpected turns. When I say passionate expression I mean an expression determined on enforcing the inner meaning of its subject, even when that subject is the contrary of passion, and when the feeling to be expressed is gentle and tender, or even profoundly calm. . . . Many people imagined that (in *L'Enfance du Christ*) they could detect a radical change in my style and manner. This opinion is entirely without foundation. The subject naturally lent itself to a simple and gentle style of music, and for this reason alone was more in accordance with their taste and intelligence. Time has no doubt developed these qualities, but I should have written *L'Enfance du Christ* in the same style twenty years earlier."

Though *L'Enfance du Christ* is an oratorio, it is, like all Berlioz's large-scale works, classically operatic in approach. There can be little doubt that he would have been a full-time opera composer had conditions in France made that possible. Even in Germany, only Wagner's colossal force of personality enabled him to realize his operatic dream. Berlioz's strength was not thus egocentric, and he had to accept the fact that the French would ignore, without even bothering to reject, his evocation of a civilization that, whether tragically or comically, once more attained the heroic. Berlioz died a broken and fatally misunderstood man. His revivified aristocracy was to renew society in the interests of the downtrodden; the search for Splendour was to be the people's instinctive protest against the spiritual tawdriness of an age dominated by trade. But the tragedy was that, having attained Power and Glory, the people, not being artists, were incapable of dealing with them. Berlioz lived to see that the rule of the people meant, not the rebirth of heroism, but the establishment of lack of thought, absence of discipline, and want of skill—the very reverse of the artistic virtues. The world which he had hoped would symbolize the Artist's triumph destroyed all that he held most dear; and he was denied even the consolation of seeing his imaginative vision adequately projected on to a stage.

Yet if Wagner triumphed and Berlioz failed, there is room, perhaps, for discrimination about the nature of failure and success. In fulfilling his dream Wagner became a part of European history. At the same time he was an end of a phase of consciousness. His art could be, and was, debased; but of itself it could lead to nothing further. About Berlioz's career, as compared with Wagner's, there is a melancholy sense of nonfulfilment. He was himself disillusioned in every creative ideal; and whereas composers all over Europe strove—both hopelessly and irrelevantly—to emulate Wagner, Berlioz did not even have any direct successors who could carry on the work he left incomplete. None the less, in the long run Berlioz has become the creative force who, as Busoni said, "pointed the way to

untold generations"; the influence of his melodic approach to
formal problems and of his polyphonic approach to orchestration has grown during the twentieth century, and is still increasing. Wagner is a climacteric point in the growth of 'the
mind'—or perhaps one should say the senses—'of Europe'; now
Wagner's music has happened we shall never be the same again.
But it is possible that Berlioz—a romantic who was rooted deep
in classical tradition while anticipating our fumbling attempts to
rescue civilization from chaos—may express the nineteenth
century more comprehensively and more deeply.

It is not a question of the relative stature of the two men,
about which argument must be as profitless as it is inconclusive.
We must take what they offer, not what they might have offered
if they, or 'things', had been different. We shall return to
Wagner because we are all preoccupied with our (significant
or insignificant) selves and, whether we like it or not, inescapably
wedded to love and death. We shall return to Berlioz because
we are all fascinated by human nature and, if we had his
imagination, would envisage the contexts in which, were we
nobler and more humane, we might hope to exist. So Wagner's
fulfilment instils into us regret for the life we ourselves have not
time enough, or capacity enough, to live: Berlioz's disillusion
fills us with hope for the unborn lives that make our passion
seem petty. The woof of hope and regret is the essence of
our being; so although Berlioz and Wagner are opposites, they
are necessary the one to the other.

The anti-Wagnerian nature of Berlioz's art is, in an indirect
sense, a key to the subsequent history of his country's music.
In his day the arbiters of taste were the complacent bourgeoisie who had made fortunes out of the new social order.
Their cultural standards were not very different from those of
their twentieth-century successors. Aristocratic hauteur and
visionary splendours and sorrows were not for them. They
wanted an art that would flatter their opulence and promote
daydreams, as a relief from the cares involved in getting richer;
the 'tired business-man' was not a twentieth-century innova-
tion. Two opera composers pre-eminently fulfilled this demand:
Gounod and, later, Massenet.

Born in 1818, Gounod [1818–1893] was close enough to the
eighteenth century to inherit—instead of Berlioz's or Cherubini's

classic nobility—a certain rococo charm. As long as he is content
to compose *opéras comiques* or little songs, his music has a delicious
frothy elegance. Eighteenth-century wit becomes rounded and
prettified in the languid symmetries of his chanson-like tunes,
and in the chromaticisms that cling like rouge to his basically
simple homophony. It is remarkable how frequently his tunes
are grouped in two-bar periods, each beginning in crochet
values, quickening to quavers, and then slowing to minims in
the 'feminine ending' that accompanies the harmonic cadence:
the melodies attempt to flow, but soon subside in cosily relaxed
sentiment (Ex. 76):

Ex. 76. Gounod: *Faust* (Cavatina)

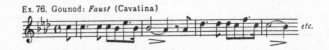

So while one does not need to be a tired business-man to be
titillated by the love-delights of *Philémon et Baucis*, one has to
admit that even Gounod's most pleasurable successes depend
on an element of deceit. This becomes still more obvious in
the work of Massenet [1842–1912], for while his operas have
very varied settings, they revolve around a single theme.
Massenet, with a sure instinct for box-office appeal, mastered
the modern equivocation and 'got it both ways': the theme
of the Repentant Whore can stimulate erotic feeling under
cover of self-righteousness. But we, unlike Massenet's public,
cannot afford to be smug: if it is true that there is a little of
Massenet at the heart of every Frenchman, we can perhaps
dispense with the national qualification. In *Manon*, at least,
Massenet's eroticism is so tenderly felt in the short-breathed,
caressing phrases and the softly lilting rhythms that we are even
prepared to accept his outmoded notion of Woman as a kind
of sensual seismograph. So apparently mild an aphrodisiac
that preserves its effectiveness after more than a hundred years
may be assumed to have something which the cruder aphro-
disiacs of Hollywood miss.

The moral duplicity of Massenet's music is part of its
insidious appeal. As the century advanced, however, moral
duplicity began to assume nastier forms: especially when it
became associated musically with the impact of Wagner.

Gounod himself, having fallen a victim to religious mania, concentrated no longer on the aspect of his talent represented by the delightful love-music in his *Faust*, but on the bland beatitudes prompted by his comically pathetic attempt to measure up to Goethe. In his innumerable oratorios, *Parsifal*-like harmony interjects a dose of 'mysticism' into the pretty, lethargic two-bar periods, and into the stolid homophony which he picked up in England from the Mendelssohnic oratorio. A genuine, if eccentric, Wagnerian force came into French music with César Franck [1822–1890]; but his influence became decisive only towards the end of the century. Around the 1850s, the spurious Wagnerism of Gounod's later operas and oratorios carried all before it: and while it was bad enough that the French should ignore their greatest genius, Berlioz, it was worse that they should worship in his stead a god intrinsically false. The falsity was not, of course, Gounod's personal responsibility. He was one reflection of the Bourgeois Dream.

Berlioz was born early enough, and had original genius strong enough, to remain creatively unaffected by the spiritually torpid conditions in which he had to work. This was not the case with the most brilliantly endowed composer whom France produced between Berlioz and Debussy: for Bizet's short career [1838–1875] is a series of false starts; and even when he ultimately solved his artistic problems, he died before he could reap the fruits of success. In 1855, when he was seventeen, he composed a symphony which expressed, with uncanny precocity, the essence of his personality. The themes have something of the lyrical suavity of Gounod in his most amiable mood: but remind one still more of the Italianate culture of Mozart and Rossini, whom Bizet admired above all other composers. The capriciousness of the modulations suggests Schubert rather than the enharmonic side-steppings of Gounod; for whereas Gounod's mildly sensual chromatics tend to oscillate around a fixed point, producing a self-regarding, narcissistic effect, Bizet's part-writing and basses have resilience and momentum. The liveliness of his texture is reinforced by his seductively individual scoring, especially for the woodwind; and although the symphony, like Schubert's boyhood efforts, is too long for its non-dramatic material, it remains an astonishing exhibition both of technique and of personality. Ironically enough, Bizet spent the next few years trying to deny the nature he had revealed in

this adolescent masterpiece: sometimes in grandiose pseudo-
Germanic symphonic music like *Roma*, sometimes in monu-
mental operas that hovered disastrously between Gounod and
Meyerbeer.

His rediscovery of his real self came by way of two com-
missions that forced him to self-discipline. Pretension was
obviously inappropriate to children's pieces for piano duet: so
in writing *Jeux d'Enfants* Bizet could concentrate on the
intimacy of his melodic gift, which was as sensuous as Gounod's
but so much more sensitive; while the chromatic and enharmonic subtleties of his harmony could gain in effect through
concentration. The delicately asymmetrical melody of *La
Poupée* is a lovely example of Bizet's lyrical flavour (Ex. 77):

Ex. 77 Bizet: La Poupée

and the kaleidoscopic polyphonic texture of *Saute Mouton*
illustrates his harmonic piquancy which leads on to Chabrier,
and ultimately to Ravel (Ex. 78):

Ex. 78. Bizet: *Jeux d'Enfants*

The relationship to these later composers suggests too how
in writing of childhood, Bizet recovered the Mozartian object-
vity of his vision. Like a child he is, even in his subtleties, simple
and single-minded; his attitude is distinct from the romantic
nostalgia of Schumann's pieces about childhood.

The other crucial commission which Bizet received was to
compose incidental music to Daudet's play, *L'Arlésienne*. Composers are apt to regard incidental music for the theatre as an

unrewarding task; it is certainly difficult to think of another composer who created his first masterpiece in this hybrid medium. But Bizet's success was not fortuitous: for in writing for a chamber orchestra, without voices, he was not even momentarily tempted to emulate the sentimentalities of Gounod or the monumentalities of Meyerbeer. He could be himself: or rather could find himself in losing himself in a play which dealt with real people in a contemporary setting. The music he creates is in fact much more dramatic than any of his earlier operas; of which the first had been an exercise in Italian *buffo* style, while the others were hampered by imbecile, inadequately motivated libretti—the inevitable product of a society that demanded no more than the easiest emotional appeal.

Each of Bizet's twenty-seven musical intrusions into *L'Arlésienne* is etched with the precision of the *Jeux d'Enfants*, though his emotional range is here incomparably wider. It is no longer a matter of entering into the self-contained hearts of children; Bizet's objectivity enables him to recreate even the love of the ageing couple who meet after fifty years' separation. The radiant tenderness of their *Adagietto* is an instance of the dependence of Bizet's harmonic originality on flexible movement in the inner parts: which again explains why his music has so much more delicate a vitality than Gounod's. The chords in both are frequently the same; the contexts in which the chords appear are very different. Gounod's melodies have charm but little character. Bizet's melodies have so personal a distinction that they communicate their vitality to the accompanying parts: and therefore to the harmony also, whether in the pathos of the suavely flowing texture of the *Adagietto*, or in the wit of the unexpected relationships created by the moving parts in *Saute Mouton*.

L'Arlésienne dealt with peasant life in Provence. Bizet incorporated a number of folk-tunes into his score, and in his orchestration achieved a translucency that, for all its sophistication, often suggests the bold colours of Provençal village bands. The earthiness of the subject, and the sunniness of the setting, aided Bizet's instinct for 'externalization'. It is significant that in his abortive operatic ventures the exotic elements had always been at once the most original and the most convincing: not because they were an escape from reality, but because they offered an alternative to Gounodesque complacence. Djamileh moves us not because she is exotic but because her exoticism expresses—through her sinuous melodic lines and ostinato rhythms, and her vivid orchestral colouring —a flesh-and-blood woman. In *Carmen* the exotic, Spanish element is likewise an approach to reality. This time Bizet knew that he had found in Merimée's story the theme which could call forth the Latin intensity of his nature.

Carmen herself provoked at the time a reaction bordering on hysteria not because she was Spanish, nor because she was a prostitute, but because she was a real woman. For Bizet's public, the operatic heroine was expected to be either virtuous and sinned against, or (better) vicious but redeemed. Carmen did not fit into either of these categories; she might be (and later was) glamourized, but sentimentalized she could never be. You cannot pretend she is a figure in a fairy tale; indeed the subject of the opera is not so much her powerfully delineated personality as its devastating effect on Don José. His tragedy was, and is, common. The initial hostility to Bizet's opera arose largely from its truth.

Musically, *Carmen* is in many ways an extension of the styles explored in *L'Arlésienne*. It is a genuine *opéra comique* with spoken dialogue which spills over into music. It is thus a play in music, the dramatic immediacy of which is weakened if sung recitative is substituted for speech. The music that flowers out of speech has all the psychological precision of *L'Arlésienne*, with a vibrant ardour appropriate to the theme of love and jealousy. The orchestral music does not in Wagnerian fashion embody subjective drama; it creates in vivid immediacy the world and atmosphere in which the characters live and move: consider the raucous, piercing passage for piccolos, cornet, and pizzicato strings at the entrance of the gamins behind the soldiers; the fatefully cumulative use of the brass in the fortune-telling scene; as compared with the magical use of low flute with horns at the of the duet '*Là-bas dans la montagne*'. In aria and arioso Bizets' style has now extraordinary plasticity. Only Micaela, a Gounodesque character, sings in conventional French lyricism; and even her music has considerably more vitality than its model. The melodies of the other characters have acquired a fervency that suggests that Verdi's example has helped Bizet to 'realize' himself in the understanding of other people. Like Verdi, he refines the banalities as well as the subtleties of human nature into 'something rich and strange'. The Toreador's Song is to be sung '*avec fatuité*'; but if the music that a fatuous man sings were really fatuous it would hardly have exerted so hypnotic a spell over so many people for so long. Even in his trivialities, Bizet has the art that hides art.

The formal lucidity of *Carmen*, despite the ferocity of its passion and the apparently episodic technique of the *mélodrame*, is typical of the French classical spirit rather than of the pretty formalities of Gounod: or perhaps it would be truer to say that that it is classical *because* of the ferocity, for the essence of classical order is that there should be something to control. *Carmen's* musical concision is thus inseparable from its dramatic force; it stands with Berlioz's operas at the furthest extreme from the symphonic operas of Wagner. We can see this in the way Bizet uses motives in association with the different characters. Wagner's leitmotives are a means of symphonic organization; Bizet uses his motives for essentially dramatic reasons. They are not subjected to symphonic development; they merely reappear, in varied harmonizations and orchestration, with uncannily powerful effect, often with ironic implications. The prevalent irony is another instance of Bizet's Latin classicality; no great artist has ever been more impervious to irony than Wagner.

Dramatic irony in *Carmen* is a counterpart of the wit which we have seen to be implicit in Bizet's harmonic texture. It distinguishes him not only from Wagner, but also from Verdi, who, though he ended his career with one supreme manifestation of wit, seldom if ever allowed irony to obtrude in his tragic operas. This is partly a difference of temperament, partly of cultural tradition: which does not alter the fact that Bizet and Verdi have one profound quality in common, beneath the superficial affinities. *Otello*, the culmination both of Verdi's work and of Italian grand opera, appeared in 1876, the year after *Carmen*. Musically and psychologically it is much richer than Bizet's masterpiece; but *Carmen* at least approaches it in the force of its impact, because it shares with *Otello* a terrifying honesty. If *Otello* is, in a sense, the end of Italian grand opera, in *Carmen* French grand opera and *opéra comique* become one. Bizet no longer thinks of the high and heroic on the one hand, the low and popular on the other: life as it is—abrupt, brutish, and short—becomes a tragic theme. The lover who kills the beloved is the eternal, and perhaps the most fundamental, human tragedy; and although Bizet at thirty-six did not see as deeply into it as did Verdi in his seventies, he too faced it without flinching.

It was this acceptance of reality that appealed to Nietszche when he reacted against his clay-footed, one-time idol, Wagner. For him, *Parsifal* was subjective mumbo-jumbo, whereas *Carmen* was Life—not in the raw, but as realized without evasion, in the lucidity of art. His dismissal of *Parsifal* now seems as superficial as his earlier idolatry of Wagner had been fanatical. Yet he was on the right lines in his appreciation of *Carmen*; for we are involved in that drama and at the same time detached from it, whereas to Wagner we must submit body and soul, if the music is to mean anything at all. Berlioz's remark that one must do coolly the things that are most fiery would apply as much to *Carmen* as to *Les Troyens*: for Bizet, even more than Verdi, has in common with Berlioz not only the wiry virility of his orchestration, but also the objectivity of his approach. At the same time, *Carmen* deflates the sublime; and it may be because it preserves the virtues of the old world while freeing them of hypocrisy that it makes so powerful an appeal to sophisticated and unsophisticated alike. In any case, no later composer revealed the tragedy of instinctive human nature with Bizet's honest precision. His natural successor was Chabrier [1841–1894], whose significant music displays a comic genius more vigorous than Bizet's in its chanson-like lyricisms, its harmonic and rhythmic ambiguities and ironies, its sharp or tender orchestral colours. But despite Chabrier's flirtings with Wagnerism, *Le Roi Malgré Lui* is essentially a brilliant extension of the French comic tradition. Ironically enough, the tragic honesty which is the core of *Carmen* led only to an operatic style as remote from Bizet's lucidity as it is from the visionary tragedy of Berlioz.

At the beginning of the twentieth century—on 5th February 1900—Debussy wrote in a letter these words, which sound a funeral knell on an epoch, apropos of Charpentier's *verismo* opera, *Louise*:

"I have been to the show of the Charpentier family. . . . It seems to me that this work had to be. It supplies only too well the need for that cheap beauty and idiotic art that has such an appeal. You see what this Charpentier has done. He has taken the cries of Paris which are so delightfully human and picturesque and, like a rotten Prix de Rome, he has turned them into sickly cantilenas with harmonies underneath that, to be polite, we will call parasitic. The sly dog! It's a thousand times more conventional than *Les Huguenots*, of which the technique, though it may not appear so, is the same. And they call this Life! Good God, I'd sooner die straight away. What you have here is something of the feeling after the twentieth half-pint, and the sloppiness of the chap who comes back at four in the morning, falling over the baker and the rag-and-bone man. And this man imagines that he can express the soul of the poor! It's so silly that it's pitiful. . . . But then people don't very much like things that are beautiful—they are so far from their nasty little minds. With many more works like *Louise* any attempt to drag them out of the mud will completely fail."

We may find this hard, and think Debussy's conclusion a bit priggish. Yet fundamentally he was right. Bizet had discovered a truth within common human nature; Charpentier [1860–1956] and the *verismo* composers journalistically exploited the commonplace to inculcate lies. Debussy's letter was intuitively prophetic; he could not have known that the musical-theatrical technique on which he comments was to become one of the bases of Hollywood's mechanized assault on our emotions. Bizet's fight against the Bourgeois Dream of Gounod would indeed seem to have been in vain: for all we are left with is on the one hand Charpentier's journalistic prostitution of truth, and on the other hand the more mechanized offspring of Offenbach's deliberate (if delightful) separation of 'entertainment' from reality. Offenbach at least never pretended that life was *really* an eternal can-can; and the music-hall turn, indulged in zestfully, may be a welcome relief from tedium. The 'decadence' lies, perhaps, in the tedium: in the fact that either deceit or escape should be necessary.

4

VERDI
AND NINETEENTH-CENTURY ITALIAN OPERA

W_{E HAVE} seen that Berlioz's approach to composition was in part conditioned by the fact that the main stream of music in France remained operatic, at a time when the German instrumental sonata dominated Europe. In Italy, conditions were in some ways similar to those in France. If the survival of the operatic tradition in France was attributable to the power of the old autocracy and of classical drama, in Italy it was due to the vigorous multiplicity of petty autocracies, and to the 'vocal' nature of the Italian language: to which we may add, perhaps, the amiability of the Italian climate.

None the less there was in Italy no lack of revolutionary fervour. Austrian tyranny encouraged patriotic feeling and a burning enthusiasm for liberty: and made national heroes out of artists such as Manzoni and Verdi, as much as out of political leaders like Cavour. It is not therefore surprising that Italian opera in the nineteenth century should have departed further from classical precedent than French opera. The nobility of *Les Troyens* is the culmination of the line that begins with the operas of Lully and Rameau; but except in so far as both are good to sing, there is little connexion between Verdi's operas and those of Handel and Alessandro Scarlatti. Only in his last works is there a (not very specific) link with the style of Monteverdi.

At first, the Italian's operatic reaction to revolutionary feeling was largely negative. Rossini dealt directly with nationalistic aspiration in *William Tell*; but that was his last opera, and was not intended for an Italian public. His native operas are mostly in the *buffo* tradition. Though they deal with real, mostly 'ordinary', people and with themes (such as the Cinderella story) which appealed to his middle-class audience, they cultivated a deliberate, and delightful, social irresponsibility; even the premonitions of romanticism in his serious Italian operas can hardly be accused of political intentions. At the further extreme from Rossini's hedonism stands the elegiac melancholy of Bellini [1801–1834]. He alone among Italian composers of his time indulges neither in *buffo* irresponsibility nor in popular patriotism. With him, a national and communal distress is submerged in personal sorrow. This sorrow is partly his own, for he possessed the consumptive's hypersensitized nerves, and died pathetically in his early thirties. But he none the less belongs to the classical world in that he expresses himself mainly through vocal melody, and objectifies his feeling in people other than himself. In *La Sonnambula* the girl who sleep-walks herself into such awkward predicaments is a young girl exquisitely 'realized' in melody; she is also Bellini himself, in the very virginal quality of her sensitivity. In *Norma*, again, we have a deeply characteristic conflict between the life of passion and the seclusion of the cloisters; from this personal theme the music derives its poignancy, rather than from the fortuitous political motive that was perhaps responsible for the opera's success.

All the music of Bellini which still lives deals with potentially tragic themes; and although he borrowed certain external features—for instance, the choral episodes—from French grand opera, his music is essentially intimate. The subject of *La Sonnambula* may seem to us suitable for the debunking technique of Rossini; yet the whole point lies in the fact that Bellini takes the girl's troubles seriously. He feels them in personal terms; and he can do so because Romani's poetry is simple, sensitive, and direct, and because his response to poetry is subtler than that of any of his contemporaries. His emotional sincerity and his literary sensitivity are related; both are inseparable from the flexible nature of his melodies, the sustained pliancy of which was admired by Verdi and even—in comparatively early life— by Wagner. Alone among his contemporaries, Bellini preserves the expressive intimacy of classical *bel canto* as it had been developed by Gluck and Mozart: making the curves more rounded, the leaps more expansive, without having recourse to rhythmically crude rhetoric such as we have commented on in Spontini, Meyerbeer, and Weber. Even when his melodies are grouped in two-bar periods, the phrases manage to preserve continuity and flow. In his greatest moments, like the famous 'Casta Diva', he achieves, in his withdrawn, valedictory manner, a lyrical span which seemed to have vanished with the heroic world: and which is recovered by no later composer except Berlioz and the Verdi of *Otello*.

The range of feeling which Bellini expresses through his lyricism is much wider than one might expect; and although his potency derives largely from his sensitive response to the text, it is not true that the harmonic and orchestral elements in his music are insignificant. There are passages in his work—such as the chains of dominant sevenths in the duet in Act II of *I Puritani*—which suggest that he was not impervious to the influence of his friend Chopin, whose *bel canto* melodies have so deep an affinity with Bellini's vocal style; and in general Bellini's technique, like Gluck's, was precisely appropriate to his intentions. He wished to express the subtlest refinements of feeling through the setting of poetry in vocal melody. If he was to concentrate attention on the vocal line, other elements must be sacrificed. The (normally) conventionalized harmony, the guitar-strumming accompaniments, the absence of polyphony are means to an end. Simplicity need not preclude subtlety; the most modest change of harmony or of accompanying figuration may, in association with a melodic phrase of peculiar poignancy, have an emotional effect disproportionate to the means employed. For instance, this transition from major to minor, followed by the modulation to the supertonic minor on the climacteric note of the phrase, harmonically complements the melody's ascending tritonal tension, answered by the declining chromaticism (Ex. 79):

Ex. 79. Bellini: Ma rendi pur contento

The structure of the melody as a whole is a series of such arch-like ascents and descents, each of which culminates a tone higher than the last: until the highest note (A flat) introduces a brief vocal cadenza which also creates the resolution of a harmonic cadence. All Bellini's melodies follow this arch-shaped contour, proceeding basically by scale-wise steps, however much vocal leaps may intensify the conjunct movement. This is why his music seems both sighfully romantic and classically poised; at once melancholy and serene.

Bellini's melody is the purest form of Italian *bel canto* in the nineteenth century. Later composers, such as Verdi and Puccini, adhered to the fundaments of this melody, though they neither achieved nor desired its refinement. Even in his own day, Bellini was an isolated figure. The most representative composer of the time was Donizetti [1797–1848], who produced sequences of comic and tragic operas designed to fulfil an insatiable demand. A comic masterpiece like *Don Pasquale* continues the tradition of *buffo* frivolity, with less vivacity than Rossini, but more grace. His tragic operas continue the romantic evasion in the cult of the extraordinary. If life seems too difficult, one can always go mad. One of the ways in which the romantics used Shakespeare was as an excuse for the Mad Scene: the difference being that whereas in Shakespeare madness is the consequence of the overwrought mind, in romantic drama and opera it becomes an end in itself—or at least its motivation is either perfunctory or synthetic. The cult of madness—like the cult of Gothick horrors and the phenomenal vogue for the novels of Scott as material for opera libretti—may have been a romantic escape, but it is not therefore contemptible. We most of us spend a considerable part of our lives trying to evade the consequences of our actions, thoughts, and feelings; Donizetti's mad scenes, especially the celebrated one in *Lucia di Lammermoor*, admit our evasiveness, and create beauty from the admission. Certainly they discover a new dramatic justification for operatic coloratura. To say that it is new is not, perhaps, entirely accurate, for there had been magnificent mad scenes in the operas of Handel. But in baroque opera madness is never the centre of the action; rather is it an aberration from man's heroic potentialities. Donizetti's vocal gymnastics, on the other hand, lead inevitably to the point where coherent melody cascades in extravagant mirth or frenzy.

There is something madly fortuitous even in his successes. He wrote so fast that he had no time to develop a lyrical gift as fecund as Bellini's, if less sensitive: or to explore a harmonic sense that might have approached the vivid immediacy of the Rossini of *Guillaume Tell*. The superb sextet from *Lucia* testifies not merely to the lyrical power of which he was capable, but also to the technical assurance of his harmonic polyphony. He owed this assurance partly to the tradition of professional craftsmanship within which he worked; yet this tradition prevented the romantic elements in his temperament from attaining comprehensive expression. So there is a melancholy appropriateness in the fact that his finest music should consist of delusions of passion, as Meyerbeer's consists of delusions of grandeur: and that, being nervously exhausted by the rigours of professional life, he should have rounded off the parable by going mad himself.

A tougher spirit than Donizetti, let alone Bellini, was needed to weather the cultural conditions of Italy in the early nineteenth century. He appeared in the figure of Giuseppe Verdi [1813–1901], who came of peasant stock and spoke soberly enough when, later in life, he said: "My youth was hard." While Verdi was growing to manhood, political affairs could hardly have been worse. With Rossini in retirement, Donizetti in the madhouse, and Bellini dead, the musical outlook was equally dismal. As a boy, Verdi exhibited some precocity and much pertinacity in acquiring a musical education in the face of odds; when he took up a professional musical career, he did so without extravagant ambitions. He wanted to compose music for the local military band, and to produce operas on the stock, saleable models. Like any other craftsman, he expected to learn his technique the hard way, partly by study, more by practical experience. The melodic clichés, the horror-struck diminished sevenths, the tremolandos—all the survivals from eighteenth-century theatrical convention which the early nineteenth century had reduced to their lowest and commonest denominator—were basic material which Verdi accepted without the faintest glimmer of shame. No more than Bellini or Donizetti did he seem to be aware that a great Austrian instrumental literature had but recently come to fruition; and as a young man he had neither Bellini's nervous refinement nor Donizetti's instinctive expertise.

Yet the exclusiveness of the tradition in which he worked had its compensations. If he was not tempted to experiment, neither was he lured from his course by extraneous distractions. Even the incompetence of the opera-house orchestras meant that in restricting the orchestra to a few theatrically effective gestures he could concentrate—as for that matter Bellini had done—on the elements that most interested him. Moreover, he had, as part of his unself-consciousness, one quality which Bellini and Donizetti had not. This was an ardent sense of a more than personal purpose. *Buffo* frivolity was not for him; nor was the luxury of personal lament. His opera was to be as serious as he knew how to make it: only its seriousness was to be inseparably linked to its popular appeal. Directly or indirectly, he had to express the passion for freedom which was to unite Italy under Cavour. He chose the historical-political theme not, with Meyerbeer, to encourage day-dreams of grandiosity, but to stimulate real people, in a real situation: perhaps even to excite them to action. Grandeur his opera hardly aimed at; power and energy it achieved—largely because its primitive technique was the servant of a passionate integrity.

Nabucco, the opera which in 1842 made Verdi famous overnight, had a historical theme to which the audience saw a contemporary parallel; they identified themselves with the enslaved Jews labouring under oppression. Yet its success, if to some extent extra-musical, could never have been so overwhelming but for the power of Verdi's music: to which the most effective testimony is that it still thrills us to-day, more than a hundred years after the event. Nor is it an accident that the greatest moments in the opera are choral. The solo vocal writing was at the time much more original than it now seems, and has great power if we accept its rhetoric and do not look to it for the languid subtleties of Bellini or the lyrical-dramatic complexity of Mozart; but it is not in itself evidence of genius, as the choral music is. It is significant that the next opera, *Ernani*—a version of the notorious Hugo play—is less impressive because Verdi has attempted more. Although in *Nabucco* the main characters are sharply delineated, it is the vehemence of the *turba* that gives the opera such momentum. In *Ernani* the fantastic embroilments of the principal characters are the centre of the action; and Verdi has not yet learnt to create, rather than reflect, the inner life of human beings in music.

As he matures, he begins to 'relive' his historical-political themes through his understanding of specific human creatures; this development coincides with the growth of his passion for Shakespeare, and with the appearance within his operatic style of dramatic techniques suggested by Beethoven. Both Wagner and Berlioz had started from an obsession, partly musical, partly philosophical, with Beethoven. As a peasant, trained in a professional tradition, Verdi did not encourage obsessions; one could not say that at any point in his career he experienced a conscious desire to modify his natural growth as an operatic composer. But if his admiration for Beethoven did not directly influence his development, it provides evidence as to the nature of that development. Nor is there anything odd in this, if we remember that from the start Verdi had been a composer of revolutionary operas.

The two operas that mark the beginning of this evolution in Verdi's work are *Macbeth* and *Luisa Miller*. He wrote *Macbeth* to please himself, knowing that its box-office appeal was dubious as compared with that of his historical-political operas. He took considerable pains over it, and preserved such an affection for the work that he revised it, nearly twenty years later, for performance in Paris. English people inevitably find it difficult to accommodate their knowledge of Shakespeare to the melodramatic clichés of nineteenth-century Italian opera; yet even as we recall Shakespeare, we cannot but be stirred by Verdi's sleep-walking scene, with its hypnotic, chromatic wail which pervades both the voice parts and the orchestra. Verdi here directed his performers to speak rather than sing their melodies —a procedure that must have seemed almost as abhorrent to his public as to his singers! One can see, however, what he had in mind; he has created an arioso style which, although it depends for its effect on being sung in time, aims at realistic immediacy. This urgency in the vocal lines is emphasized by the scoring, which, though never complex, is highly atmospheric: consider the sepulchral use of the low registers of the clarinet. Shakespeare has evoked in Verdi a power to 'realize' characters such as he had not previously possessed; and as a corollary of this his music begins to acquire a Beethovenian trenchancy. The first act in particular reminds us of the more rhetorical aspects of early Beethoven—both in the contour of the phrases and in the persistent syncopated *sforzandos*.

Verdi had dealt imaginatively with the burning political issues of his day; Shakespeare had revealed to him some of the darker depths of the human heart. Now, in *Luisa Miller*, Verdi's political consciousness and his interest in the human psyche meet in a story of immediate contemporary relevance. For Luisa is an ordinary middle-class girl sacrificed to bourgeois convention. Her tragedy is gloomy indeed, but never—like earlier bourgeois opera—sentimental. Verdi's passion is here not heroic, like Gluck's or Berlioz's; but it is no less powerful for being intimate. If the melodies lose something of the earlier Verdi's brutal force, they take a further step towards the sinewy flexibility of the creations of his maturity.

Maturity certainly arrived in *Rigoletto*, which, first produced in 1851, was to remain one of the peak points of Verdi's career. The story, based on Hugo's *Le Roi s'amuse*, is as complicated as it is melodramatic, but being admirably constructed, is continuously gripping. In so far as it deals with human relationships warped by environment and circumstance, it was again close to Verdi's heart; it is worth noting that the theatre management wanted to transform Rigoletto into a handsome young man, and that Verdi had to fight strenuously to preserve him as a physical, as well as spiritual, cripple. One would not immediately think of the vital energy of middle-period Verdi in association with the subtle humanity of Mozart; and it is true that Verdi has none of Mozart's civilized irony. Yet *Rigoletto* is in conception a Mozartian opera, and not merely for the superficial reason that the famous minuet is modelled on the minuet from *Don Giovanni*. It is significant that Verdi refused to compose an additional aria for a vainglorious singer on the grounds that *Rigoletto* was an opera not of arias, but of duets. Like Mozart's operas, it is conversation in music. The conversation may be rhetorical, flamboyant, even crude compared with Mozart's wit and tragic pathos; but its sincerity and dramatic impact carry all before them. The thrilling quartet is, again, closer to Mozart than to the quintet in *The Mastersingers*. Wagner's ensemble is a static set-piece. Verdi's is dramatic movement, in which the interlocking passions of the characters create unity from tension, the Duke's nonchalant tune and Maddalena's chatter being counterpointed against Gilda's sustained, lamenting phrase and Rigoletto's gloomy ostinato (Ex. 80).

Verdi's intensifying imagination has learned, too, how to make even the 'hit-number' dramatically relevant. It would never have occurred to him to call '*La Donna è mobile*' or any other of his tunes vulgar; but he knew that it had every quality essential

Ex. 80. Verdi: *Rigoletto*

for popular appeal without being, in its rhythmic blatancy, a tune of profound subtlety or beauty. He also knew that it expressed to perfection the Duke's cynicism; and most of all he knew that its effect when sung off-stage to a Rigoletto who has murdered his own daughter in mistake for the Duke would be shattering. A 'better' tune would not have served. Only a tune such as this could have expressed the appalling indifference of life to the sufferings of its blind, deluded creatures.

The Elizabethan, if not Shakespearean, immediacy of Verdi's imagination in *Rigoletto* fulfils the promise of *Macbeth*. Similarly, *La Traviata* raises the more intimate manner of *Luisa Miller* to a higher plane. The theme is neither heroic nor rhetorical. It deals with the conflict between the real life of human emotion and the life of Society. Violetta is the outcast who yearns to 'belong' to the glittering world to which she is pretty butterfly and parasitic gadfly, and is thereby denied the love which alone would give her life meaning. All the characters—in Dumas' play as in Verdi's opera—dramatize themselves and are, in their very theatricality, true to human nature; indeed, the characters seemed so faithful to some aspects of French provincial life as to provoke offence—especially since Piave presented them in a more or less contemporary setting. Donizetti had used operatic coloratura to express madness; Verdi here gives it a much subtler dramatic propriety, for Violetta's *fioriture** express the feverishness both of the *demi-mondaine* and of the consumptive; her gaiety is melancholy as much because she is spiritually rootless as because she is soon to die. Again, Verdi merges personal feeling into a being remote from himself; and the growing depth of his insight is reflected in the music's 'psychological' fusion of aria and recitative. Moreover, the orchestra no longer, as in the earliest operas, reinforces the excitement with theatrically effective cliché, nor provides, as in *Macbeth*, an atmospheric background. Although it never, in Wagnerian fashion, subverts the pre-eminence of the voices, it becomes an intrinsic part of the psychological drama. The tender preludes and interludes extend our understanding of character and situation, apart from serving the baser theatrical function of providing time for scene-shifting.

Rigoletto and *Traviata* are the culminating points of what we have come to think of as Verdi's 'middle' period. The operas that follow—notably *Simone Boccanegra*, *Un Ballo in Maschera*, and *Don Carlo*—are a transition between the middle period and the last. Verdi here returns to the historical-political theme: the setting of *Un Ballo* had to be transferred from contemporary Sweden to a highly improbable Boston in order to avoid trouble with the censor. The theatrical vehemence of early Verdi now comes to terms with the psychological intimacy of *La Traviata*; and if these operas have not the terrific impact of *Rigoletto*, they manifest a distinct advance in symphonic organization. Verdi has mastered the art of building whole scenes on the evolution of instrumental figurations prompted by the action. One no longer thinks of the music as a setting of the drama (as with Monteverdi), or of the drama as an illustration of the music (as with Wagner); instead, music and drama become synonymous (as with Mozart). *Un Ballo* is especially interesting in that it introduces in Oscar a character whose glinting, fragilely

---

* Fioriture: literally flowerings, flourishes. Ornamental figurations decorating a melodic line, in the vocal style usually referred to as coloratura.

scored music suggests a rebirth of the *buffo* spirit. This is the
first appearance of any quality that could be called wit in the
gloomy violence of Verdi's world. It provides evidence of a
widening emotional range, from which alone the glories of
Verdi's old age could have sprung. In this opera too Verdi
employs extended passages of fugato—dramatically justified,
since they symbolize the machinations of the conspirators.

The greater orchestral and scenic richness of these transitional
operas was in part prompted by emulation of the Grand Manner
of Meyerbeer: which Verdi can recreate with none of Meyerbeer's self-consciousness. Certainly Meyerbeer never composed
a 'grander' opera than *Aida*, which Verdi produced in 1871 for
festival performance at Cairo. The Amneris story is the peak
point thus far of Verdian passion, the Aida story of his
lyrical amplitude: a comparison of the duet in the last scene
with any of the duet scenas in *Norma* will reveal how Verdi
preserves the arching contours and stepwise evolution of
Bellinian *bel canto*, even while incorporating into the phrases
ecstatic leaps of seventh and ninth. The grandiose choral
elements now grow cumulatively, along with the unfolding
of the personal drama. Even the dances—and Verdi had
seldom advanced beyond the conventional except when
stimulated by voices and a human situation—acquire poetic
richness: Verdi's orchestration now has a translucence, especially in its handling of woodwind, which is a no less personal
achievement than Wagner's massive horn-pervaded sonority.
In the last scene the ethereal scoring for divided strings, flute,
harp, and clarinets surrounds the ever more tenuously cantabile
melodies like a halo: the music is the more deeply moving
because it follows the cataclysm of Amneris's altercation with
the priests. Passion disintegrates as the lovers' physical bodies
die, until nothing remains but the low monotone of Amneris's
repeated D flats, praying for peace. The rest is silence. The
Hamlet-like melancholy that hides beneath Verdi's flamboy-
ance has made *Aida* a 'grand' opera to end grand opera. He
was to write one grander still: but not in external magnificence,
only in the terrifying honesty of its response to the perversities
of the heart.

At the height of his fame Verdi had bought a farm, retired
to the country, and adopted the life of a squire. During the
years in which he was, as a composer, a national hero, he was

also on a modest scale a man of affairs, engaged in local govern-
ment and politics. Wagner, who talked so much about the
divinity of the Folk, really meant the divinity of himself; Verdi
refused even to write his memoirs, on the grounds that the
public which had put up with so many of his notes deserved to
be excused the perusal of his prose. Verdi's nationalism was
expressed practically in his love of the countryside and of the
peasant community; in his work as landlord and parliamen-
tarian; in the fact that many of the tunes he created became part
of popular tradition; in his reverence for the musical traditions
of his country.

This last point is evidence of the sense in which, like Berlioz,
he stands at the opposite pole to Wagner. His human interests
were centred in the multifarious variety of people other than
himself. His musical interests embraced most creative aspects
of contemporary music; his immediate predecessors, especially
Rossini, whom he greatly admired; and—increasingly as he
grew older—the Italian masters of the sixteenth and seventeenth
centuries. "Everybody should preserve the characteristics of his
own nation," he said. "You are fortunate in that you are still
the sons of Bach. And we? We too once had a great school of
our own, but it has become bastard and looks like perishing
utterly." He once gave Boito a list of composers whom he
thought it profitable to study. They included Palestrina,
Carissimi, Marcello, Scarlatti, Pergolesi, and Piccinni—but,
significantly, not Gluck. All these composers thought primarily
in terms of vocal melody; and when Verdi advised students to
return to the old if they wanted to progress, he meant what he
said. He did not mean that archaic models should be imitated
passively; he meant that respect for traditional principles would
lead to the only true creative development. He proved it
himself: for no composer thought less about problems of technical and spiritual evolution, or showed a more continuously
stimulating growth from the first creative years of a long life to
the last.

This becomes clear in the church music which Verdi composed during a pause in his operatic activity between *Aida* and
the two final Shakespearean operas. His *Requiem Mass* was
prompted by a particular occasion—the death of a great artist
and patron, Manzoni. It is an act of homage to human greatness, not fundamentally a religious work: for although Verdi

lived in a Catholic country, he was, like Wagner and Berlioz —
and to the deep distress of his wife—an agnostic. He expressed
his humanist creed when he said: "Music needs youthfulness of
the senses, impetuousness of the blood, fulness of life"; and it
was inevitable that one who believed so vehemently in life as
self-justificatory, should have been subject to recurrent pessimism. "Life is suffering," he said; "when we are young, the
exuberance of living, activity, and amusement torment and
fascinate us. We shoulder our portions of good and ill as they
come and do not notice life at all. As we grow old we may be
tormented less, we may even achieve our ambitions; then we
wonder what our ambitions are worth." Verdi's own life, after
the tragic death of his first wife and children, was outwardly
sane, happy, uneventful; yet in his music he expressed through
the personalities of other human beings the wildest extremities
of passion, desire, and despair. The turmoil is perhaps more real
than the placidity. Hamlet-like, he oscillates between violent
activity and spiritual torpor; and though he fears death no more
than he fears suffering, he hates it because for him death is the
end of strife, and therefore of hope.

We would, therefore, hardly expect that Verdi, in composing
a requiem, would attempt to emulate, however much he
admired, the devotional serenity of Palestrina. The only
occasion on which Verdi directly approached the manner of
Palestrina was in the little *Ave Maria* included in the *Pezzi
Sacri* of 1898. Even here Verdi employs not an ecclesiastical
mode, but an invented 'enigmatic scale' which offers to the
part-writing strange harmonic potentialities; and Verdi regarded the piece as an experiment outside the main line of his
music. In the *Requiem* there is a slight flavour of modality in
the Agnus Dei and Offertorium, and occasionally a use of
harmonically unrelated concords which may have been
prompted by sixteenth-century practice: consider the moving
intrusion of the G major chord into the B flat amens of the Dies
Irae (Ex. 81):

Ex. 81. Verdi: *Requiem*   (Chorus) A   men

In general, however, any recollections of sixteenth-century technique—or of the monumental choral style of Carissimi and Marcello, or the nobly operatic church music of Cherubini —are absorbed into the operatic style that was Verdi's spontaneous language. The *Requiem* deals with living and dying—with the same immediacy and splendour as does *Aida*. The passion of its soaring cantabile themes, of its violent harmonic and tonal oppositions, of its glowing, even garish orchestration is so intense as to seem sublime: though the music has none of the enigmatic, visionary singularity of Berlioz's *Requiem* (which Verdi knew and admired). The sobs of the Lachrymosa are grander, but identical in spirit and technique with the sobs of Violetta in *Traviata*, for this requiem is of the earth, earthy. Perhaps it is also of the sun, sunny; the fury of the Dies Irae terrifies us because, when death shuts out the sun, we become 'a kneaded clod'. The opposition between being alive and the suspension of movement which is death, is the core of the Requiem, as it is of Verdi's greatest work, *Otello*.

It seems probable that Verdi's response, in his church music, to the scope of the Italian tradition had something to do with the final maturing of his operatic style. A more richly civilized musical technique came to meet the texts not of a hack librettist, however theatrically astute, but of a poet who had the literary talent, and the musicianship, to release the Shakespearean range of Verdi's genius. The Othello story, as a fight between instinctive passion and destructive intellect, between over-exuberant life and irremediable death, was quintessentially Verdian; and Boito's poetry, often closely modelled on Shakespeare, is beautiful enough to prompt Verdi to seek the 'justest delineation' of the words in his power. In *Otello* there is no single element that is new. There are passages in *Simone Boccanegra* which effect as powerful a fusion of recitative and aria, of vocal lyricism and orchestral drama, of melodic and symphonic organization; certainly there is no justification for maintaining that the enhanced cogency and continuity of *Otello* had anything to do with the example of Wagner. What has happened is that the aged Verdi's dramatic imagination now functions on so consistently intense a level that even the survivals of melodramatic convention—like Iago's inverted Credo—become moments of revelation which forward, rather than disrupt, the action. Only in Mozart can we find a fusion of music and drama as complex, and seemingly as inevitable, as this; and we could pay Verdi no greater compliment than to say that whereas in *Macbeth* our acquaintance with Shakespeare is an embarrassment, in *Otello* we accept Verdi's drama as different from, but parallel to, Shakespeare's.

Perhaps the most remarkable, and Shakespearean, quality about *Otello* is its restraint. Verdi never wrote wilder music than the physical and psychological storm scene, or Othello's arioso of hysteria. Yet the ultimate climax comes in the eternal quietude of the Willow Song and Ave Maria: and in Othello's unaccompanied, almost Monteverdi-like sob: '*Come sei pallida, e muta e bella*' (Ex. 82):

Ex.82. Verdi: *Otello*

That which was quick and glowing is motionless, silent. It is not so much that Othello (like Verdi himself in the *Requiem*) cannot accept this, as that he cannot believe it. Nothing could be more remote from the end of *Tristan und Isolde*. The mutual self-destruction of those lovers is a merging into oneness; the fulfilment of love offers them no choice but death. But Verdi's Othello and Desdemona had no choice but life; and Othello can but gaze dumbly at the being who was living and is now dead: and in death eternally other than himself, separated. He does not fulfil himself in dying; he atones for what was for Verdi the only cardinal sin. His tragedy moves us so deeply because we have all—Verdi among us—at some time destroyed what we love through blindness, perversity, or masochistic malice. In so doing we— or the Iago within us—kill a part of ourselves. The greatest of Italian grand operas owes its grandeur to the fact that it offers, not romantic evasion, but a fearless admission of our stupidity and our guilt.

Otello is the culminating point of Verdi's career, but it was not his last word; its Mozartian and Shakespearean restraint leads on to a development as logical as it is unexpected. Having expressed the essential Verdian tragic situation with unflinching honesty, the octogenarian composer can at last contemplate life ironically. In extreme old age, he writes his first comic opera: in which the relationship to Mozart—and to Rossini, Cimarosa, and the minor *buffo* composers—becomes for the first time explicit in musical technique. Of course, the man who had created *Otello*, not to mention the lurid sequence of operas from *Rigoletto* onwards, could not merely revive *buffo* gaiety; once more, to return to the past is for Verdi a step forward. So although he insisted that *Falstaff* was unambiguously comic, that is not how it affects us. Ford's jealousy recalls the madness of Othello; the music of the young lovers relives with virginal grace the first magical love scene between Othello and Desdemona; even Falstaff himself is a figure of fun who is fundamentally tragic, in so far as his 'youthfulness of the senses, impetuousness of the blood' are all too obviously subject to age and decay.

But the passions of mortal life, as Verdi had experienced them with so acute an immediacy, are now viewed from a distance. The ultimate objectification of experience occurs in this exquisitely wrought score into which is distilled the quintessence of Verdian lyricism, while the linear orchestral texture becomes as kaleidoscopic as life itself. Apart from Fenton's tender love song, there are no arias; and the sequence of moods is so continuously flexible that although most of the music moves rapidly, the opera seems suspended in time. The unreality and artifice of the old *Commedia* here reaches its consummation; for the opera is a dancing dream which is not a substitute for reality, but a microcosm of the passions of a long life. The plot against Falstaff is not a crude parody of, but a deliciously ironic counterpart to, the many conspiratorial scenes in the earlier operas; even the fairy music is a distillation of human wit, not an evocation of a world of fancy like the fairy music of Weber or Mendelssohn. Perhaps it is no accident that, whereas Verdi's middle-period works had suggested some relationship to the rhetorical aspects of Beethoven, in the complex interrelations of the through-composed score of *Falstaff* we can detect some kinship with the cryptic linear organization of Beethoven's last quartets. (Consider especially the first movement of opus 135.) Though the 'philosophical' significance of Verdi's music may be far removed from that of late Beethoven, both have in common a release from the domination of Time.

From this point of view it is worth noting that *Falstaff* ends with a fugue. In some ways one can think of this as the last breath of the *buffo* spirit, comparable with the sextet that

ironically concludes *Don Giovanni*. But it is not just a *buffo*
ensemble; it is a fully-fledged fugue with a witty, rhythmically
complex theme (Ex. 83):

Ex. 83 Verdi: *Falstaff*

which in polyphonic development creates a subtly fluctu-
ating harmony. In this agile counterpoint all the contradictions
and perversities of life become one. The fugue does not deny
Verdi's belief that life is suffering: only suffering itself becomes
a kind of joy; or suffering and joy together make sense. They
coalesce in this great fugal laugh, which is the reverse of *buffo*
irresponsibility, because it is an affirmation of life.

Verdi once said: "I admit the past and the present, and I
would admit the future too, if I knew it and found it good." If
it were not for his music, that might seem an odd remark from
a man who held that life was suffering. Knowing his music—
and in particular the fugal epilogue to *Falstaff*—we can see
what he meant: in the profound subtleties of his old age, no
less than in the powerful banalities of his youth, his strength lay
in his self-sufficiency. In 1875 he wrote in a letter:

"I am unable to say what will emerge from the present
musical ferment. Some want to specialize in melody, like
Bellini; others in harmony, like Meyerbeer. I am not in favour
of either. I should like a young man, when he begins to write,
never to think about being a melodist or a futurist or any other
of the devils created by this kind of pedantry. Melody and
harmony should be only means to make music in the hands of
the artist. If ever the day comes when we cease to talk of melody
and harmony; of Italian and German schools; of past and
future, etc., etc.—then perhaps the kingdom of art will be
established.

"Another calamity of the present time is that all the works
of these young men are the products of *fear*. Everybody is
excessively self-conscious in his writing and, when these young
men sit down to compose, their predominant idea is to avoid
antagonizing the public and to enter into the good graces of
the critics.

"You tell me that my success is due to a fusion of the two schools. I never gave either of them a thought."

One could not wish for a more moving tribute to the advantages of being born into a living tradition. But when tradition is in decay, it takes uncommon genius so unquestioningly to assume one's ability to renew the past. Verdi was justified in pitting his intuitive self-sufficiency against our self-conscious fears. Perhaps the measure of his greatness, however, is that he understood our fears while being himself as unafraid as any man who ever lived.

Otello and *Falstaff* would seem to round off the Italian tradition of tragic and comic opera, leaving no more to be said. The relation of Verdi's successors to *Otello* is, indeed, comparable with the relation of Bizet's successors to *Carmen*: both prostituted the truth which their master had discovered. Mascagni [1863–1945] and Leoncavallo [1858–1919] and the Italian *verismo* school degraded Verdi's immediacy to cinematic sensation, making journalistic fiction out of the appearance of truth. But Verdi at least had one successor who, though he may have prostituted truth, did so with insidiously fascinating genius.

At first, Puccini's ambition was unambiguously to follow his idol, Verdi. Even in his earliest operas, however, we find that he combined Verdian lyricism with harmonic and orchestral techniques suggested by the 'expiatory' operas of Wagner and by the sentimental lyric dramas of Massenet. This is significant, because it soon became clear that, Italian though he was, Puccini [1858–1924] had none of Verdi's dramatic objectivity— his ability to understand and to create people utterly different from himself. Though he had not Wagner's sublime egomania, his music comes to life only when he can, even if momentarily, identify himself with his characters. Since the range of experience which genuinely moved him is extremely narrow, his plots and operatic conventions tend to be stereotyped: he went to great pains to persuade his librettists to produce—if necessary, to contrive—the kind of situation which interested him.

If we compare his *Manon Lescaut*—his first really representative opera—with Massenet's *Manon*, we can see at once that there is a core of personal feeling in Puccini's work which Massenet's lacks. Massenet is like his Manon, easy-going, sensually wanton, emotionally coquettish; sincere enough, but not deeply engaged. Puccini becomes his Manon, whose eroticism is not merely a surface titillation like Massenet's fragmentary phrases and tripping rhythms, but a melancholy obsession that flows into lyricism. The characteristic Puccini melody has already emerged. Italian *bel canto* still soars in scale-wise moving arches, but with little of Verdi's virility: for the phrases now tend to droop further than they rise. Moreover, Puccini's themes, lyrical though they may be, have in common with Massenet's a partiality for feminine endings; they tend to split up into clauses rounded off by falling appoggiaturas, or even fifths—an interval which, since it usually implies cadential finality, slows down the lines' momentum (Ex. 84):

Ex. 84. Puccini: *Turandot* Act I

In order to counteract this drooping tendency, Puccini frequently groups the clauses in sequences which rise: so that the melodies produce an effect at once limp and hysterically wrought. The more sophisticated harmony—as compared with Verdi—emphasizes the subjective emotionalism of the melodies: especially since Puccini's fondness for the neutral 'Tristan' chords tends to deprive his harmony of the sense of movement. When in later years he picked up from Impressionism the devices of parallel fifths, sevenths, and ninths, and whole-tone progressions,* they all tended to reinforce this harmonic neutrality, creating a more potent form of the narcissistic quality we commented on in Gounod. This harmonic aspect of his work is thus associated with his fondness for pentatonic figurations which deprive melody of the sense of progression, for long sustained pedal points, and for ostinato rhythms. All tend either to induce hypnosis or to provoke hysteria.

One might almost say that Puccini did not use these techniques because he dealt with exotic subjects; he chose exotic subjects because these were the techniques through which he

---

* THE WHOLE-TONE SCALE : that consisting of whole-tone steps only: e.g., C, D, E, F♯, G♯, A♯, C. It contains no perfect fifth and no feeling of tonality.

could say what he had to say. In his later work his limp but nervously strained melody, his obsessional harmonies and ostinato rhythms, are associated with his preoccupation with physical suffering, whether sadistic or masochistic; and while this type of neurotic experience is the genuine element from which Puccini created a language, it is also paradoxically the source of a quality inherently synthetic. Having so narrow a range of experience, he is tempted to resort to any expedient to stimulate it; and stimulation may become simulation, as his hysteria becomes self-induced, and sentimental, because in excess of the object. We can see this even in his mastery of theatrical effect. His sense of the theatre is consummate, in that his effects usually strike home. But he is not a great musical dramatist, for his effects are seldom subservient to an artistic purpose. So long as he is excited, he can excite others. It did not occur to him that theatrical excitement, though necessary, is not an end in itself.

Madame Butterfly is probably Puccini's most successful full-scale opera because the theme of passive suffering is here unambiguously the core of the action, while the final catastrophe is executed with comparative restraint. *The Girl of the Golden West* is probably his worst opera because, having chosen a fashionable theme that did not accord with his emotional interests, he had to drag in those interests by hook or crook (for he could never produce the pot-boiler in which his feelings were unengaged). Something similar happens in his last opera, *Turandot*, in which Puccini tries to extend his range by dealing with a heroine who was neither frail nor passively suffering. But sadism is an inversion of masochism, hardly a richer experience; and although *Turandot* contains some of Puccini's most powerful and remarkable music, it is—not merely in the sense which Puccini intended—a monstrous work. It is revealing both that the scene of the torture of Liu is gratuitous, being without dramatic justification: and that Liu has the most personal and beautiful music in the score.

Artistically, Puccini's most impressive work is the sequence of three one-set operas in which he as it were segregated the melodramatic, sentimental, and comic aspects of his talent. *Il Tabarro* is the most powerful of *verismo* operas (unless one counts *Carmen* as such) because, although it tells a sordid murder tale journalistically, it presents 'the facts' with horrid authenticity.

We (and Puccini) are involved in what the newspapers call 'the tragedy' because murder is necessarily sadistic; but in this trenchantly nasty little piece Puccini offers the minimum of emotional indulgence. *Gianni Schicchi* succeeds because, being inspired by Verdi's *Falstaff*, it is funny. The comic elements in Puccini's full-length operas exist mainly to enhance the pain and pathos by contrast. But *Gianni Schicchi* is comic, even witty, in its own right: as are the satirical impressions of convent life in the third member of the triptych, *Suor Angelica*, which describes, with unexpected simplicity and reticence, a girl's attempt at repentance after an illicit love affair.

The comic and satirical music in *Il Trittico* suggests that the theatre lost a brilliant operatic comedian in Puccini's slavery to his neuroses—and to their box-office appeal. Yet it is unfair to accuse Puccini of cynicism in his self-exploitation; if the qualities on which his commercial success depends were not also the most genuine thing about him his works would have lost their kick long since. What is sad is that, while Verdi's career had proved how arduous is the process of growing up, Puccini takes us back to adolescence—and leaves us stranded. He has something to say; but what he says unmans us. He panders to our weakness, and scares himself in scaring us. At the time, we may find the experience exciting. But we have to turn again to Verdi, to rid our mouths of the ashes of fear.

Comparisons between Wagner and Hitler have been discouraged because Wagner's imagination functioned on a plane at once more profoundly human and more sublime; yet the fact that *Tristan* is one of the greatest works ever created by the mind of man does not alter the fact that resemblances between Wagner and Hitler exist. Puccini is as much above the horror comic as he is below Wagner; yet if we think of him as standing somewhere between the two we shall understand better the potency of his appeal. It is a tribute to his perverse genius that he still has the lure of danger: and that we can no more 'reject' him than we can reject our subconscious minds.

INDEX OF MUSIC EXAMPLES

VOLUME III (from *c.* 1750)

GENERAL INDEX